Heritage
of
Music

THE MUSIC OF THE JEWISH PEOPLE

Heritage
of
Music

by Judith Kaplan Eisenstein

Union of American Hebrew Congregations · New York

LIBRARY OF CONGRESS CATALOGING IN PUBLICATION DATA

Eisenstein, Judith (Kaplan)
  Heritage of Music: The Music of the Jewish People.

  SUMMARY: A guide to the history and appreciation of Jewish music. Includes simple arrangements for many of the songs discussed.
  Includes bibliographical references.

  1. Music, Jewish—History and criticism. [1. Music, Jewish—History and criticism] I. Title.
II. Title: The Music of the Jewish People.
ML3776.E48   781.7′2′924   73-92164

Union of American Hebrew Congregations
838 Fifth Ave.
N.Y. 10021

PRODUCED IN THE U.S. OF AMERICA

To Ira

who guided wisely, encouraged
patiently and helped in every
possible way—my love

ACKNOWLEDGMENTS

Unless otherwise stated, all translations and musical arrangements in this book are by the author.

I wish to express my deep gratitude to the following: ACUM Ltd. (The Society of Authors, Composers and Editors of Music in Israel) for permission to include *"Hiney ha-Stav Avar"* by Yizhar Yaron (Popper) and *"Yom ha-Shevi-i"* by Yitzhak Edel; the Central Conference of American Rabbis for permission to include the hymn "Father, See Thy Suppliant Children" from the *Union Songster;* the Jewish Publication Society of America for permission to include a long excerpt from Soma Morganstern's novel *Son of the Lost Son,* translated by Joseph Leftwich and Peter Gross; the Jewish Reconstructionist Foundation for permission to include the arrangements of *"Kol Mekadesh Shevi-i"* and *"Le-Koved Shabbes"* from the cantata *Seven Golden Buttons* by Ira and Judith Eisenstein and the arrangements of *"Yovo Adir"* and *"Af Bri"* from the cantata *Reborn* by the same; Mills Music, Inc. for permission to include *"Ki Mi-Tziyon"* by Emanuel Amiran and the melody of *"El Ginat Egoz"* by Sarah Levi-Tanai;

Maurice Samuel for his gracious permission to include excerpts from his translations of *"Ha-Matmid"* and *"Ben Nehar Prat,"* both by H. N. Bialik; Ben Aronin for his kind permission to include his translation of "The Courting Song" from Goldfaden's operetta *Shulamith.*

I am also indebted to the then reading committee of the Commission on Jewish Education: Rabbis Leon Fram, Samuel Glasner and Alexander M. Schindler; Cantors Arthur Asher, Joseph Portnoy and Joseph Rosenfeld; and Mrs. Samuel Cook.

I also wish to thank Ruth Sumliner who typed the original manuscript; sincere appreciation to Ralph Davis for the beautiful format of this volume and to Annette Abramson for her indefatigable work on manuscript and proofs.

Above all, my deepest gratitude is extended to Edith Samuel for her unlimited and creative assistance in the final stages of preparing the manuscript for publication.

J. K. E.
New York, 1969

CONTENTS

LIST OF MUSICAL EXAMPLES

FOREWORD

According to a hasidic tale, the Ladier *rebbe* once noticed a confused look on the face of one of his elderly congregants. He called to the man and said: "I can see that you do not understand my sermon. Listen to this melody, and it will teach you how to cling to God." The *rebbe* began to sing a song without words. It was a song of Torah, of trust and love for God. The old man listened and soon understood.

This story explains why the Commission on Jewish Education endorsed the publication of this book as part of the curriculum on both secondary and adult levels. There are many ways of communicating the values of our heritage. Across the span of Jewish history, one of the most potent ways has been through song. Religion, according to Whitehead, cannot exist without music. In the same way, religious education is inadequate without musical programs and activities.

One book, however, cannot develop deep and abiding appreciation for the meaning of Jewish music, just as a single course in liturgy does not produce a worshipful Jew. This appreciation must be cultivated from a child's first experiences of Jewish tradi-

tions. But, assuming that the mature student has thus been taught the musical heritage of Judaism, this book can help him understand how Jewish music expresses the values and visions of his people. It is another way of teaching, which the Ladier *rebbe* fully utilized.

The author, with her skill as a teacher and her sensitivity as a musicologist, provides many opportunities for actual participation by the student: playing instruments, singing, creating, sharing. Merely learning *about* Jewish music would be insufficient for the inherent purpose of music itself. The major goal, therefore, is to evoke feeling and expression and to communicate ideas through emotions.

In the following pages, the author explores the meaning of Jewish music not as an intellectual exercise but as a source of emotional enrichment. We can understand our heritage with the heart as well as the mind. And music is the clearest language of the Jewish heart as it is the oldest language of the Jewish people.

JACK D. SPIRO
NATIONAL DIRECTOR OF EDUCATION

PREFACE

One Passover, my husband and I had the pleasure of attending a *seder* at the home of Ira and Judith Eisenstein, and it was a memorable experience.

The company, the atmosphere, the food, the spirit—all were impressive. But the songs that punctuated the evening—songs ancient and new, songs barely remembered and songs never forgotten, songs heavy with associations accumulated over centuries and songs light with the lilt of the young State of Israel, songs in different languages from different lands and different ages and musical traditions—these songs sung out lustily and appreciatively by the company made the *seder* moving and unforgettable. I remember wondering at the time how many Jewish families, gathered at the *seder* table in homes around the world, were singing as we were. How many knew these songs, how many felt the weight of their history, how many cherished them as a part of the heritage they were at that same moment honoring?

It is a curious thing: When Jews speak about the "heritage," they may mean the vast literary heritage of the Jewish people—the Bible, the Talmud, the legends, commentaries, poetry, philosophy, prayers, responsa, grammars, lexicons, guides to moral conduct; or they may be thinking of the extraordinary history—the great persons, dates, places, movements, persecutions, wars, the central fact of survival; or they may intend "the way of life," "the outlook," the folkways and the observances. Or, again, they may have in mind the religious ideas, concepts and ritual practices; or perhaps certain values as the Jewish love of learning, the Jewish reverence for life, the Jewish tenacity in survival; or possibly even those human traits which have been associated with Jews at their best—the "wit," the "intellectual curiosity," etc. The curious fact is that few of the observers of Jews and Judaism over the ages have dwelt at length—or, in many cases, at all—on one point: Jews are a *singing* people. Since the earliest times, long before King David, the sweet singer of Israel, a love for music—perhaps it may even be called a deep need for expression in music—has existed in the people.

The documentation is ample, and in this book Judith Eisenstein explores the music of the Jewish people and shows us some of the whos, the hows, the whats, the wheres and the whens. But the *whys*—why do Jews have such a love for music, why do they have such a need to express themselves in music (for example, King David and his temple orchestra; or those tragic captives who hanged up their harps by the rivers of Babylon and, like caged songbirds, could not sing in a foreign land; or Levi Yitzhak of Berditchev; or the musically untutored *klezmorim;* or the young pioneers breaking the soil and their backs in pre-State Israel)—the *whys* must be left open to speculation by readers for there can be no real or sure answers.

Heritage of Music had its beginning in a series of short articles, "Words and Music," which *Keeping Posted* invited Mrs. Eisenstein to write in 1964. The editor found herself captivated by the subject and suggested a larger work. This present volume is the outcome.

This is *not* a song book, but it is a book containing more than 100 musical selections. Some of them are available to laymen for the first time, many of them are translated newly and freely into English for easy comprehension and singing and most of them are presented by the author in fresh arrangements which carry the melody and are simple enough for amateurs to play and sing.

This is *not* a history of music although Judith Eisenstein is obviously more than qualified to write such a work. She is a noted musicologist, composer, author and teacher (at the present time, she is an instructor in music at the Hebrew Union College-Jewish Institute of Religion, School for Sacred Music, New York) who believes—with the Department of Jewish Education of the Union of American Hebrew Congregations—that a purely chronological approach to this lively subject will not tempt a new Jewish generation to want to investigate its heritage of music and to experiment with creative ideas for song and dance.

Having ruled out the chronological historical method, Mrs. Eisenstein has managed nevertheless to include a great quantity of historical data which readers should find stimulating as well as informative. She ranges throughout time and space for examples of music sung by the far-flung Jewish people over the millennia, touching down now in Bokhara, now in Jerusalem, now in Salonika, now in Yemen, now Safed, now Second Avenue in New York, now Odessa or the Negev or sunny Andalusia. For those who want an historical trajectory, she has prepared a "Time Chart" which appears at the end of her book.

Heritage of Music is being published at a time when there is a vast explosion of interest—especially on the part of young people—in creating, singing and performing music. Mrs. Eisenstein offers innumerable suggestions for musical activity in religious schools, in youth and adult camps, in the home—guitar chords, instrumental ensembles, elementary choral arrangements, piano arrangements, to name a few—which should excite those who love their heritage and who love making music. For those less young or less innovative or less eager to perform but with a deep and abiding love for their people and for the music of their people, she provides an extensive list of sources for additional reading, study and listening opportunities.

This is the first book of its kind—in so far as we are aware—that deals with the music of the Jewish people *topically*, that is, under broad topics of wide appeal and concern. Anyone who has the capacity to tap his foot to compelling rhythm or the urge to sing out—off key or on—or the curiosity to dip into a rich and incredibly varied musical culture or the desire to enjoy what is for many an entirely new area of musical experience—in short, anyone of whatever age, station and interest in life today—will find himself drawn into *Heritage of Music: The Music of the Jewish People.*

And what a heritage it is!

EDITH SAMUEL

KEY TO PRONUNCIATION

The Hebrew pronunciation indicated by transliteration in this book is generally that of modern Israel. However, there are exceptions to this when the Ashkenazic pronunciation is an inherent and inseparable feature of a particular song. The system of transliteration is a modification of the standard scholarly transliteration. This will involve reading vowels as they are pronounced in all European languages which use the Latin alphabet:

a = "a" as in large, or like "o" in lock
e = "e" as in let
ey = "a" as in way
i = "i" as in hid; at the end of a word, "ee" as in seek
o = "o" as in song
u = "oo" as in look; when it stands alone as a syllable, "oo" as in room
ai = "i" as in like

The consonants are like the English with the following exceptions:

h = both "h" as in hand and the guttural (the letter ח in Hebrew) like the "ch" in the German "ach." At the end of a word the "h" is silent.

kh has the same sound as the guttural "h" but represents the letter כ , ך .

The transliteration of Yiddish follows the same general pattern with the following exceptions:

ay = "a" as in way
ei = "i" as in hide
ch = the guttural "h" like the "ch" in the German "ach"

Heritage
of
Music

One
RESTORING
LIVING CONNECTIONS

LET ME tell you about the music of a people. Let me tell you of the music which the plain Jew of my parents' generation heard and sang and of the songs sung by the generations before them. Let me tell you of the music of my own generation and something of the music which the generation of my children is hearing, singing and playing. It will not begin with a scientific "definition" of Jewish music. I'd as soon try and define a Jewish face!

This will not be a history of Jewish music. It will not be a systematic march through the centuries, year by year, country by country. No, this is not my plan—or my purpose.

I want to restore connections.

We have today a large store of music which to many modern Jews seems totally unrelated to them. The tunes apparently lack any association with the Jewish experience; at least, we cannot seem to remember them or to identify many of them as songs we once sang and loved and taught to new generations. The songs are not necessarily dead; many of them are very much alive and are sung, or could be sung, with pleasure.

I want to sort out from this confusing jumble of music a number of chants, songs, theater pieces, choral music and symphonic suites and to restore their living connections with the Jewish experience.

My own generation has been a careless, at times even a destructive, guardian of its heritage of music. We have failed to protect the life line between the people and the music; in many cases we have even cut off that life line so that the vigor and energy which once flowed through that vital link have ebbed away. The people gave the music life, and the music in turn pulsated in the people, passing from parent to child, and from land to land. The joys and triumphs, the tenderness and warmth, the agony and sorrows, the prayer and the protest, which were shared by Jews and made them one, were poured into music; and, wherever they are still felt, that process continues today. When

we live for a moment with that music, we are touching the pulse itself, and our own is quickened in turn.

In our time we have a great advantage over our forebears. However closely knit they may have been, however great their love of their musical heritage, their musical memories were restricted largely to their own immediate communities, even when those communities stretched far back in time. My own grandparents, for example, lived in the *shtetlach* of Poland and Lithuania. They probably never saw a page of written music in their lives and, if they had seen it, they could not have read the notation in any case. What they learned in their homes, what they sang in their synagogues, what they heard in the streets, at their weddings—this was all they knew. Some threads of melody may have been carried from ancient Palestine to Rome or Germany. There some new strands were picked up and woven in: Teutonic folk songs, troubadour songs, even fragments of church chant. The folk moved eastward and gathered in Russian drinking songs, Roumanian dance tunes and even a new thread of Oriental melody which had come into Eastern Europe by way of Byzantium. The total fabric of their music could be labeled "Ashkenazic (German)—East European."

We can, if we wish, be far richer than our forebears in musical memories and associations. A century of exposure to Western techniques of writing, composing and recording music has made it possible for us to know the music of other Jewish communities, in all their vast dispersion to the four corners of the world. Perhaps it would not be amiss to stop for a moment and recall the extent of that dispersion. The great Ashkenazic community spread westward, as well as eastward. France and England, and what is left of the German community itself, are still sources of "Ashkenazic song, Western version." The Sephardic community, once of Spain, long ago suffered its own dispersion to the New World, to the Netherlands and England in the West; and to the East, across North

Africa, into Greece, Turkey, the Balkans, over to Syria, Iraq and Iran, down to Egypt. There are the Jews who moved directly from the homeland deeper into the Orient down to Yemen at the tip of the Gulf of Aden, to ancient Persia, and thence up into the mountains of Afghanistan, Daghestan, Bokhara, some as far as Cochin, India, and even into China.

We should, under the best of circumstances, find it impossible to visit these remote centers of Jewry. Today many of them have been liquidated; some may still exist as entities behind the Iron Curtain where they are completely inaccessible to us. But many have carried their memories and their music to America. Many are part of the new ingathering in the land of Israel. Like their clothes, their customs, their folkways, their music is often strange and exotic to our ears. But it is being recorded, written down and absorbed into the consciousness of a new generation of composers who are fashioning the music of our future.

This book tries to bring you a small sampling of all the musical memories. In such a sampling, all of the material will not be of the same musical quality. Tastes change from era to era, and you may find that great favorites of the nineteenth century are less appealing to you than archaic chants from the Middle Ages, or that a composition from the Italian Renaissance has more enduring quality than one from the very decade in which you are reading this book. The writer has tried not to impose her own personal predilections on the selection of examples but to present a wide variety, from which you will make your own choices. In a few instances, the historic memory is more poignant than the melody associated with it. Occasionally, the poetry of the words may overshadow the lyricism of the musical setting. You will find that you like some music instantly but that your own tastes expand with an increased understanding.

For the sake of that understanding, you will need a modest vocabulary of basic technical terms. Read through the first few chapters, and then you will be ready to go on with the story without interruptions for further definitions and translations. Also, if you

wish to get the full flavor of the samplings in this book, you really ought to sound them out for yourselves. Most of them are presented in arrangements simple enough for you to spell out, with a minimum of musical training, either as individuals or as a group. Some of our music is too large in scope or too difficult for this, but you will be able to hear it in records. Since records have a way of going in and out of print, you will have to look up those referred to in the book in the Schwann catalogues as they are published. You will probably find many new recordings as well. Keep yourselves up to date by watching for the names of composers mentioned here. Also, follow the new listings of recorded folk music.

You may wish to explore for yourselves beyond the limited range of this book. To help you, we have included a section at the back of the book called "For Further Exploration." As you read this book, you will often notice a small symbol ‡ inserted into the text. This symbol means that you will find more information in the back of the book—information such as suggestions for further reading, references to more musical examples than are provided in our text, sources for finding still others, additional recorded material, etc.

If you are interested in a chronological presentation of the examples provided in the various chapters, turn to the "Time Chart" at the back of the book. There you will find references to pages in the text, where historical information is provided, and to musical examples by number.

Listen, play, sing, form small ensemble groups for choral music and chamber music. Play your guitars, make your own arrangements, and by all means try to compose your own music. Plan small concerts, song fests, musical plays. But, above all, perhaps you will realize that the music of a people lives only when that people lives, when it has not only memories in common but also hopes, dreams and purposes which are continually alive and expanding, just as you yourselves are alive and growing and changing and seeking new worlds.

Two

SEARCHING FOR
LOST SOUNDS

WHAT'S WRONG with this story? Students at a synagogue are rehearsing an original play about the patriarch Abraham and, in a scene showing him entertaining his mysterious guests, the director suddenly suggests to the actors: "Sing *Ma-oz Tzur* (Rock of Ages). That would be a nice touch."

You don't have to be a scholar to recognize the first error: the hymn is a *Hanukah* song referring to the victory of the Maccabees who lived almost two thousand years after the time of Abraham. The song is thus inappropriate for chronological reasons.

The second error is more subtle. When you reread the familiar Hebrew or English words (which are not really a translation from the Hebrew but rather a paraphrase), you find that either version is strictly metrical—that is, it has a regular beat and a definite rhyme scheme, a type of verse which did not appear in Jewish literature until the tenth or eleventh century. Now recall the tune. No musicologist has to guide you; your own common sense tells you that *Ma-oz Tzur* sounds suspiciously like a church hymn. In fact, it is; the tune comes from an old German Protestant chorale combined with a bit of German folk song. Thus *Ma-oz Tzur* is utterly inappropriate for reasons of style, content, form and religious spirit.

However, if you were asked: what kind of music *did* the ancient Hebrews sing? Or even the not-so-ancient Hebrews in the time of the Kings, or, still later, the Maccabees themselves, or the students of Rabbi Akiba, or the farmers and tradesmen who gathered in the academies of Sura and Pumbedita in Babylonia in the days of the *Geonim?* The answer is: no one really knows!

Questions about other aspects of the life of our distant ancestors—what they ate, how they dressed, what sort of houses they built, what occupations they followed, what ideas they had about God, about government, family life—are far less difficult to answer. We have, first of all, the written record, beginning with the Bible itself. We have, second, enormous quantities of additional data provided by modern archaeologists—ancient records preserved in clay, ruins of buildings, coins, tombs, pottery, tools, crumbling scrolls and other fragments describing the life, poetry and laws of our remote forefathers.

But nobody made any written record of music. Sounds cannot be preserved in caves or tombs or dust. They vanished into the air forever.

We shall never know exactly what the music sounded like in those ages before the invention of musical notation. However, the scholars of music, in cooperation with the historians and archaeologists, have been able to do some detective work and to furnish us with approximations of the way some of the ancient music may have sounded. There are certain "skeletons," preserved from the distant past, on which an expert can construct a body of music in much the same way that a paleontologist can reconstruct an entire dinosaur—which, of course, he has never seen in life—on the framework of a few ancient bones or fossilized tracings.

The first set of remains, and the most obvious, is of course the Hebrew Bible itself. Scriptures provide the words of songs of all kinds—war songs, love songs, victory songs, dirges. One great archaeologist suggests that many of the stories in the opening chapters of the Bible were originally sung by bards, who spread

An ancient Middle Eastern harp

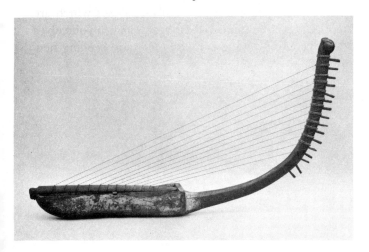

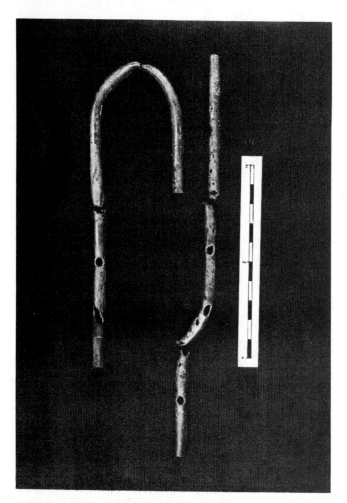

Ancient silver flutes photographed with scale

names appear in the text of a poem. The names were studied and compared to those of instruments used in other lands at the eastern end of the Mediterranean Sea—of Egypt, Assyria and Greece, for instance. Some of those instruments were depicted in excavations and identified by archaeologists. The ancient Greeks wrote some specific explanations of how their instruments were played, and we have those explanations. In more recent years, archaeologists have discovered parts of musical instruments—the mouthpiece of a trumpet, the frame of a drum, etc.—in places where ancient Hebrews were known to have lived.‡ (See Chapter Twenty-Eight for all references.)

The scholar can surmise from this kind of information what type of sound came out of an instrument—the twang of strings, the shrill wail caused by blowing through a reed, the clash of metal struck by a hammer, the blare of wind through brass. What is still hard to know is how the strings were tuned, or

An ancient Middle Eastern lyre

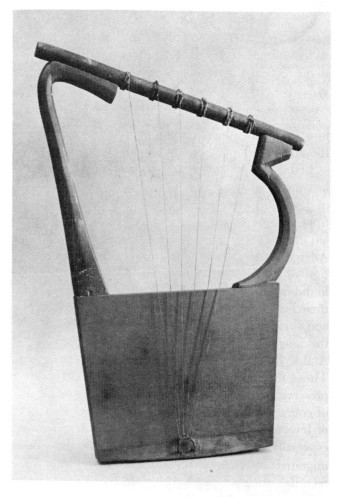

them throughout the Hebrew tribes long before they were written down. The Bible also mentions collections of songs which are lost to modern man, collections such as the *Book of the Wars of the Lord* (see *Numbers 21: 24*) and the *Book of Jashar* (see *II Samuel 1: 17*).

Later in this book we shall encounter some of the songs of the Bible. Sometimes the rhythm and the pattern of the words give us a clear idea of the rhythm and pattern of their accompanying melodies, but the melodies themselves have totally vanished.

Another set of "bones" is our increasingly growing information about the instruments of Bible days. For hundreds of years, our knowledge was limited to the names of those instruments. Sometimes they are mentioned in passing, as part of a biblical story; at other times, they are listed as the actual instruments of an orchestra in the temple; and, at still other times, their

Instruments pictured on ancient coins: Six-stringed lyre, 1st century C.E.; two trumpets, Bar Kokhba's time; three-stringed lyre, Bar Kokhba's time

how the holes were placed in the flute, or what scales the ancients played.

Living people can furnish us with clues about the lost music of the past. There are some communities of Jews still alive today who never strayed very far from their homeland. The Jews of Yemen, in particular, lived in the East, on the shores of the Gulf of Aden, for the nineteen centuries between the destruction of the Second Temple in the year 70 and the founding of Israel in 1948. In their everyday songs, their love songs and their work songs, their lullabies and their dance songs, the Yemenite Jews took over the language and the tunes of their neighbors, the Arabs. But their religious songs are something else. Those they seem to have kept strictly apart—to have preserved from change or outside influence. They are, of course, sung in Hebrew, as are the religious songs of Jews all over the world. In the last several decades, especially since nearly all the Yemenites have now migrated to Israel, students of music have tape recorded their songs or have written them down in

modern notation. They have been comparing the Yemenite prayer chants to the songs of ancient Eastern churches, churches which had their beginnings in the land of Palestine in the last years of the Second Temple. From the songs of ancient communities like the Yemenites, from the instruments they play, scholars can gain more information about the sounds heard by our ancestors.

Occasionally, there is a dramatic discovery, the kind that every scholar dreams of but knows he must never really expect. One such discovery came in the wake of that lightning flash which startled the world of Jewish scholarship, namely the Cairo *Genizah*. The story of the discovery by Dr. Solomon Schechter of a vast collection—ancient manuscripts hidden over a five-hundred-year period in the attic of a Cairo synagogue—is told elsewhere.‡ Poetry, philosophy, biblical narrative, codes, innumerable varieties of writings on countless pages or fragments of parchment and papyrus—all these were piled up together in no semblance of order. Most of the documents and fragments were removed early in this century to the library of the Jewish Theological Seminary of America and to Cambridge University in England. After all these decades, scholars today are still sorting and examining

One of the Genizah fragments

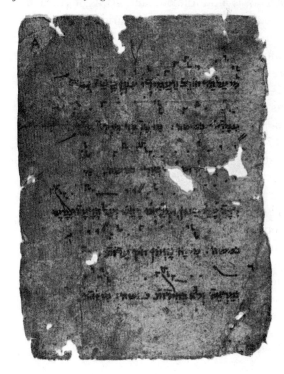

the material, attempting to decipher and to date every fragment.

In both the English and American collections, scholars found some scraps of parchment containing Hebrew words, and over the words were some signs which they recognized as a very old form of music writing. They handed the fragments over to musicologists, who soon recognized the notes. They were exactly like those which had already been deciphered in the writings of monks in the monasteries of northern Italy in the eleventh century. The scraps were compared with each other and were found to be in the same handwriting. Some of the scraps contained portions of well-known prayer texts. One fragment contained a poem not found anywhere else, *Eulogy on the Death of Moses*. A number of different scholars, working together, finally agreed that the scribe who wrote these manuscripts was a man named Obadiah, a convert to Judaism of the eleventh century, who had lived in northern Italy and had studied, before his conversion, in a monastery. It was there that he had learned to write the musical notation of his day, notation called *Beneventine neumes*. He moved to Cairo, where he probably heard the music from some *hazan* (cantor) of the time—and now we can be quite sure of at least a few of the sounds dating from the early Middle Ages.‡

A second dramatic discovery—this one by Israel Adler—was a bundle of manuscripts of music from the sixteenth and seventeenth centuries, hidden in the cellar of an Amsterdam synagogue. This was a collection of music for chorus, orchestra and soloists, individual pieces and cantatas with original Hebrew texts in the style of the Baroque era in which they were written. Words and music, indeed, the very existence of these pieces, had been unknown until very recently. They have been studied and are now published in suitable form for performance, and we shall read about them in later chapters.

But musical archaeology, like other forms of archaeology, is not all a matter of astounding discoveries. The archaeologist has to spend long years patiently sorting and patching and classifying thousands of tiny fragments of shattered clay jars, tablets or other artifacts. In the same way, the musicologist must sift through thousands of tiny fragments of melody, melody written down at different times, by different people, in different places. In order to date them, he will compare them with fragments of melody from Christian chant, troubadour song and *minnelieder, cantigas* and *romanzas* from Spain, all of them written down long before the Jewish song, and all of them now dated by experts.

This may give you some small idea of the kind of searching and study which is going on in our time. The greatest laboratory for research right now is Israel, where scholars are busily making tapes of the music of Jews brought with newcomers from all parts of the world. They have to work fast, before these Jewish immigrants become so much part of modern Israeli culture that they neglect their old songs in exchange for the new. Some of their old songs are absorbed into the new music of the land and take on a new life. (See Chapter Twenty-six.)

Three
MODERN EXPERIMENTS
IN MAKING ANCIENT MUSIC

MOST OF US are not apt to find ourselves among the professional searchers for lost music. We are all capable, however, of performing some amateur experiments which will to a degree recapture for us some of the sounds of the ancient Jewish world. In this chapter we shall describe two such experiments as they have been carried out by young students. Later chapters will provide suggestions for still more.

1.

The first experiment consisted of an attempt to build sounding models of the instruments of Bible times. The easiest to construct were the percussion instruments: the *tof,* a drum or a timbrel or a tambourine, which was used, mainly by women, to accompany dancing and processionals; the *metziltayim,* or cymbals, which were used to punctuate the order of sacri-

A homemade sistrum

fice in the temple; the *mena-anim,* or sistrum, a variety of shaken instrument, used in ancient times on occasions of rejoicing and merrymaking. *Pa-amonim,* bells, were omitted because they were described as being attached to the hem of the priests' garments. Wind instruments were more difficult to reproduce. The most ancient of them all, the *shofar,* did not need to be reproduced. A *shofar* belonging to the synagogue was available. For the ancient trumpet of brass (or silver or gold), a cornet was substituted. This trumpet was called *hatzotzerah,* and the *hatzotzerot* (plural) were usually played in pairs, especially in the temple service, where they frequently introduced and concluded the singing of psalms. The woodwinds mentioned in the biblical text, such as the *ugav,* a primitive oboe, and the *halil,* the ancient form of clarinet, were represented in our model orchestra by soprano and alto recorders.

The string instruments—the most highly regarded of all instruments in biblical times, which served as the principal voices in the temple orchestra—were the *nevel,* a harp, and the *kinnor,* the lyre. Our modern student experimenters at first used conventional autoharps to simulate these instruments. They could have used dulcimers or zithers just as well. Some members of the group actually built their own on the basis of illustrations which they studied in various articles on the instruments of the Bible.‡

Page 10 contains sketches of the four instruments made by the students and furnishes brief descriptions of the method of making them.

Before the group could proceed to improvise melodies on their string instruments, they had to agree about how to tune them. The majority preferred to tune according to the conventional pitches to which their ears were accustomed. Those were assuredly not the pitches used in ancient times in the land of Israel.

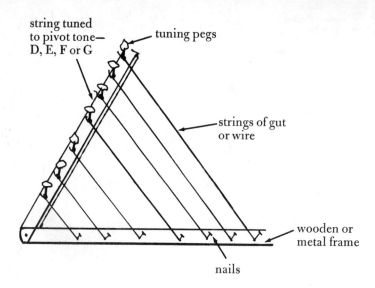

string tuned
to pivot tone—
D, E, F or G

tuning pegs

strings of gut
or wire

wooden or
metal frame

nails

KINNOR

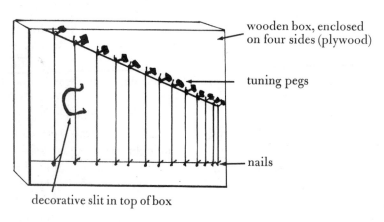

wooden box, enclosed
on four sides (plywood)

tuning pegs

nails

decorative slit in top of box

NEVEL

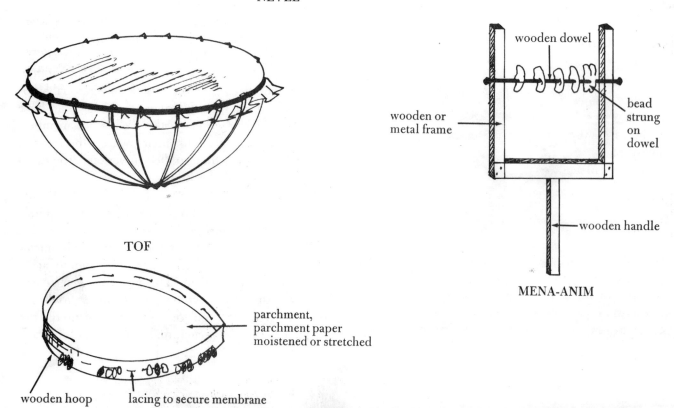

TOF

wooden dowel

wooden or
metal frame

bead
strung
on
dowel

wooden handle

MENA-ANIM

parchment,
parchment paper
moistened or stretched

wooden hoop

lacing to secure membrane

They are the pitches which European musicians long ago selected and fixed for their music, the pitches of the "tempered scale" which we find on our pianos. However, the full range of our Western tone repertory was not used. An old system of building scales seemed more appropriate. The group worked out the scale building at the piano and used only the tones of their scale when they played their autoharps. They strung their homemade instruments with seven strings and matched the pitches of their strings to the selected scale.

Beginning on D above middle C, the scale was built by playing only white notes, up four tones to G and then from the same D down four notes to A like this:

In that instance D was chosen arbitrarily as the pivot tone. They could have proceeded in exactly the same way using E, F or G as pivot tones. The resulting scales would have been as follows:

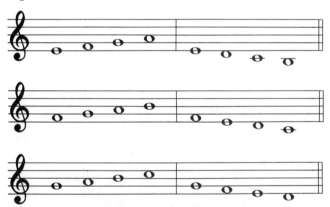

Another possible tuning which was taken into consideration was the pentatonic (five-tone) scale. This very old scale is the basis for melodies sung and played in many parts of the world. It corresponds to the succession of black notes on the piano, like this:

Whether you build your own instrument or choose to play a conventional instrument, you may choose to use any of the scales described above. However, your ears may have become accustomed to different types of tuning. Many of you have listened to the

A homemade harp

sounds of the Indian sitar. The music of the sitar and of other East Indian instruments consists of tones which do not correspond to those of our tempered scale and which could not be reproduced by our piano. This is equally true of instruments used in the Middle East today, by Arabs and by Jews of the Eastern communities. You are free to be adventurous. Tune your strings to any pitches you wish. Assign a number to each string, so that you can use the numbers to notate your improvisations. (Our musical notation will have no symbols for the pitches you are playing.) Use bar lines and rests to indicate rhythm, if you wish. You will not be concerned with the notating of chords, because your music, like that of the ancients, will have no harmony and no counterpoint. It will be *monophonic* (one-voiced). Principally, the instruments will be used to accompany singing, playing the same melody as the voice, with here and there an additional flourish or trill.

2.

This brings us to the second experiment, the reconstruction of a temple psalm. The psalms were originally sung as part of the order of sacrifice by the professional temple musicians, who also played the accompanying instruments. These musicians, members of the tribe of Levi, were called Levites. They inherited their positions in the Temple and at the same time inherited the secrets of making music, playing and caring for their instruments—secrets which they guarded jealously. The words of their songs—at least a good many of them—were collected in ancient times and have come down to us today in the *Book of Psalms*. Some of the psalms have headings which tell us they were to be sung to certain popular tunes of the day, *To the Lilies of the Sharon, To the Morning Star* and others. Others carry headings like *To the Instrument of Ten Strings* or *For the Conqueror*. Some headings are descriptive: *A Meditative Song* or *A Rapturous Song*. Many psalms are entitled in Hebrew *Shir ha-Ma-alot*, usually translated as *A Song of Ascents*. These were probably pilgrim songs.

As we have already noted, the melodies are lost. What is more, the original melodies referred to in the psalm headings were probably lost in the period between the destruction of the First Temple (in 586 B.C.E.) and the building of the Second Temple—the period when the Jews were living in exile in Babylonia. It was in this Second Temple that the type of singing called psalmody was initiated. The very shape of the poems as they appear in the Bible must have produced the form of the ancient psalmody. The poems have no meter; that is, one cannot beat time to them or count the number of syllables. They have no rhyme either. But they do have their own kind of rhythm. This is obvious in the original Hebrew of the psalms. But it is also apparent in the English translation. Let us take, for example, the 92nd psalm, the psalm for the Sabbath day, which was used for the experiment to be described in this chapter. First, we have as the opening line the title: *A Psalm, A Song. For the Sabbath Day*. Then the poem begins:

2. It is a good thing to give thanks unto the Lord
   And to sing praises unto Thy Name, O Most High.
3. To declare Thy lovingkindness in the morning
   And Thy faithfulness in the night seasons
4. With an instrument of ten strings and with the psaltery;
   With a solemn sound upon the harp.

If we read those verses aloud, we begin to hear how each half-verse divides itself into three parts: "It is a good thing / to give thanks / unto the Lord / And to sing praises / unto Thy name, / O Most High." The second half of each verse seems to repeat the idea stated in the first half in different words. This form is called "parallelism" . . . the ideas and rhythms in the two lines are parallel. Presumably, if the verses were

sung, the tunes, too, would tend to be parallel. Also, the form suggests that the singing was either responsorial or antiphonal. Responsorial singing means the alternating of lines between a leader and a choir. Antiphonal singing is the alternating of lines between two choirs.

Our student experimenters chose to use the antiphonal style of singing. The boys formed the first choir and the girls the second. Several of the participants held autoharps. They were not used at first. The group read the first three verses quoted above antiphonally. Then they chose a string of the autoharp, a tone which would be comfortable for their voices, the D above middle C. Using this one note, they intoned the three verses antiphonally, and the autoharpists played along. This proved to be very monotonous (literally, on one tone). To help vary it, they tried to find some method which would indicate the end of a full verse. The girls sang their half-verse. An autoharpist then suggested that they change the last note, shifting up two tones of the scale to F. The verse now sounded like this, when sung from the beginning:

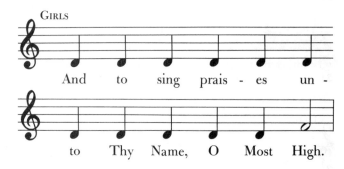

At this point, a boy proposed that they find some way of indicating the end of the half-verse—the end of the boys' share of the antiphonal singing. His idea was to move up one tone, from D to E, with this result:

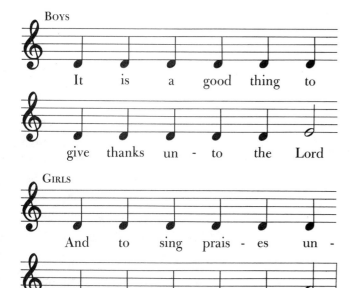

This scheme was applied for the full three verses. The effect was still uninteresting. To vary it still more, the group decided to move away from **D** (now referred to as the "reciting tone"), at an agreed-upon point in the middle of the half-verse. They chose the important word "thanks" in the first half of Verse 2 to move up to **F**, and in the second half-verse the word singled out for emphasis was "name." A boy sang out "name" on the tone **G**, and it was matched by the string on the autoharps. Now Verse 2 sounded like this:

One more variation seemed to be needed. Instead of starting the verse on the reciting tone (**D**), they would lead up or down to it and reach the **D** only at the first accented word, "thing." The group tested a variety of approaches, preferring this one:

Now the group felt they were ready to sing through the psalm. They found that they could proceed without any difficulty to find the first accented word and also the important word in each half-verse and to accompany themselves on the autoharps. But when they reached Verse 8 of Psalm 92, they hit a snag. Suddenly the Psalmist broke his two-part verse pattern and without warning brought in a verse using *three* parts:

When the wicked spring up as the grass,
And when all the workers of iniquity do flourish;
It is that they may be destroyed for ever.

The method they used to solve this problem will be easy to see in the notation of the entire psalm in **Ex. 1.** Before we get to that, however, we should notice one more device which the group invented to give a finishing touch to their psalmody. At the very last verse—Verse 16 of Psalm 92—on the final word "unrighteousness" they agreed to put in a decorative flourish, to produce an effect of actual finality. They extended the accented syllable, "right," over a little melody of five tones before settling back to the reciting tone, like this:

Ex. 1 is the complete Psalm 92 as composed and performed by the group. (Because the psalm is so long, Verses 9 to 12 have been omitted.) The autoharps were played throughout, following the voice parts.

Any group can compose its own psalmody. (Of course, an individual can do the same, except that the choral effect will be missing.) Choose any psalm that appeals to you. Psalm 30, entitled *A Psalm; a Song at the Dedication of the House of David,* is particularly appropriate for *Hanukah,* when we celebrate the rededication of the Temple after the Maccabean victory. Use any tone from D to G as your reciting tone and, when you approach or leave the reciting tone, move no more than four tones away in either direction. An autoharp is not essential; even the piano will be helpful, although it will not have the sound of the "stringed instruments." Your own homemade instruments in any tuning will supply a feeling of authenticity. You increase the interest and color when you add introductory clashes of the cymbals or fanfares of trumpets. Take especial notice, if the mysterious word *selah* should occur in the psalm of your choice. Nobody knows exactly what that word means, and it is never translated from the Hebrew. One theory about it is that it was a signal to the cymbal players. Take advantage of the theory, and punctuate your psalmody with a good, vibrant clash!

Ex. 1

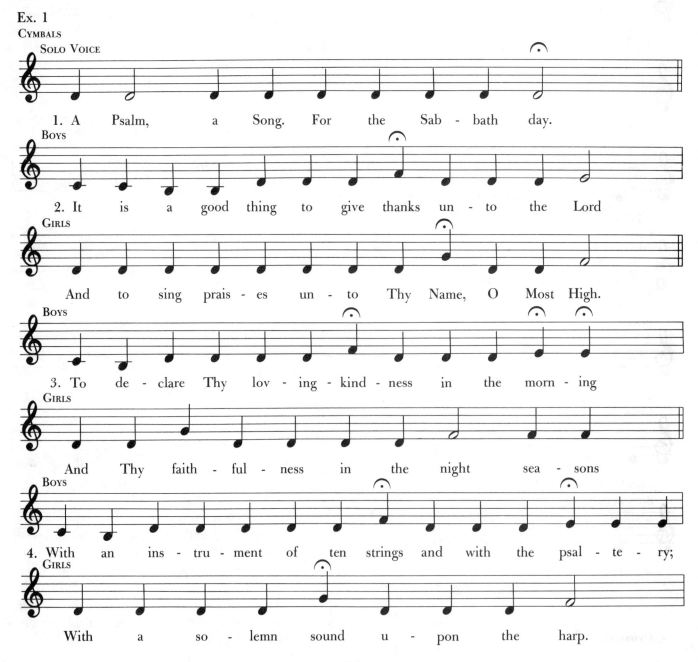

1. A Psalm, a Song. For the Sab - bath day.

2. It is a good thing to give thanks un - to the Lord

And to sing prais - es un - to Thy Name, O Most High.

3. To de - clare Thy lov - ing - kind - ness in the morn - ing

And Thy faith - ful - ness in the night sea - sons

4. With an ins - tru - ment of ten strings and with the psal - te - ry;

With a so - lemn sound u - pon the harp.

Boys

5. For Thou, Lord, hast made me glad through Thy work;

Girls

I will ex - ult in the works of Thy hand.

Boys

6. How great are Thy works, O Lord

Girls

Thy thoughts are ve - ry deep.

Boys

7. A brut - ish man know - eth not

Girls

Neith - er doth a fool un - der - stand this;

Boys

8. When the wick - ed spring up as the grass

Girls

And when all the work - ers of in - i - qui - ty do flour - ish

Boys & Girls

It is that they might be de - stroyed for - e - ver

Cymbals

15

13. The right - eous shall flour - ish like the palm - tree;

He shall grow like the ce - dars in Le - ba - non

14. Plant - ed in the house of the Lord

They shall flour - ish in the courts of our God.

15. They shall still bring forth fruit in old age;

They shall be full of sap and rich - ness,

16. To de - clare that the Lord is up - right

My Rock, in whom there is no un - righ - teous - ness.

CYMBALS

Four
THE OLDEST
SURVIVORS

THE METHOD of composing psalmody described in Chapter Three produces melodies which must be at least reminiscent of the ancient melodies. We can demonstrate this by comparing them with some shreds of melody, still being sung today, which might very well be remnants of temple song.

Even before the Second Temple was finally destroyed in the year 70 C.E., Jews had begun to build a new type of house of worship. These were Jews who lived in distant corners of the land, or in such far-off countries as Egypt and Babylonia, and who found it difficult to make frequent pilgrimages to the Temple in Jerusalem. They built local houses of gathering where they did not perform the sacrifices but took

over the benedictions, prayers and psalmody of the Temple. The Hebrew name for one of these houses was *Bet ha-Knesset*. Our English term, "synagogue," comes from the Greek form of the word, "synagoge," meaning "assembly." There was one such synagogue right within the very walls of the temple compound itself. It was called the "Hall of Stones." Representatives of this Hall, and of other synagogues throughout the dispersed communities, were sent to stand by and witness the temple service. These "standing men" were expected to learn the essentials of the service and take them back to their own communities.‡

This was no simple task. There were no printed books in those days to carry home and study. If the words of some of the service had been written down at all, on parchment or papyrus, the "standing men" would have had to copy them out carefully. The greater likelihood is that they memorized both words and music. Returning home, they became leaders of their congregations and were honored with the title of *"shaliah tzibur"* or "representative of the community." Their knowledge was handed down, again, by word of mouth, to younger scholars or apprentices.

What was never transmitted was the temple practice of using musical instruments. The orchestra had been one of the great glories of the Temple. With the final destruction of the Temple, the instruments were stilled. The Levites kept the secrets of their order to the very end, and the art of making and playing the *nevel* and *kinnor,* the trumpets and the instruments of ten strings disappeared with the Temple. Only the old signal horn, the *shofar,* survived. In later centuries, the absence of instrumental music was accounted for, by the rabbis and by the folk, as a sign of mourning for the Temple and the lost land of Israel. But no mourning was able to still song itself. It lived on in the memories of leaders who tried to pass it on as faithfully and as accurately as they could.

From Psalm 92, handwritten in an old Italian Bible

מִזְמוֹר שִׁיר לְיוֹם הַשַּׁבָּת׃
טוֹב לְהֹדוֹת לַיְיָ
וּלְזַמֵּר לְשִׁמְךָ עֶלְיוֹן׃ לְהַגִּיד בַּבֹּקֶר
חַסְדֶּךָ וֶאֱמוּנָתְךָ בַּלֵּילוֹת׃ עֲלֵי עָשׂוֹר
וַעֲלֵי נָבֶל עֲלֵי הִגָּיוֹן בְּכִנּוֹר׃ כִּי
שִׂמַּחְתַּנִי יְיָ בְּפָעֳלֶךָ בְּמַעֲשֵׂי יָדֶיךָ
אֲרַנֵּן׃ מַה גָּדְלוּ מַעֲשֶׂיךָ יְיָ מְאֹד
עָמְקוּ מַחְשְׁבֹתֶיךָ׃ אִישׁ בַּעַר לֹא יֵדַע
וּכְסִיל לֹא יָבִין אֶת זֹאת׃ בִּפְרֹחַ
רְשָׁעִים כְּמוֹ עֵשֶׂב וַיָּצִיצוּ כָּל פֹּעֲלֵי אָוֶן
לְהִשָּׁמְדָם עֲדֵי עַד׃ וְאַתָּה מָרוֹם
לְעֹלָם יְיָ׃ כִּי הִנֵּה אֹיְבֶיךָ יְיָ כִּי הִנֵּה
אֹיְבֶיךָ יֹאבֵדוּ יִתְפָּרְדוּ כָּל פֹּעֲלֵי אָוֶן׃
וַתָּרֶם כִּרְאֵים קַרְנִי בַּלֹּתִי בְּשֶׁמֶן רַעֲנָן׃
וַתַּבֵּט עֵינִי בְּשׁוּרָי בַּקָּמִים עָלַי מְרֵעִים
תִּשְׁמַעְנָה אָזְנָי׃ צַדִּיק כַּתָּמָר
יִפְרָח כְּאֶרֶז בַּלְּבָנוֹן יִשְׂגֶּא׃ שְׁתוּלִים

17

Ruins of one of the oldest synagogues at Capernaum in the Galilee

In some parts of the world where the Jewish communities were never exposed to the great development of Western music, in places like Yemen, as we have seen, or in Bokhara, high in the mountains of western Asia, the chant survived in its ancient form without—as far as we know—significant change. Thus we can consider the melodies used by the Jews in such remote settlements to be the oldest survivors of song once heard in the temple.

Ex. 2 is the way the Yemenites still chant Psalm 92 in the original Hebrew. This was recorded on old wax records early in this century by Abraham Zevi Idelsohn, first of the scholars to explore the history of the music of the Jews.‡ Compare this ancient chant with our modern version in Chapter Three.

There is yet another source for acquiring some idea of the sound of the old psalmody. The first Christian churches were Jewish houses of assembly—that is, synagogues—in the land of Palestine. Much of the old synagogue ritual was taken over into the church service. The psalmody, in particular, was preserved and carried over to Europe, where it became an important part of the service in the Church of Rome. Listen to a few verses of the Roman psalmody for the same Psalm 92. The Latin translation is used, but that translation, too, keeps the rhythm of the words; and the form of the music, you will find, is very similar to the psalmody of the Yemenites and to the modern example given in Chapter Three—and also to the one you may attempt to compose. (Ex. 3)

Psalm 92: 1-9

Miz - mor shir le-yom ha - shab - bat; Tov le - ho - dot la - a - do - nai ul' - za -

mer le - shim - kha e - le-yon; le - ha - gid ba - bo - ker has - de - kha ve - e -

mu - na - te - kha ba - le - y - lot; a - ley a - sor va - a - ley na - vel a - ley

hi - ga-yon be - khin - nor: ki si - mah - ta - ni a - do-nai be - fo - o - le - kha

be - ma - a sey ya - de-kha a - ra-nen; mah go - de - lu ma - a - se-kha a - do -

nai me - od o - ma - ku mah-she - vo - te - kha: Ish ba - ar lo ye -

da u - h'sil lo ya - vin et zot; bif - ro - ah re - sha-im ke - mo e -

sev va - ya - tzi - tzu kol po - a - ley a - ven

le - hi - sha - me - dam a - dey ad: va - a - tah ma-rom le - o - lam a - do - nai.

Bo - num est con - fi - ta - re Do - mi - no

Et psal - le - re no - mi - ni tu - o, al - tis - si - me.

Ad an - nun - ti - an - dum ma - ne mi - se - ri - cor - di - am tu - am

et ve - ri - ta - tem tu - am per noe - tem

In de - ca - chor - do, psal - te - ri - o

Cum can - ti - co in ci - tha - ra

Hebrew psalmody in Western Europe was changed over the centuries. The reciting tone began to give way to a more tuneful kind of chanting, but the general form remained the same: uniform endings for the half-verse and the whole verse; special endings in three-part verses; and *"melisma"* (a syllable stretched out over several tones) at the very end. Ex. 4 is a portion of the chant for Psalm 92 as it is sung in Spanish and Portuguese synagogues.

In the traditional Ashkenazic synagogue, psalmody was somewhat neglected. Psalm 92 would be chanted on Friday evening in the service called "Receiving the Sabbath" (*Kabbalat Shabbat*) according to the prayer mode for that service. We shall learn more about prayer modes in Chapter Seven. Meanwhile, Ex. 5 is a sample of how Psalm 92 would be chanted in the Ashkenazic synagogue at that particular service.

The contemporary composer, in setting the psalms to music for a synagogue service, may at times utilize the principles of psalmody, much as did the amateurs of Chapter Three. The first principle is that of alternating voices, using either the responsorial form (that

Psalm 92: 1-5

Miz-mor shir le-yom ha-shab-bat: Tov le-ho-dot la-a-do-nai

u-le-za-mer le-shim-kha el-yon. Le-ha-gid ba-bo ker has-de-kha

ve-e-mu-na-te-kha ba-ley - lot: A-ley a-sor_____ va-a-

ley_____ na - vel a-ley_____ hi-ga-yon

ba-kin - nor: ki si-mah-ta-ni a-do-nai be-fo-o-

le - kha, be-ma-a-sey ya-de-kha a-ra-nen

21

Psalm 92

Tov le - ho - dot la' - do - nai u - le - za - mer le - shim - kha el - yon

Le - ha - gid ba - bo - ker has - de - kha Ve - e - mu - nat - kha ba - ley - lot

Ish ba - ar lo ye - da, u - khe - sil lo ya - vin et zot

Bif - ro - ah re - sha - im ke - mo e - sev ve - ya - tzi - tzu kol po - a - ley

a - ven le - hi - shom - dam a - dey ad ve - a - tah ma - rom

le - o - lam a - do - nai.

Thirteenth-century synagogue of Toledo, now used as a church

is, a single voice and a choir) or the antiphonal form (two choirs). The responsorial form is used more frequently because most synagogues have a single choir and one cantor. The second principle is that of using a reciting tone and also of making the second part of each verse run parallel to the first. The composer may relieve the monotony of a single reciting tone by introducing several different reciting tones, varying them from section to section, or verse to verse, or even within one verse. He can also add interest by abandoning the reciting tone briefly and substituting instead a more melodic passage at certain points during the course of the psalm, or in the very last verse.

A good example of this approach to composing psalm settings may be found in the version of Psalm 96 in the *Friday Evening Service* by the American composer, Yehudi Wyner.‡ In his setting, the chorus sings in unison except in two short passages, when the alto section has its own part. The new alto part produces an archaic sound. The organ plays a role, too: at some points, it utters punctuating chords; at other points, it sings along with the voices; and just once, for exactly one measure, it swerves off into a rapid *fortissimo*.

Wyner's highly irregular rhythms generate great excitement. He uses no time signature. The accents of the music are determined entirely by the accentuation of the Hebrew text. The total effect is fresh and joyous. His composition has been published, and any group who is interested may sing it. It is particularly appropriate for young, vigorous voices.

Five
SING
HALLELUYAH!

Ex. 6   *Halleluyah!*   ROUND

Hal - le - lu - yah,   Hal - le - lu - yah,

Hal - le - lu - yah,   Hal - le - lu - yah!

THIS IS an easy round to be sung in two parts. Sing it several times, starting very softly, building up a *crescendo* and then dropping in a *diminuendo* to a soft finish. The Hebrew word *"Halleluyah"* is a musical sound in itself and always has a joyous lift. It combines two words, *"Hallelu"* (praise ye) and *"Yah"* (the Lord), and occurs frequently in the psalms. In any translation of the Bible, whatever the language, the word is left in its original Hebrew. Sometimes the opening H is dropped, as in Latin, and the word becomes *"Alleluia."*

Halleluyah occurs in the texts of a great variety of music over the centuries. The familiar *Michael, Row the Boat Ashore, Halleluyah* is only one of the many spirituals in which the word figures. The great marching song of American Civil War days, *Battle Hymn of the Republic,* has as its powerful refrain, "Glory, glory, Halleluyah!" There are even popular songs which feature the word *Halleluyah!* In Palestine of the twenties and thirties, before the State of Israel was established, the Jewish settlements celebrated the harvest of first fruits, *Shavuot,* and with it revived the *Halleluyah.* One of the happiest of the pilgrimage songs composed for the occasion has a short verse which calls out, "Arise, let us go up to the mountain of the Lord our God!" and then a refrain of Halleluyahs.‡

Great composers of the Western world in every age have been fascinated by that word, *Halleluyah*. Listen to the famous *Halleluyah Chorus* from Handel's *Messiah*. Hear how the word is passed from voice to voice, how it sounds in sharp staccato chords, sometimes interrupting the flow of the text, sometimes continuing simultaneously with the text, insistent and brilliant. Listen also to the second movement of Mozart's motet for solo voice, *Exsultate, Jubilate*. Here the soprano sings only the one word *Alleluia* over and over and over again in what seems like an unending outpouring of joy.‡

The word first took on importance, scholars believe, in those very first synagogues where, as our last chapter told, the practice of psalmody had been carried over from the Temple. There were no professional choirs to chant the psalms in the synagogues—only the leader, the *shaliah tzibur*, and the congregation. The plain people were unable to remember the verses of the psalms and, of course, those were the days before printed books. The leader would sometimes chant a verse and the people would repeat it after him. Even that was not too easy, for the psalms were in Hebrew, and Hebrew was not the spoken language of the Jews. Their "vernacular" was Aramaic. Some psalms carried their own refrain, *"Ki le-olam hasdo"* (His lovingkindness endures forever), after every verse. This the people would be able to sing. Whenever a psalm began—as many of them did—with *Halleluyah*, the people would sing the word after every verse. This last form can still be heard among Yemenite Jews, as the following section of a *Hallel* psalm reveals.‡

The *Halleluyah* response of the synagogue was taken over by the early Church, and the *Alleluias*—they were sung in the Latin form, of course—became very important in Christian religious services. Sometimes they were stretched out into great long melodies, with many notes for each syllable. (The technical term for this kind of singing is "melismatic.") As the years passed, the *Alleluias* became so protracted and complex that the monks, who were supposed to sing them, couldn't remember them. As an aid to their memories, their leaders wrote new words to the *Alleluia* tunes. Then they added new voices to sing new melodies

above the *Alleluia* tunes, and in this way a whole new kind of music arose among the Christians of Europe.

The *Halleluyah* of the Yemenite psalmody in Ex. 7 is only mildly melismatic. Without being a student of musical composition, you can still improvise original *Halleluyahs*, some strictly syllabic, some melismatic, just as our ancestors did. Beat out the rhythm of the word on a large drum, slowly. Beat it out on a tambourine, fast. Try it out on your *mena-anim* or a pair of maracas, or any other percussion instrument at hand, even if it is only your pencil tapping on a desk. Remember that, in Hebrew, the accent must fall on the *last* syllable. Make a score for playing *Halleluyah* rhythms.

Now stretch the word out in a melody. Give each syllable several tones, prolonging each separate one: *Ha-----le-----lu-----yah!* The last syllable should be a longer *melisma* than the others. You can improvise this tune by singing or, if you'd prefer, by playing on any tuned instrument. If you have trouble remembering your improvisation, perhaps a tape recorder will help. Alternate your melismatic melodic *Halleluyahs* with your percussion *Halleluyahs*.

For a more ambitious project, try this: Select a *Halleluyah* psalm, for instance, Psalm 150, last in the collection in the Bible, and make up a psalmody. Introduce it with one of your melodic *Halleluyahs*. Repeat the *Halleluyah* at the end of each verse. Substitute percussion *Halleluyahs* at the end of some verses. Psalm 150 itself is packed with ideas. "Praise Him with *nevel* (harp) and *kinnor* (lyre)," Verse 3 declares, and, after that verse, play *Halleluyah* on your stringed instruments as you sing it. "Praise Him with stringed instruments and the *ugav* (oboe)," Verse 4 says. Combine strings and recorder. For *tziltzeley shama*, the "loud-sounding cymbals" in Verse 5, strike one cymbal with a stick; for the *tziltzeley teruah*, or "clanging cymbals," clash two cymbals together. "Praise Him with the blast of the horn," Verse 3 opens, and you can sound your *Halleluyah* rhythm on a trumpet. When you put this all together, you should have a very exciting composition.

Many composers have written settings for Psalm 150. The best-known setting of the Hebrew words was composed by the nineteenth-century composer, Louis Lewandowski, whose name we shall meet in later chapters of this book. Lewandowski was a great

Psalm 118: 13, 14, 22–24

Halleluyah

Yemenite Chant

Hal - le - lu - yah! Da - ho da - hi - ta - ni lin - pol va' do - nai a - za -

ra - ni hal - le - yu - yah! O - zi ve - zim - rat yah vay' hi

li li - shu - ah, Hal - le - lu - yah! E - ven ma - a - su ha -

bo - nim ha - ye - tah le - rosh pi - nah, Hal - le - lu - yah!

Me - et a - do - nai he - ye - tah zot, hi nif - lat be - e - ne - nu,

Hal - le - lu - yah! Zeh ha - yom a - sah a - do - nai

na - gi - lah ve - nis - me - hah vo, Ha - le - lu - yah!

admirer of his contemporary, Felix Mendelssohn, and his *Halleluyah,* Psalm 150, is in the style of the Mendelssohn oratorios.‡ The composer César Franck wrote a setting for a French version. The composer who perhaps comes closest to the spirit of the ancient psalm is the modern Igor Stravinsky, whose Latin setting comprises the third movement of his *Symphony of Psalms,* a great composition for orchestra and chorus, full of strong, clashing dissonances. The third movement starts with the word *Halleluyah* sung slowly (not melismatically)—just one great chord to each syllable. After that, each verse has its own interpretation, beginning with the word *"Laudate"* (Latin for Praise ye) *"eum"* (Him). Much of the music is fierce and strong. Only at Verse 4, "Praise Him with timbrel and dance," do we hear a brief passage of gentle lyric singing. If you can hear a performance or a recording of Stravinsky's work, notice that contrasting passage.‡

Six
MUSICAL
HIEROGLYPHICS

AARON COPLAND, the gifted contemporary composer, has often based his music on the folklore and folk music of America. His familiar *Rodeo, Appalachian Spring* and *A Lincoln Portrait* are uniquely American works expressing the country's spirit. Less familiar, perhaps, but no less American is his composition called *In the Beginning*.‡ He wrote it for *a cappella* chorus—that is, for voices without instrumental accompaniment—and he took his words straight from the opening of the *Book of Genesis*. To Copland the Bible text was as much a part of America's heritage and folklore as the legends about Lincoln, the tales of cowboys and the customs of the Shakers. And, indeed, he was right, for the Bible has been an enormous influence in shaping America's character since the first Pilgrim settlement.

Copland builds his composition verse by verse on the creation story told in Chapter 1 and the beginning of Chapter 2 in *Genesis*. He gives each day its own special character, portraying musically the creation step by step. The piece ends with a great paean to the appearance of man, the climax of the creation. But, before reaching that climax, Copland weaves in the beat of jazz—and you can hear it without the aid of any drum or bull-fiddle behind the voices. He also introduces fleeting echoes of phrases from Negro folk songs (for example, "the anklebone connected to the shinbone"). When the chorus reaches the end of Chapter 1—"And it was evening and it was morning, the sixth day"—the tempo slackens. The work of creation is finished, and now it is time for rest. The music quiets down, the Sabbath mood takes over. This passage is so expressive of the Jewish idea of the Sabbath that it could almost be used as a synagogue song.

The words in this passage opening Chapter 2 of *Genesis* are, of course, known to any Jew who has observed the Sabbath ritual: "And the heaven and the earth were finished . . ." They are sung in the synagogue and in many homes on Friday evening, just before the *kiddush* or sanctification ceremony. The traditional melody sung in Ashkenazic congregations has been preserved for us in writing by Louis Lewandowski who arranged it with accompaniment. (Ex. 8)

Now if you were in the synagogue on a certain Sabbath morning—the first Sabbath following the fall festivals of *Sukot* and *Simhat Torah*—you would hear a different tune for this passage from Chapter 2 of *Genesis*. The annual cycle of Torah readings in the synagogue starts on that Sabbath, and the story of creation is chanted to the congregation from the Torah scroll. The reader has learned the chant—or cantillation—from a strange-looking set of signs, a sort of musical hieroglyphics called "accents" or, in Hebrew, *ta-amey neginah*.

These accents do not appear in the Torah scroll itself, and only a person experienced in scroll-reading can unroll it to the correct place and point to the location of a particular passage. Even very familiar sections are difficult for the novice to find because

The story of creation, in the Torah scroll

Va-yekhulu

L. LEWANDOWSKI

i mi - kol m'lakh - to a - sher a - sah. Vay' - va - rekh e - lo -

him et yom ha - sh'vi - i vay' - ka - desh o - to, ki vo sha -

vat mi - kol m'lakh - to a - sher ba - ra e - lo - him la - a - sot.

there are no chapter or verse numbers or punctuation of any kind in the sacred scroll. In fact there are no vowels, only consonants.

Verse 1 of Chapter 2 in *Genesis* appears this way:

וכלו השמים והארץ וכל צבאם

The English equivalent of this verse would be: *"Nd th hvn nd th rth wr fnshd, nd ll th hst f thm."*

Now turn to a prayer book, in which the same passage is quoted as part of the worship service. It will look like this:

וַיְכֻלּוּ הַשָּׁמַיִם וְהָאָרֶץ וְכָל צְבָאָם

The dots and dashes are the *vowel signs*. In any printed Hebrew Bible, the verse appears as:

וַיְכֻלּוּ הַשָּׁמַיִם וְהָאָרֶץ וְכָל צְבָאָם

These accents came into usage beginning about the year 600 C.E. when the Masoretes, the copyists of the Bible, started to insert them into the unmarked text primarily as a punctuation and grammatical device. They showed readers where to pause and where to come to a full stop, and they marked off groups of related words into phrases. But, long before 600 C.E., the custom of chanting the Bible text in the synagogue had been firmly established. The order of Bible readings had also been established.* For centuries, the chants had been taught by rote. They consisted of little bits of melody arranged to suit the natural pauses, stops and word-phrasings. When the accents were attached to these bits of melody, they served two purposes: they were punctuation marks and they were also "pictures" of distinct tone-groups. Thus, musical notation was at a stage of development which language notation had outgrown centuries before, a stage where a sign symbolized an idea.

Each accent bore a name. The traditional way of learning how to chant a particular passage was, first, to sing the names of the accent and, second, to apply the *tunes* of the accents to the words of the text. Here is a step-by-step illustration of how one would learn to chant *Genesis 2: 1*, which begins with the Hebrew word *"va-yekhulu"*:

*Selections from the *Torah*—that is, from the *Five Books of Moses* or the *Pentateuch*—and from the *Prophets* are read out in the synagogue on every Sabbath and Jewish festival. Certain books from the *Writings* section of the Bible are read on fixed occasions—e.g., *Song of Songs* on *Pesah*, *Esther* on *Purim*, *Lamentations* on the Ninth of *Av*, *Ruth* on *Shavuot* and *Ecclesiastes* on *Sukot*.

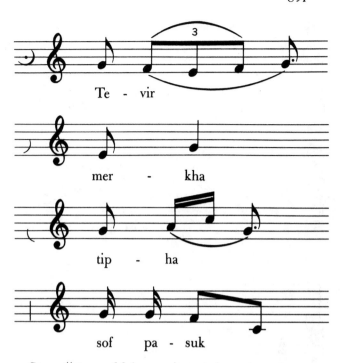

Te - vir

mer - kha

tip - ha

sof pa - suk

Step #1 would be to sing each name:

Te - vir   mer - kha

tip - ha   sof pa - suk

Step #2 drops the names of the accents and in their place substitutes:

Ex. 9

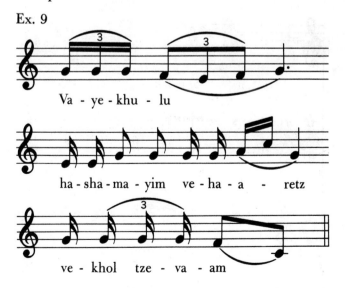

Va - ye - khu - lu

ha - sha - ma - yim ve - ha - a - retz

ve - khol tze - va - am

As it happens, this Verse 1 of *Genesis 2* is not completely typical. It is one of the few verses in the Bible which has only one part. If we continue in the text to Verse 2, we will see that it consists of two sections, with a half-pause in the middle. (The two sections are not perfectly balanced like those of the psalm verses. Neither do they have parallelism of idea.) Here, then, is a table of the accents in Verse 2:

Mah - pakh

pash - ta

tip - ha

mu - hah

et - nah - ta

pash - ta

za - kef   ka - tan

mu - nah   (like tip-ha)

sof - pa - suk

Omitting step #1, we drop the accents and proceed to step #2 to sing the Hebrew words of the verse as follows:

Ex. 9a

Va - ye - khal   e - lo - him

ba - yom   ha - sh'vi - i

me - lakh - to   a - sher

a - sah   va - yish - bot

ba - yom   ha - sh'vi - i

mi - kol me - lakh - to

a - sher a - sah

We could continue with Verse 3 in precisely the same way. However—and it is here that the experienced *ba-al keriyah*, or Torah cantillator, becomes indispensable—the third verse is the concluding verse of a

32

parashah; that is, the small portion of the total reading for which a congregant has been called up to the Torah. The *sof pasuk* and its preceding *merkha* have a different musical interpretation, with a more definitely final sound:

tip - ha   sof pa - suk

Here then is Verse 3:

Ex. 9b

Va - ye - va - rekh e - lo - him

et yom ha - sh'vi - i

va - ye - ka - desh o -

to, ki vo sha - vat

mi - kol me - lakh - to

a - sher ba - ra e - lo

him la - a - sot.

Earliest known notation of the Torah chant‡

This system of notation is obviously cumbersome, imprecise and difficult to transmit. Compared to modern notation, it is like ancient hieroglyphics in relation to the alphabet. Each accent was a symbol of a tone-group or musical idea. Individual tones had no symbols as they do today, in the form of notes placed carefully on a staff. One had to learn each separate tone-group by ear and remember it and teach it *exactly*. This turned out to be physically impossible, and it is one reason why there is such a variety of chants for the same biblical passage. A simple experiment will dramatize how this variety came about. Play the game of telegraph, using a little tune of four or five tones. The first player sings the tune softly into the ear of his neighbor, who repeats it in turn to his neighbor, and so on around the room. By the time the last player has heard and sung it, the little tune will have undergone considerable change. And when this can happen inside one room in the space of a few minutes, consider what could—and actually did—happen over the centuries of Jewish history. Even within a given locality, there could be changes in the chants over the years. And when the little chant tunes —or *motives*—had to travel about in the world in the wanderings, settlements and forced migrations of the Jewish people over 2,000 years, they underwent many transformations. The Jews living in Central and Eastern Europe evolved their distinctive Ashkenazic chants. The Jews of Yemen and of Oriental lands produced their own chant varieties, and the Jews of Spain developed their Sephardic chants which, after the expulsion of 1492, were scattered throughout the world. Ex. 10 is an example of the Spanish and Portuguese chant for the *Va-yekhulu* passage.

Va - ye - khu - lu ha - sha - ma - yim ve - ha - a - retz ve -

khol tze - va - am, va - ye - khal e - lo - him ba - yom

ha - she - vi - i me - lakh - to a - sher a - sah

va - yish bot ba - yom ha - she - vi - i mi - kol me - lakh -

to a - sher a - sah va - ye - va - rech e - lo - him

et yom ha - she - vi - i va - ye - ka - desh o - to,

ki vo sha - vat mi - kol me - lakh - to a - sher

ba - ra e - lo - him la - a - sot.

One of the interesting characteristics of Jewish cantillation is that each of the various sections of the Hebrew Bible has its own distinctive melody. In other words, the section called *Torah* (variously known as the *Pentateuch,* the *Five Books of Moses,* or the *Humash*) has its own cantillation; the second section, *Prophets* (consisting of all the books from *Joshua* through *Malakhi,* and known in Hebrew as *Ne-vi-im*), has its unique cantillation. In the third section, *Ketuvim* (*Writings* or *Hagiographa*), there are individual books, or scrolls or *megillot,* each of which, in turn, has its own melody.

Thus far, we have considered two examples—one Ashkenazic, the other Sephardic—of the cantillation of *Genesis 2: 1–3,* which, of course, is in the Torah section of the Hebrew Bible. Here is an example of the cantillation of a verse in the prophetic section. It is a verse (*Isaiah 43: 5*) out of the prophetic portion (*Haftarah*) which is read on the same *Shabbat Bereshit* when the *Genesis* passage is read. The prophet is comforting his people and says, in the name of God: "Fear not, for I am with thee; I will bring thy seed from the east, and gather thee from the west." In the Hebrew Bible it looks like this:

אַל־תִּירָא כִּי־אִתְּךָ אָנִי מִמִּזְרָח אָבִיא זַרְעֶךָ וּמִמַּעֲרָב אֲקַבְּצֶךָּ:

The names of the accents applied to that verse are sung as follows:

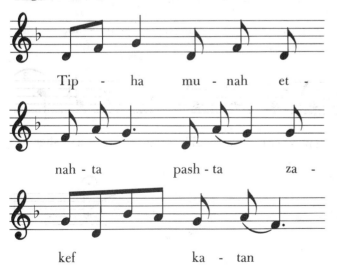

Tip - ha mu - nah et - nah - ta pash - ta za - kef ka - tan

tip - ha sof pa - suk

Now, applying the tune to the text, we have the following:

Ex. 11

Al ti - ra ki it' - kha

a - ni mi - miz - rah a -

vi zar' - e - kha

u - mi - ma - a - rav a - kab - tze - kha

There will be examples of other cantillations in subsequent chapters, examples from various portions of the Bible and from many different communities. All of them will share certain features: they will be in free rhythm, without bar lines; and every verse (with only one or two exceptions) will have a semi-cadence (a half-pause) and a full cadence (a complete stop). However, this chapter and those that follow will not equip the reader for the practice of cantillation. In order to master the practice, one needs to know the full roster of accents, many of which are not included in the illustrations provided here; one also must know how to adapt the motives to varying numbers of syllables and how to make smooth connections between one motive and another.‡

Even on the basis of the information in this chapter, however, you might want to try your hand at composing your own cantillations. You can use the traditional cantillations as a basis, if you wish. Take each motive, follow its directions—that is, its ups and downs—and exaggerate those ups and downs by using notes which are farther apart in pitch (technically, increasing the intervals between the notes). Following the roster of accents preceding Ex. 9a, this is a sample of that sort of exaggeration:

There is no need to use the traditional chant tunes, even as a basis for your own composition. Invent your own semi-cadence (*etnahta*) and full cadence (*sof pasuk*). Devise several pairs of motives, the first of each a "questioning" tune, the second an "answering" tune. Make up a leading tune, *tip-ha,* which will take you directly into your cadence tunes. Keep away from the usual major and minor modes. Try using some of the scales suggested in Chapter Three.

When you have your set of motives, select a favorite verse from the Bible and set it to your own cantillation. Sing it slowly. Now transpose the whole melody to a lower pitch. Sing it faster. Try experimenting with the sounds on different instruments, at different pitches and different tempos. Exaggerate your own cantillation the way that was suggested for the traditional cantillation. This type of experiment is being carried on by a number of young composers in Israel. Their works are not available in scores or in recordings at this writing. Perhaps, if you visit Israel and attend a concert of modern works, you will be able to hear this interesting kind of music for yourselves.

Seven
SONG OF
THE HAZAN

In his novel, *Son of the Lost Son,* Soma Morganstern gives this moving description of a learned Jew of Poland, sometime between the two world wars, as he started his day:

He stood still for a while at one of the four open windows against the green wall. It surprised him that after so warm a night there should be so much dew on the grass and on the branches of the trees. With a glance at the birch, whose delicate silver rose in the midst of all these beeches, he saw that it must have rained during the night. He began to say his prayers.

He wrapped himself in his yellow black-striped prayer shawl and softly murmured the opening words with ardent lips. His left arm came out of the sleeve of his silk caftan, with the swift movements at which a thousand days of prayer had rendered him adept. He pulled up his shirt sleeve as far as the shoulder, baring the arm for the leather straps of the phylactery which he removed from its velvet bag and kissed. Murmuring the blessing, he wrapped the phylactery around his arm and over his fingers in the prescribed manner. He then placed the second phylactery on his forehead, pulled the prayer shawl over his head and stood there, God's steed, harnessed for prayer.

Now he sang many songs to the Eternal, old and ancient songs; ancient, old and new melodies. The ancient were sad and mournful and solemn. They are the melodies of those prayers that are as rigorous for the weekday as they are for the Sabbath or for the highest festivals. The old were sprightly, bizarre, joyful. Such are mostly the melodies for those prayers that serve also the Sabbath day. Nor were the new really new. These are the prayers for every day, the garb for the ordinary working-day prayers. They are like the dress of the Jews of this sad Galician land. These clothes hang on restless, humbled, undernourished bodies in which there runs old, proud blood; they are cut according to the old-fashioned style of a distant land, with its colors and folds, pockets, patches and stains, yet they are so acclimatized to the Slav gloom of this landscape that they could not be imagined apart from it.

He sang the melodies as his people sings its songs. He did not catch at the songs by their note, he took hold of

them by the word. For the melodies are humble and modest like the people; but the words of the prayers, as a part of God, are great and tremendous. Many a melody seems blinded by the glory of the word. It gropes its way to the light but without attaining the sense. "And a redeemer shall come to Zion and to them that turn from transgression

The Chant, by Issachar Ryback (1897–1935)

37

in Jacob." The word rejoiced, but the melody lamented, just as much as the melody which sobbed, "O God, look upon our sunken glory among the nations and the abomination in which we are held as of utter defilement." Did the melody err? Or the man who prayed? "Exult in the Lord, O ye righteous; praise is seemly for the upright!" The word exults, the melody sobs. "For we are like ears of corn scattered in the wind, we are like sheep driven to the slaughter." On Sabbath days, on festivals, the same prayers may robe themselves in joyous garb of melody; on ordinary days these notes suit them better, notes of affliction and of mourning, or mourning and humiliation.

Though otherwise calm and gentle, Velvel prayed with the zealousness of those who burn themselves up in prayer, as the Hasidim pray. He prayed as he had learned to pray from his father, as a child, as a young lad. The voice of Judah Mohilevski who was long dead lived on in the prayers of his son. And whenever the worshipper, now in a solemn mood before his journey, was in danger of straying from the melody or even from the word, the voice of his father came to him and—as a man might rise in the darkness of the room to take hold of a newcomer by the hand as he enters the room—led the voice of his son in the right path. Spirit and body of the worshipper seemed to share equally in the fervor of his prayer. He paced up and down the room as though the words and the sentences stood in some secret relation to the number of his paces; as though these were precisely measured to fit the beat of the songs. A word came that was welcomed with a slight bow of the upper body, like a good friend who is allowed to pass with a cursory greeting. Another came before which the worshipper stood still and bowed ceremoniously with bent knees as before an invisible throne. Then came a song which he welcomed by dancing towards it like a jubilant victor. And one came and went from which he parted with mournful, painfully outspread arms, as from one dead. A melody brought a note that expired like the sigh of one dreaming. And another bore a note that broke from his breast like the wild cry of a Cossack on the steppe. Once he stopped still before the Ark of the Law, drew the hood of the prayer shawl over his face as though to shut himself away in that silence where God dwells, and after the passage was said he flung his arms up in the air and clapped his hands, like a child that has suddenly caught sight of a beautiful strange bird in the garden. For the Eighteen Benedictions he stood still against the east wall. He stood there within the magic circle of the three paces, motionless with rigid legs, in blissful devotion, as though a little bird had settled on his left arm where he wore the phylactery. Then his upper body shook wildly from right to left, from left to right, and he bowed like a swaying stalk before the wind, swept here and there like a leaf in the storm.

An hour passed. When Velvel at last emerged from the chapel into the hall that was now flooded with bright daylight, he looked fresher in body and spirit, as though he had just come out of an invigorating bath.*

Morganstern does not put the music of those prayers into his novel. But we can easily surmise what some of them sounded like, because Reb Velvel (fictional character though he is) is very much a real Jew who did not invent his tunes. He learned them from his father before him, or in the communal religious services which he would attend on occasions when a *minyan* or quorum of ten men was required. Some of the ancient tunes described by the author undoubtedly resembled the Ashkenazic chant in Ex. 12.

O Lord our God, make the words of the Torah pleasant in our mouths and in the mouths of Thy people, the house of Israel. May we, our children, and our children's children, know Thee, and study Thy Torah. Blessed art Thou, O Lord (blessed is He, and blessed His name) who dost teach the Torah to His people, Israel. (Amen)

Other of Reb Velvel's melodies may have echoed the folk songs of his Polish neighbors. Since he was a *Hasid* (and we shall learn more about the *Hasidim* in a later chapter), Reb Velvel perhaps added a few measures of his own improvisation. But basically the Ashkenazic chant was undoubtedly what he sang. Reb Velvel was not a rabbi or a cantor. He happened to be a fairly prosperous farmer. But he, or any one of his Jewish friends, would have been able to lead the prayers in a communal service not only on an ordinary weekday morning or afternoon or evening but also on the Sabbath and on festivals and the High Holy Days. He would know which chant to use for each occasion, and his fellow worshippers would know how to respond properly with the words, "Blessed be He and Blessed be His Name," or the final "Amen." In fact, every literate Jew knew how to *daven*. (Nobody knows exactly where this word comes from, but it is widely used by Ashkenazic Jews. It is the practice of chanting the prayers correctly.)

None of this was learned from music books. It was passed down from generation to generation, purely by imitation. Without consciously doing so, the pious Jew was able to follow certain musical guidelines

*From Soma Morganstern, *Son of the Lost Son*, translated by Joseph Leftwich and Peter Gross, Phila. Jewish Publication Society of America, 1946.

Ve-ha-arev Na

V'ha - a - rev - na a - do - nai e - lo - he - nu

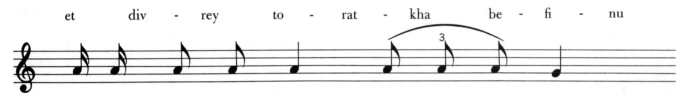

et div - rey to - rat - kha be - fi - nu

u - be - fi am - kha bet yis - ra - el

ve - nih - yeh a - nah - nu ve - tze - e - tza - e - nu

ve - tze - e - tza - ey am - kha bet yis - ra - el

ku - la - nu yo - de - ey she - me - kha ve - lom' - dey to - ra - te - kha

ba - rukh a - tah a - do - nai (Ba - rukh hu u - va - rukh she - mo)

ha - me - la - med to - rah le - a - mo yis - ra - el. (A - men)

which made it possible for all the Jews of a given community, or even of a different Ashkenazic community, to join in communal prayer.

These guidelines we call *modes*. Everyone has heard of the major and minor modes. They are more correctly called "scales." They are only two scales most commonly used in Western music, left over from a great variety of scales that were the basis for music in the Middle Ages. Some of these medieval scales can still be heard in folk song and, upon occasion, modern composers have revived them.

To understand what a mode is, we must first have an idea of what other scales are possible. Try this exercise at a piano: begin with D above middle C and play all the white notes in succession up to the next D. You will hear a scale different from either major or minor. Do the same on E, on F, on G and on A. The A scale will sound like the familiar "natural minor" scale. Omit a scale on B. For reasons too complicated to discuss here, the scale on B was never used. And, of course, if you play the scale from C to C you will have the familiar "major" scale. A scale is not necessarily a series of seven tones. There is, for example, as we have already seen, a five-tone scale which has been used by many peoples from earliest times.

Modern composers have used new scales. Try playing *every* note (black and white) from C to C. You will have a *twelve-tone* scale. The French composer, Claude Debussy, invented still another scale called the "whole-tone scale." It consists of a series of tones, each of which is one whole tone higher than its predecessor:

Now look back to the fragment of the morning prayer we quoted above (Ex. 12). The scale in which it is sung is the one on E with only white notes. Play the scale. If we play the tune, without repeating notes, it will sound like this:

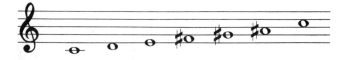

You will see that each phrase of the prayer has its own little melody or motive.

Let us experiment with another passage from the morning prayer, the Priestly Blessing (taken from the ancient temple ritual and found in the Bible, *Numbers 6: 24–26*):

The Lord bless thee and keep thee;
The Lord make His face to shine upon thee and be
    gracious unto thee;
The Lord lift up His countenance upon thee and give
    thee peace.

Take the motives of Reb Velvel's prayer and apply them in any order you wish to the Priestly Blessing, just making sure to begin with motive #1 and end with #7. It might work out like this:

Ex. 13

gra - cious un - to thee;

The Lord lift up His coun-te-nance

up - on thee and give thee peace.

You have now chanted the Priestly Blessing in the mode of the weekday morning service. If it were being chanted by a leader in a communal service, the congregation would respond to each part with the words, "May it be Thy will." They would sing it in the same mode, this way:

May it be Thy will

Here is the Priestly Blessing in the original Hebrew:

Ex. 14   TRADITIONAL

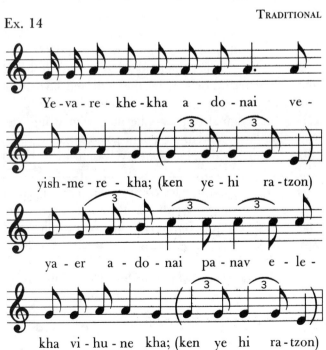

Ye-va-re-khe-kha a - do - nai ve -

yish-me-re-kha; (ken ye-hi ra-tzon)

ya - er a - do - nai pa - nav e - le -

kha vi-hu-ne kha; (ken ye hi ra-tzon)

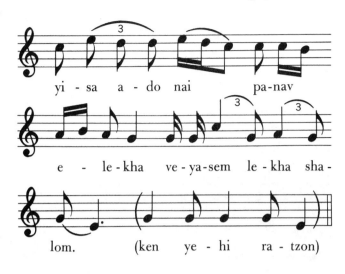

yi - sa a - do nai pa-nav

e - le-kha ve-ya-sem le-kha sha-

lom. (ken ye - hi ra - tzon)

The very same Priestly Blessing is sung on the morning of the Sabbath in a different mode. The scale of that mode is as follows:

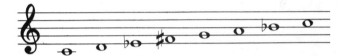

Here are some of the motives in that scale which make up the mode for the Sabbath morning service:

41

The Priestly Blessing sounds like this:

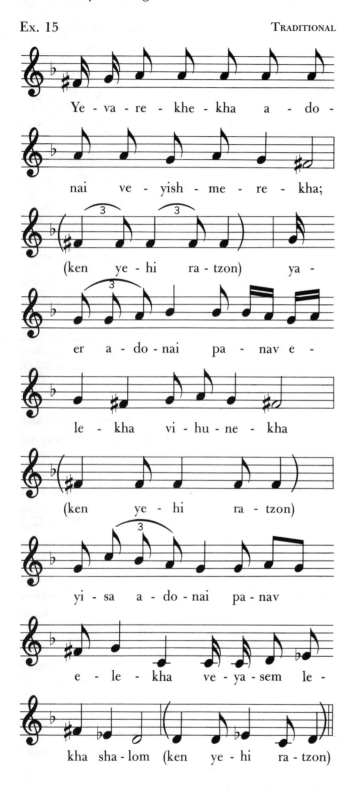

Ex. 15   TRADITIONAL

Ye - va - re - khe - kha   a - do -

nai   ve - yish - me - re - kha;

(ken   ye - hi   ra - tzon)   ya -

er   a - do - nai   pa - nav   e -

le - kha   vi - hu - ne - kha

(ken   ye - hi   ra - tzon)

yi - sa   a - do - nai   pa - nav

e - le - kha   ve - ya - sem   le -

kha sha - lom (ken   ye - hi   ra - tzon)

The Hebrew word for this type of prayer mode is

nusah (plural, *nus-ha-ot*). There are many other *nus-ha-ot*—that is, sets of motives in their particular scales—each for its special occasion. Two examples were presented earlier in this book in Chapters Four (Ex. 5) and Six (Ex. 8). The Ashkenazic version of Psalm 92 is in the mode of the service for welcoming the Sabbath, the *Kabbalat Shabbat* service. Its scale can be played on the piano from G to G on white notes. (In Chapter Four it is written in a lower key to make it easier to sing.) Here are some of the important tone groups of that mode:

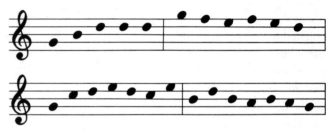

The second example is the melody notated by Lewandowski for *Va-yekhulu* (see Ex. 8). This mode is in the "natural minor" scale on A. but midway it moves to C major (we call it *modulating to* C major). Then it modulates back to A minor. This mode is used in the evening service of the Sabbath eve, the *Ma-ariv* service.

We shall be coming upon other *nus-ha-ot* in later chapters. In this book are presented only the simplest forms of the modes, the way they might be chanted (*davent*) by a learned traditional Ashkenazic Jew like Reb Velvel. However, you may have occasion to hear them sung with many additional trills and turns. You must understand that the modes have been preserved and elaborated upon not by the educated laymen of the community but by what in our day would be called professional cantors—the men who would devote their time and their talent to synagogue song; those men who, in times gone by, would travel, from town to town, to lead an occasional Sabbath service, a High Holy Day or a festival service. The cantor or *hazan* was, and still is, the professional singer who, with his special ear for music, his sweet voice and his understanding of the words, would improvise long, involved, enriched songs on the basis of the simple modes. Many cantors also introduced new and foreign elements into their chants, bits of song which they picked up in their travels. Some of these additions became so much a part of the service that they were accepted as *nusah*. Later chapters will provide some examples of these elaborations.

In most communities of the West today, the *hazan* is no longer a free-lancing and wandering minstrel like his predecessors. Very probably he is a permanent member of the synagogue professional staff, thus making it unnecessary for a layman to lead the service. The professional cantor today is thoroughly familiar with all the techniques of Western music; he knows how to read it, write it and sing it. Indeed, the modern *hazan* gets his training not only in Jewish and secular music but also in every phase of Jewish lore and learning, at special cantorial colleges. But this was not always true. For centuries, the *hazan,* like the layman, learned his art by ear, simply by listening and imitating the older *hazan;* and then if he had the talent for it, he added his own flourishes and modifications. The first *hazanim* were probably the select men in those earliest synagogues—gifted men who were able to remember not only the music but also the words because there were no books or scores.

Beginning in the sixth and seventh centuries in Palestine and in Babylonia, the *hazan* was not only the leader of the service but often a poet who composed new prayers. When the Muslim civilization conquered the Middle East and spread across the Mediterranean to Spain (the high tide of the Arab empire was about the middle of the eighth century), the Arabic language and Arabic literature, and particularly the Arabic form of poetry, a poetry of meter and rhyme, swept over all the subject peoples. The Jews, living in the midst of this Muslim Arab civilization, cultivated the new literary forms, and the *hazan* began to improvise his prayers in meter and rhyme, often even setting his words to melodies which he heard sung by his Muslim neighbors. These new prayers were called *piyutim* (sing. *piyut*) meaning simply "poems." The authors were given the name *payetanim* (sing. *payetan*) meaning "those who write poems."

Not until the middle of the eighteenth century did some individual *hazanim* in Europe begin to learn to read and write music. The first music they were exposed to was probably the instrumental music of the Baroque period, and so impressed were they by it that they took the style over into the service and began to write minuets, gavottes and other dance forms as settings for the most solemn prayers.

They learned something of harmony, too. They didn't have real choirs—perhaps at most two assistants, a bass and a boy soprano (or grown man who sang falsetto). Women had no part at all in the traditional synagogue. For these assistants they would write simple harmonic parts—parts often better suited to the instruments of a military band than to human voices. The *hazanim* were more likely to have heard band music or gypsy orchestras than fine choral singing. The *hazan* in Europe before the days of the Emancipation had to make his music into something of a performance. In Eastern Europe, where the Emancipation came very late, the synagogue, in addition to being a house of worship, was the one gathering place for the Jews—their concert hall, opera house, study, recreational, social and meeting hall. The *hazan* provided their principal entertainment. He would try hard to move them to tears or to awe and admiration at the tricks and turns of his voice. Sometimes he actually sang operatic arias set to the words of the services. This very often earned the disapproval of rabbis and worshippers who objected to such tampering with the tradition. However, there were always some *hazanim* who retained as much as possible of the pure modes, and, thanks to them, we can today separate the ancient from the eighteenth- and nineteenth-century threads in the traditional service.

About the middle of the nineteenth century, a number of well-trained musicians who were also *hazanim* started to compose a new type of music for the first Reform synagogues. Solomon Sulzer in Vienna, Louis Lewandowski in Berlin (not a *hazan* but a choral director) and many others began the work of writing music which was appropriate for the synagogue, with truly singable parts for their soloists and choir singers. They also began, in the course of the years, to write down some of the old chants to keep them from being forgotten. By the end of the century, cantors in Russia and Poland also learned to compose music in the manner of the Western world. Dunajewsky, Weintraub, Nowakowsky are some of the celebrated East European cantor-composers who combined their knowledge of the old chant with Western techniques in writing their synagogue music. They all lived into the first decades of the twentieth century.‡

Today there are Jewish composers who write for both the Reform and the Conservative synagogues. They are not themselves cantors, but they understand the requirements of the cantorial style and are able to use the kind of modern harmonies and counterpoints which have developed in the West. Most of these composers are now living in America.‡

Eight
SOUND OF
THE SHOFAR

‖‖‖   ‖≋≋   ‖‖≋≋

תקיעה שברים תרועה תקיעה
תקיעה שברים תקיעה
תקיעה תרועה תקיעה

THIS mysterious-looking diagram appears in the original manuscript of one of the oldest Hebrew prayer books in existence—the *Siddur* compiled by Saadyah Gaon, the brilliant tenth-century Jewish philosopher and scholar of Babylonia.‡ The diagram, read from right to left, is meant to represent the calls of the *shofar,* or ram's horn. The Hebrew words underneath the diagram are the names of the different calls in the order in which they are sounded as part of a synagogue service. Transliterated, the lines read:

Tekiah	*Shevarim*	*Teruah*	*Tekiah*
Tekiah	*Shevarim*	*Tekiah*	
Tekiah	*Teruah*	*Tekiah.*	

The traditional *shofar* has no mouthpiece. In order to sound the calls, one blows across the hole at the narrow end of the instrument, tightening the lips as in the case of blowing a bugle, to reach the overtones. The *tekiah* is a long, steady blast represented in the diagram by a straight vertical line. The *shevarim* is a wavering, sobbing sound represented by three horizontal wavy lines, one above the other. The *teruah* is a series of short, staccato blasts represented by a vertical jagged line.

Shofarot (plural of *shofar*) come in many sizes and shapes. The most commonly found shape is this:

From Germany, 19th century

Pictures of *shofarot* in that shape appear on ancient coins and wall-carvings. However, occasionally a ram's horn is twisted and looks like this:

From India, 18th century

The size of the *shofar* determines the pitch of the calls. The smaller the instrument, the higher the pitch.

Even at the time when the ingenious diagram was devised for Saadyah Gaon's *Siddur,* the ram's horn was already an ancient instrument, a survival of the earliest biblical days when it was an instrument used for sounding an alarm, rallying troops or for frightening the enemy. There was a time when it was thought to have a kind of magical power. The ram's horn figured prominently in the story of Joshua and the battle of Jericho. (See *Joshua,* Chapter 6.) The *shofarot* were blown as the children of Israel marched around the city; and, on the seventh day, after seven marches and loud blasts, the walls came tumbling down.

In Saadyah's day, the *shofar* no longer served its ancient functions. It had become what it is today, an instrument purely for Jewish rituals. The custom is still practiced in modern Israel of blowing the *shofar* to announce the beginning of the Sabbath. It is also blown on very special occasions. During the Six Day War of 1967, for example, when the Western Wall was captured by Israeli forces, throngs of soldiers and citizens watched in solemn joy as a great blast was sounded on an enormous *shofar.*

However, for most Jews outside of Israel, the *shofar* is associated chiefly with *Rosh Hashanah,* the New Year, which is sometimes called *Yom Teruah,* the Day of the *Shofar* Call. In Orthodox communities, the *shofar* is blown daily throughout the whole penitential

From Ethiopia, 19th century

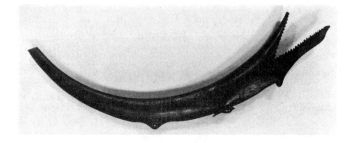

season which begins a month before the Jewish New Year and ends at sundown on *Yom Kippur.* In all synagogues the *shofar* is sounded according to the order designated in Saadyah's diagram on the morning of *Rosh Hashanah.* Some modern synagogues in America have substituted a trumpet or cornet for the original ram's horn. For these instruments the calls can be written in modern notation, like this:

Ex. 16 *Shofar Calls*

The clearly defined tones of the trumpet cannot duplicate the eerie, piercing quality of the *shofar.* Saadyah's diagram is better suited to the inexact pitches of the primitive instrument. Indeed, the calls are interpreted differently in different parts of the world. Oriental Jewish *shofar*-blowers invert the sounds as we know them, starting with the high overtones and dropping to the low, fundamental tone somewhat like this:

It is not easy to blow the *shofar.* The person who is granted the privilege of blowing it in the synagogue usually needs to practice for some time before the High Holy Days. His lip and his breath control will determine the tone-quality or timbre of his performance, for the *shofar* can sound shrill or mellow, keening or triumphant. He must also keep his instrument impeccably clean. One tiny dust mote inside the narrow tube can stop the sound entirely. When this has happened during the service, it has given rise to folk tales in the old world of how Satan himself gets inside

45

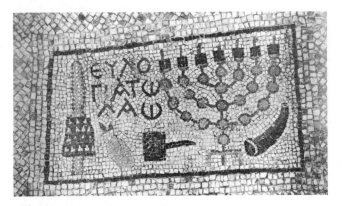

Shofar together with lulav, etrog, shovel and menorah, detail from floor pavement, 6th-century C.E. mosaic‡

the *shofar* to prevent its voice from reaching the ear of God.

The first time the *shofar* is sounded on the morning of *Rosh Hashanah,* the blower precedes the ceremony with a blessing in which he gives thanks to God for having sanctified us with the commandment to hear the voice of the *shofar.* The melody he uses (in the Ashkenazic tradition) is itself an imitation of a trumpet call:

Ex. 17   *Shofar Blessing*   TRADITIONAL

Ba — rukh a ——— tah
a - do - nai   e - lo - he - nu
me - lekh ha - o - lam   a - sher ki -
de - sha - nu   be - mitz vo - tav   ve -
tzi - va - nu lish - mo - a kol sho - far.

Blessed are Thou, O Lord our God, King of the universe, who hast sanctified us with Thy commandment, and bidden us to harken unto the *shofar.*

Then the cantor or the rabbi pronounces the ancient names of the calls one by one, and the blower sounds them. After they have all been sounded, the congregation sings a passage from the prayer book, a joyous response at having heard their ancient rallying cry once more:

"Happy is the people who knows the sound of the *shofar,* They shall walk in the light of Thy countenance!"

They follow this immediately with Psalm 84:5 which follows in the traditional order of prayer:

"Happy are they who dwell in Thy house, They are ever praising Thee, Selah!"

Ex. 18 is the traditional music.

The *Rosh Hashanah shofar* service is somewhat revised in the American Reform synagogue. Using the text of the *Union Prayer Book,* the American composer, Herbert Fromm, has made a striking setting for chorus, organ and trumpet.‡ His piece is made up of four brief sections. Part I, written for the traditional words, "Happy is the people, etc.," quoted above, forms an introduction. If you listen to it carefully, you will hear a suggestion of the same traditional melody (Ex. 18) in the opening phrase (the subject) with which each voice enters in turn. This is called a *fughetto.* That means that the voices follow each other as in a round, but the first voice sings "the subject" in the key of A flat, the *tonic,* or the home-key of the piece; the second sings it in E flat, the *dominant,* the key of the *sol;* the third voice enters in the key of the *tonic;* and the fourth in the *dominant.* The voices weave in counterpoint, coming together on the final words, "Thy countenance."

Part II is introduced by the trumpet playing all the calls of the *shofar* in the traditional order (in the key of E flat). "The Lord reigneth, He is clothed with majesty; the Lord is girded with strength!" all the voices shout out in unison. Then they drop to a whisper, "Thy throne is established of old; Thou art from everlasting to everlasting." Part III, introduced

Ashrey Ha-am

by the *Shevarim* call of the trumpet, repeats the music of Part II, "For the mountains shall depart, and the hills be removed," sung *forte,* and the *piano* response, "But My kindnesses shall not depart from thee, neither shall My covenant of peace be removed, saith the Lord that hath compassion upon thee." Part IV is introduced by the *Teruah* call of the trumpet. The same powerful unison melody as that of Parts II and III is applied now to "All ye dwellers on earth, when the *shofar* is sounded, and the great trumpet is blown." The trumpet interrupts with a high blast. "Hark ye!"—another trumpet blast—"Hark ye!" The voices again drop to a whisper, "Come ye and worship the Lord at the holy mountain," and rise in crescendo with "The Lord of Hosts shall be a shield unto you!" These last words are repeated in a broad, powerful passage, while above the voices the trumpet sounds out a *Tekiah Gedolah,* a great *Tekiah.*

A fairly advanced amateur chorus can perform this composition by Fromm. If no cornet player is available, Fromm himself suggests that the trumpet calls may be played on the organ.

Nine
KOL NIDRE

THE ARK is opened. The elders of the synagogue remove the white-clad scrolls of the Torah and hold them up before the hushed and waiting congregation. It is sundown, the beginning of *Yom Kippur,* and the first notes break the solemn stillness:

Ex. 19

It may be the *hazan* or the organ or the choir who will utter those first awesome sounds. But the notes are the same in synagogues across the land and across the seas, and they are probably more familiar to more Jews than any other notes in the whole repertory of Jewish song. They seem to well up out of the ages and to take on a life of their own which is independent of the very ancient Aramaic words to which they are sung. Those words are the *Kol Nidre,* a formula of absolution from vows, a text which has been subject to disapproval and to dispute and to a variety of interpretations over the centuries since the days of the *Geonim* in Babylonia. The melody itself awakens emotional memories of the past—the past of each individual listener as well as the past of the entire folk. It stirs a hope that the New Year will be better than the old, that all of us will be given the strength to shed old weaknesses and to rise to new crises in life with vigor and courage.

Like other synagogue song, this great, virtually universal chant has come down to us in a variety of forms. It is not sung exactly in the same way by all those who sing it. However, certain basic elements of the

chant invariably occur. Those first descending tones followed immediately by a rising melody are always present. They are in the minor mode. But, as the melody proceeds, it always modulates at some point to the major mode, returning to the minor for the finish. Sing or listen to some of these fragments—they are the basic elements of the *Kol Nidre* chant. (Ex. 19 provides the familiar opening strains.)

Ex. 20

Motives of Kol Nidre
TRADITIONAL

Nobody knows exactly when or where the *Kol Nidre* was first sung. It is not known to the Jews of the Sephardic and Oriental communities. They have their own chants to the text, chants which have never taken on the depth of meaning and association of this melody. The familiar *Kol Nidre* melody is of Ashkenazic origin. The stress upon singing the text originated in northern France, Germany and Bohemia as far back as the eleventh century. In *Yom Kippur* prayer books written in the eleventh and twelfth centuries, there are specific instructions to sing a set tune rather than to improvise a chant for *Kol Nidre*. Some books direct that it be sung three times beginning softly and increasing the volume with each repetition; other books suggest that the text be sung several times with a different melody each time. We have no record of the melodies to which the writers of that time were referring.

The first version of the *Kol Nidre* melody as we know it appeared in 1785 in a collection of synagogue chants notated and published by Ahron Beer, then a *hazan* in Berlin. His notation contains most of the elements of the song with which we are familiar. But the melody continued to be changed even after it was written down and, a hundred years later also in Berlin, Louis Lewandowski wrote it as it appears in Ex. 21.

Even this version is not the last word. Many variants have been written and sung. Various composers have made arrangements of the *Kol Nidre* for *hazan*, choir and organ. Perhaps the melody will continue to change as it is put into new choral and instrumental settings in the harmonies, counterpoints and rhythms of our times.

It has already found its way into concert music. The nineteenth-century composer, Max Bruch, wrote a *Kol Nidre* for 'cello and orchestra which became a favorite showpiece for virtuoso 'cellists.‡ His composition starts out with the recognizable elements of the synagogue chant and then digresses into lyric romantic passages that have no relationship to the original. Far

Yom Kippur, Germany, 1726

less frequently performed but much closer in musical material and in spirit to the great *Yom Kippur* chant is the *Kol Nidre* by Arnold Schoenberg, one of the greatest of the twentieth-century composers. Written in 1938, it had its premiere of performance in 1958, some seven years after the death of the composer.

This is a work for chorus, orchestra and a "speaker" who must be able to read his part in precise rhythm and inflections—that is, with a rising and falling pitch close to singing—prescribed by the composer in the score. The German word *sprechstimme* is the technical term for this kind of speech; Schoenberg first used the device in his native Vienna.

Schoenberg's composition has an interesting history. The composer had been born a Jew but in his youth had become converted to the Christian faith and subsequently had shunned all religious affiliation. Nevertheless, he was always deeply concerned with religious themes and occasionally expressed his searching and probing feelings in music with his own texts. On one or two occasions he based those texts on the Hebrew Bible. An early work of this nature was his *Jacob's Ladder*. A later work, begun in 1928, was his monumental unfinished opera, *Moses and Aaron*, written in the "twelve-tone-row" system which was his own unique contribution to the technique of musical composition and which is one of the most influential innovations in contemporary music. The Nazi terror drove him, along with many other great artists, to find refuge in the United States. Schoenberg settled in Los Angeles, and there he encountered the late Rabbi Jacob Sonderling, a mystical and poetic soul, who stirred his Jewish feelings to the degree that the composer resolved to return formally to Judaism.

His "act of contrition"—symbolic of his thoughtfully pondered reconversion—was this *Kol Nidre*. He used an English text provided for him by Rabbi Sonderling. It begins with a legend from the *Kabbalah*, the lore of mystical Judaism, leading to the words, "A light is sown for the righteous!" This is followed by a traditional text which interprets the *Kol Nidre* as dispensation for anyone who has taken vows of conversion, "Let him repent, and we give him leave to worship with us this day." Finally, there comes the translation of the *Kol Nidre* itself, with great emphasis on the words, "We repent."

Schoenberg's music carries out the mystical quality of Sonderling's interpretation. But from the very shimmering, amorphous beginning to the final, decisive

Kol Nidre

TRADITIONAL
NOTATION OF L. LEWANDOWSKI

Kol nid - re ve - e - sa - re, va ha - ra - me ve - ka - na -

me ve - khi - nu - ye ve - ki - nu - se ush' - vu - ot

din _____ dar - na ud' - ish - ta -

ba - na ud' - a - ha - rim - na u - di - a - sar -

na al naf - sha - ta - - - - na,

mi - yom kip - pu - rim zeh ad yom kip - pu - rim ha - ba a - le - nu le -

to - - vah, kol - hon i - ha - rat na ve - hon

kol hon _____

ye - hon sha - ran, she - vi - kin she -

vi - tin be - te - lin um' - vu - ta - lin la she-

ri - rin ve - lo ka - ya - min. Nid - ra - na la____

_____ nid - re

ve e - sa - ra - na la e - sa - re,

u - sh' vu - a - ta - na la_____

_____ she - vu - ot.

"We repent," we hear fragments, and fragments of fragments, of the *Kol Nidre* chant. The first motive in Ex. 19 is heard almost immediately, stripped of any ornament, reduced to its barest outline, like this:

The first two notes of that illustration become a motive in themselves. Motive #4 in Ex. 20 appears over and over in different keys, in different rhythmic patterns, as for example:

The themes are inverted (high notes become low notes and vice versa), played against each other, re-versed (begin with the last note and sound them backward), but they are always present as the vital musical leavening of the whole work.

Schoenberg's *Kol Nidre* was for him, in addition to a religious reconversion, a musical reversion as well —a reversion to a more traditional style of composition than the great bulk of his work. That is, it has a key signature, and it comes home to a "tonic" at the end. However, it has a purely twentieth-century sound and none of the sweet romanticism of Max Bruch's *Kol Nidre* composition. It is now possible to hear the *Kol Nidre* of Schoenberg on a recording.‡ By listening closely, one can discern the traditional themes within the powerful dissonances and feel the impact of the religious fervor in the entire work. Careful and repeated listening to the record would be the most desirable preparation for the experience of hearing a live performance.

Ten

THE THEMES
OF THE
NEW YEAR

THE KOL NIDRE is the most famous theme of the Jewish liturgy, but it is only one of a large repertory of musical themes associated with the High Holy Days. The Days of Awe—*Rosh Hashanah* and *Yom Kippur*—are observed in the synagogue with an elaborate and impressive musical liturgy, a rich fabric woven of fragments of melody drawn from many periods of Jewish history. Sometimes they appear in the solo chant of the *hazan* and in the responses of the congregation. At other times they are developed into compositions for choir and organ. The liturgy is interspersed with metric hymns (*piyutim*) which have been given a variety of settings for congregational singing.

Rosh Hashanah, 16th-century woodcut

As far back as the Middle Ages, *hazanim* introduced special songs for *Rosh Hashanah* and *Yom Kippur* which became the basis of new modes, or *nus-ha-ot*. These have been kept alive over the centuries down to our own day and are known in the tradition as *Mi-Sinai* chants, chants descended "from Mount Sinai." This exaggeration of the antiquity of the songs illustrates the veneration in which they have been held. Modern composers writing music for the High Holy Day services usually have managed to retain some of the elements of the chants even when they employ the most contemporary techniques of composition. The composer, Herbert Fromm, used a fragment of traditional chant in his very modern *Shofar Service*, as we saw in Chapter Eight.

Here are a few of the most important liturgical themes of the solemn Days of Awe. The first, which is used to introduce the whole penitential season at the service of the evening of *Rosh Hashanah*, sounds like this:

Basic Motive
Ex. 22 ## Eve of Rosh Hashanah

(ba-rukh hu u-va-rukh she-mo)

ha-ma-'riv a-ra-vim.

Ex. 22c *Mi Khamokha*

Mi kha-mo-kha ba-e-lim a-do-nai,

mi ka-mo-kha ne'-dar ba-ko-desh,

no-ra te-hi_____lot o-sey fe-le.

We know that this theme is no older than the Middle Ages because musicologists identify it as a "borrowing" from a song of the medieval German Catholic Church. However, the melody has become so much a part of the Jewish heritage that it immediately sets the mood of solemn contemplation. More than that, it serves as the theme for the entire service of *Rosh Hashanah* eve and is repeated as the theme of the evening service for *Yom Kippur*. Notice the way the melody is adapted to different parts of the prayer:

Ex. 22a *Barekhu*

Ba_____re-khu et a-do-

nai ha-me-vo_____rakh.

Ba-rukh a-do-nai ha-me-

vo_____rakh le-o-lam va-ed.

Ex. 22d *Uf'ros Alenu*

U-f'ros a-le-nu su-

kat she-lo-me-kha. Ba-rukh

a-tah a-do-nai (ba-re-khu u-

va-rukh she-mo) ha po-

Response:
Ha-Ma-ariv Aravim
Ex. 22b

Ba-rukh a-tah a-do-nai,

res   su - kat   sha - lom

a - le - nu   ve -

al   kol   a - mo   yis - ra -

el   ve - al   ye - ru - sha - la - yim.

A second theme which is laden with memories of the High Holy Days is made up of just three tones:

Those three tones form the nucleus of many responses in the High Holy Day service. In some synagogues they are sung by the congregation, in others by the choir. Here they are used for the "Amen" in the *Amidah* (or "standing" prayer):

From the Amidah—
Ex. 23 *Musaf of Rosh Hashanah*

Me - lekh   o _____ zer

u - mo - shi - a   u - ma - gen

Ba -

rukh   a - tah   a - do - nai

(ba - rukh hu   u - va - rukh   she - mo)

ma - gen   av - ra - ham.   (A - men)

The great *Kaddish* or Sanctification which opens the *Musaf* service (the "addition" to the morning service) ends with the same three notes on the word *Shalom* sung by the cantor and echoed with *Amen* by choir or congregation. This great *Rosh Hashanah Kaddish* has been arranged as an art song with a rich piano accompaniment by the French composer Maurice Ravel. Many fine singers have recorded it. If you are a student of voice, this might be added to your repertoire.‡

The three descending tones of the response form a *minor* chord. Three similarly descending tones forming a *major* chord introduce one of the most impressive moments of the entire *Rosh Hashanah* service—the passage "*Alenu*" which appears in the section of the prayers declaring the Kingship of God. The same text appears in every weekday and Sabbath service of the year. In the Reform synagogue it is usually recited or sung in English translation ("Let us adore . . ."). During the course of this prayer a memorable passage reads, "We therefore bow and bend the knee . . ." On *Rosh Hashanah* in traditional synagogues, when those words are reached, the congregation or, in many instances, the rabbi and the *hazan* actually do get down on their knees, put their hands to the floor and then touch their foreheads to the floor to bow in true Oriental fashion. That musical passage follows.

Va-Anahnu Kore-im
Musaf of Rosh Hashanah

Ex. 24

ASHKENAZIC TRADITIONAL

The custom of kneeling in prayer is reserved only for High Holy Day services, and the actual act of kneeling is not practiced at other times of the year. The traditional Jew at most will bow low from the waist when he recites *Va-Anahnu Kore-im.* But, during the High Holy Days, he has a second opportunity to prostrate himself. This occurs during a dramatic portion of the *Musaf* service of *Yom Kippur* when worshippers relive the ancient ceremonial practiced on *Yom Kippur* in the Temple of Jerusalem. That was the one time of the year when the High Priest entered the inner sanctuary, the Holy of Holies, while the other priests and the people waited, assembled in the court. When he came forth out of the Holy of Holies, the High Priest pronounced aloud—just this one time

in the whole year—the ineffable name of God. Upon hearing this holy Name—so sacred that it could never be uttered by anyone and only once annually by the High Priest alone—all the priests and the people fell on hands and knees, bowed their heads to the ground and called out, "Blessed be the Name of the Lord forever and ever!" (Ex. 25)

This ancient ceremony is recalled by the *hazan* (and at times by the choir) with a long, florid, rolling melody, stretching each word over many notes, interpolating the syllable "ah." When the cantor arrives at the words, "They would bend the knee and bow, and fall on their faces," the traditional congregation or their leaders actually do so. At the words, "Blessed be the Name," the people, representing the worshippers in the old temple court, rise and sing out loud and strong, syllable for syllable, with no frills or flourishes. This section of the service is called the *Avodah* (temple worship).

The *Avodah* melody is still another of the important musical themes of the High Holy Days. Like other such themes, this melody too becomes *nusah* for other parts of the service. It has been arranged in many forms, sometimes for the *hazan* who may improvise his own elaborations or sometimes for choir and organ (in which case it is necessarily forced into a strictly metrical form). Here is a relatively simple version of the *Avodah* as chanted by a cantor and congregation. The arrangement is by Eliezer Gerovitch, one of the great Russian cantors of the late nineteenth century. (See Chapter Eight.)

Ex. 25

Avodah

TRADITIONAL
ARR. E. GEROVITCH

V'ha ko———— ha-nim v'ha am ha-om'-dim ba-a-za-rah ke-she-ha-yu shom'-im et ha-shem ha-nikh, bad ve-ha-no——ra me-fo-rash yo———tzey mi-pi kho-hen ga-dol bi-k'du-shah u-ve-to-ho——rah ha-yu ko-re-im u-mish ta-ve-om-rim ha-vim v'nof-lim al p'ney-hem ve-om-rim

Special music frequently comes at points of the synagogue service when there is a certain amount of action. One such moment in every synagogue service occurs just before the Torah is read. The sacred scroll has just been removed from the ark and the *hazan* holds it up before the people. He sings, *"Shema Yisra-el, Adonai Elohenu Adonai Ehad!"* ("Hear, O Israel, the Lord our God is One!") The congregation repeats it. Then he sings, *"Ehad Elohenu, gadol Adonenu, kadosh venora Shemo!"* ("Our God is One, our Lord is One, holy and awesome is His Name!") and the people sing that after him. On *Rosh Hashanah* and *Yom Kippur*, this *Shema* is sung to a melody different from that of the ordinary Sabbath. It goes:

Ex. 26

Shema
Torah Ceremony, High Holy Days

E - had e - lo - he - nu, ga - dol a - do - ne - nu,
ka - dosh ve - no - ra she - mo.

E - had e - lo - he - nu, ga - dol a - do - ne - nu,
ka - dosh ve - no - ra she - mo.

ga - zal - nu, di-bar-nu do - fi

Another of the highly dramatic features of the *Yom Kippur* service is the Great Confession. Here the *hazan* recites the list of the community's sins—they are given in alphabetical order in the Hebrew and use the plural pronoun to denote *collective* sins—and the congregation repeats each sin after him. In the very traditional synagogue, the worshippers will frequently beat their breasts with clenched fists, one beat for each sin. The melody is very plain, very stark, with none of the musical decorations of other parts of the *nusah*. Here are the opening bars which are merely repeated to complete the passage:

Ex. 27 *The Great Confession* TRADITIONAL

A - sham - nu, ba - gad - nu,

Finally, we have a chant which touches off the most awesome emotions in the heart of the Jew. The closing section of the *Yom Kippur* service occurring at the end of a long day of fasting when the sun is nearly down is called *Ne-ilah* (Conclusion). To the pious Jew this is the last opportunity to appeal to the "ear" of the Almighty with a final plea for forgiveness, for mercy and for a new year of life and blessing. A special *Kaddish* introduces *Ne-ilah*. The melody of this sanctification becomes *nusah* for the prayers following it. A portion from that *Kaddish* follows.

Kaddish for Ne-ilah

Yit - ga - dal v'yit - ka - dash she - mey ra - ba A - men.

Be - o - le - ma di - ve - ra khir' u - tey ve - yam -

likh mal - khu - tey b'ha - ye - khon uv' yo - me - khon u' - ve - ha -

yey de - khol bet yis - ra - el de - khol bet yis - ra - el

ba - a - ga - la u - viz' - man ka - riv ve - im' ru A - men.

A - men, ye - hey she - mey ra - ba me - vo - rakh le -

o — lam u - le - ol' - mey ol - ma - ya yit - ba - rakh

Eleven
SONG
OF RAIN

A NEW settlement is being built. The scene is Palestine; the time, the late nineteen-thirties. The land is lifeless, parched, rock-strewn, forbidding. Before this desolate spot can support any kind of life, there must first be provision for water. Some young pioneers are assigned to dig a well. They make several bad starts. Suddenly their cry goes up, *"Mayim!* Water! We have struck water!"* All hands get to work and the well is dug. Now they can proceed with the buildings—the watch tower, the children's house, the huts for the grown-ups. At night they celebrate. This same scene recurs in many parts of the long-neglected country. Before long someone has made a song to celebrate and, immediately after, someone invents a dance to go with the song. The song maker in this case was Emanuel Amiran, who took as his text a prophecy made twenty-five hundred years ago by Isaiah, "Therefore with joy shall ye draw water out of the wells of salvation" (*Isaiah 12: 3*). The song and the dance spread like wildfire from settlement to settlement across Europe and America. You have probably sung it and danced the simple folk dance that accompanies it.‡

For people living in sun-baked desert, the discovery of water always calls for celebration. One of the oldest

Mayim, mayim!

songs the Jewish people produced (that is, the words only) is preserved in the Bible *(Numbers 21: 17).* The people of Israel at the time were still wandering in the wilderness. Led by Moses, they at last reached Be-er.

That [Be-er] is the well whereof the Lord said unto Moses: "Gather the people together, and I will give them water." Then sang Israel this song:
"Spring up, O well—sing ye unto it—
The well, which the princes digged,
Which the nobles of the people delved,
With the sceptre, and with their staves."

Since there is no known melody for this poem, you will have to provide your own. This type of celebration song, when sung by early peoples, was sure to have started with dance, with strong rhythm, with the beat of drums or the striking of tambourines. Such songs also were likely to begin with a high-pitched triumphant shout, dropping in pitch from line to line. To create your own "Song of the Well," you would do well to follow their pattern. Pronounce the words with exaggerated accents. Clap your hands, once for

Well in the desert

each syllable. Stamp your foot at the accented sylla-bles. Move into a round dance, intoning the words of the poem. Use the forms of the *Mayim* dance, but change the steps, invent new motions. Last of all, improvise your own melody, and accompany both melody and dance with drum, tambourines, cymbals.

The original Hebrew poem has a crisper, brighter sound than any translation. Perhaps you would prefer to base your song on it. Here is a transliteration, with the accents marked for you:

Ali be-er̀ ènu làh
Be-er̀ ha-fa-rù-ha sa-rìm
Ka-rù-ha ne-di-veẏ ha-am̀
Bi-me-ho-kek̀ be-mish'a-no-tam̀.

Water and well and rain continued to be matters of critical importance in the many centuries the people lived in the land. In the time of the Second Temple in Jerusalem, a special day of feasting was devoted to the significance of water. This was called *Simhat Bet ha-Sho-evah,* or *Water-Drawing Festival.* It took place in the outer courts of the Temple immediately after the autumn harvest festival *Sukot,* while the pilgrims were still gathered from all over the land.

The symbolic drawing of water from a well in the court was supposed to help end the long drought of the arid, hot summer and to bring on the much-needed rainy season. It was followed by wild celebration, with sword and torch dances, drinking of wine and carnival. This festival was dropped after the destruction of the Second Temple. It has been revived once or twice in modern Israel as a dance festival but has not been taken very seriously.

The Second Temple was leveled in the year 70 C.E. and the people of Israel were exiled from their land. They found themselves in different climates, in lands of four distinct seasons instead of merely a dry and a rainy season. In eleventh-century Spain, a great Jewish poet composed two prayers, one for rain and one for dew, not for Spain but for the far-off land he never saw. To this day in Sephardic synagogues, Solomon Ibn Gabirol's prayer for rain is sung on the Eighth Day of Solemn Assembly *(Shemini Atzeret)* which follows the *Sukot* festival. His prayer for dew is sung on the seventh day of Passover, when the rainy season is ending and the long hot dry summer begins. "Rain," "dew," "water"—these words mean life for the land. This is Ibn Gabirol's *Song of Dew.* His prayer for rain is sung to the same melody.

Ex. 29

IBN GABIROL

Song of Dew

TRADITIONAL SEPHARDIC MELODY

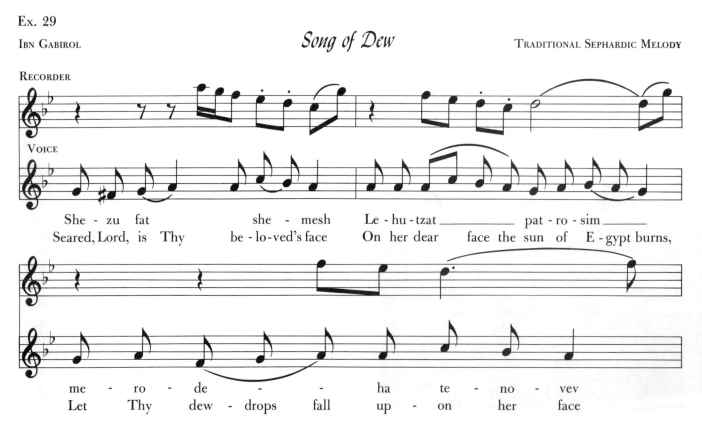

RECORDER

VOICE

She - zu fat she - mesh Le - hu - tzat pat - ro - sim
Seared, Lord, is Thy be - lo - ved's face On her dear face the sun of E - gypt burns,

me - ro - de - ha te - no - vev
Let Thy dew - drops fall up - on her face

be - tal - le - lay _____ re - si - sim.
on her sweet face which un - to Thee turns.

Ha - el ha - o - neh be - et ra - tzon a - mu - sim _____
Lord, when men cry bit - ter - ly on - ly from Thee comes an an - swer true,

Ma - gen _____ hu le - hol ha - ho - sim _____
Shield of those who trust in Thee, Ans - wer with Thy re - freshing dew.

The Jordan Valley

Other Jewish poems of prayer for rain and dew were written elsewhere and were sung to their own melodies. For example, in Germany, not long after Ibn Gabirol's time, some unknown singer composed a prayer for rain *(tefilat geshem)* with a melody that he gathered up partly out of some *minnelied* which he heard in his travels (a *minnelied* is the song of a *minnesinger,* the German counterpart of a troubadour, a knightly composer of love songs), partly out of folk tunes and partly out of the traditional chant or *nusah.* The tune became popular and was used also for a prayer for dew *(tefilat tal).* These prayers are still sung in the traditional Ashkenazic synagogue, the former on *Shemini Atzeret,* the latter on *Pesah.* Ex. 30 is an English adaptation of the *Geshem* prayer. (The words, and this version of the melody, are from the article, "Geshem," by Rabbi F. L. Cohen, in *The Jewish Encyclopedia.*)

63

1. Thou_____ hast ap - point - ed. the

pow'rs of Na - ture that ga - ther wa - ter to bring the rain.____

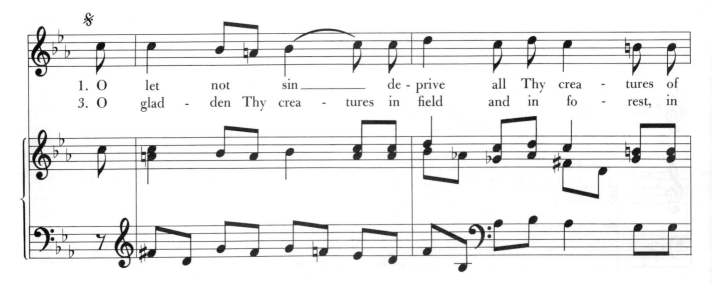

1. O let not sin____ de - prive all Thy crea - tures of
3. O glad - den Thy crea - tures in field and in fo - rest, in

this need - ful bless - - ing, but crown all Thy val - leys with
vale and on moun - tain, and bright - en the green - wood, and

Fine

fresh smil - ing ver - dure, that they may live who ask for rain.
strength - en the har - vest by send - ing down a plent - eous rain.

2. Ga - ther, and dis - trib - ute the wa - ters to moist - en the

D.S. al Fine

hard and thirst - y soil, and ba - nish pain.

This *Geshem* song has itself become a kind of theme for the synagogue services conducted on the day the Prayer for Rain is sung. It is *nusah* for the prayers which precede and follow it. Similarly, the Prayer for Dew gives its melody to the prayers which precede and follow *it*. In particular, the *Kaddish* introducing the *Musaf,* or additional section of the service, is chanted to variants of the same melody. The *hazan* refers to this setting of *Kaddish* as the *Geshem* or *Tal Kaddish.* The first part of it is in Ex. 31.

Long after this *Geshem* melody had become part of every Ashkenazic service, an Eastern European Jew took it over for his own song, a song about autumn, using words from his own everyday language, Yiddish. To this Jew, whose name has been long forgotten, the *Geshem* melody was the symbol of the sadness of autumn, the end of summer warmth and comfort. It brought premonitions of cold winds and bitter hunger. The melody held the same meaning for his neighbors and for the Jews of other East European villages not only during his own lifetime but for later generations. The songs of the synagogue formed their

The Jordan Valley

entire musical vocabulary, and they could find a melody in the tradition for almost every mood. In later chapters there will be other examples of Yiddish folk song based on synagogue chant. Ex. 32 is the song of autumn. Its first words *Af Bri* are Aramaic, quoted from the prayer in the liturgy.

Ex. 31   *Geshem-Tal Kaddish*   TRADITIONAL ASHKENAZIC MELODY

Af Bri

"Af bri _____" Es iz nit do vos tzu ge-ben es-sen di kin. Der
"And send the rain!" There is - n't a - ny grain! The

zum - mer iz a - vek un der vin - ter iz tzu-rick, un kein
sum - mer is gone and the win - ter's here a - gain and I

gelt iz als nit do. Di shti-vel zein-en tze-ris-sen,
have-n't a penny to my name. The cold winds are bloom-ing,

ei   ei   ei   ei   ei, un kein gelt   iz als   nit do.
ei   ei   ei   ei   ei, and I have-n't a pen -ny to my name!

How different is the song of rain of the Jewish farmer once more restored to the soil of Israel. Once again the Jew awaits the rainy season, no longer with foreboding but with joy and hope. The Israeli folk composer, Matityahu Shelem, wrote his own *Geshem* song with words that describe a glorious harvest. His refrain is a quotation from Psalm 126, "They that sow in tears shall reap in joy." In the following English translation of Shelem's song, the refrain has been changed slightly in order to fit the melody.[‡]

Song of Rain

1. Rain is coming, blessed rain,
   To the golden fields of grain,
   To the grass on every rill,
   In each valley, on each hill.

Refrain: Have no fear, have no fear,
         All ye who sow in tears!
         With a song, with a song
         Soon shall ye be reaping.

2. Reaper, soon will come the day
   When your barns are filled with hay,
   Sheaves of corn from far and near,
   Yellow tassels on each ear.

Refrain.

3. Let your heart rejoice, O brother!
   Earth is yielding, Earth the mother,
   Vineyard keeper, make your wine,
   Grapes are heavy on the vine.

Refrain.

Twelve

SONG OF
THE STUDENT

IN ONE of his most memorable narrative poems, the great Hebrew poet Bialik (1873–1934) recorded his own feelings of protest against the traditional life of Jewish study as it had long been practiced in Eastern Europe. For many centuries, gifted Jewish boys—boys still in their early teens—who had completed *heder* (Jewish primary school) and had absorbed everything their local rabbis could teach them were sent off to Jewish academies of higher learning to master all the tractates of the Talmud. These academies called *yeshivot* (sing. *yeshivah*) were located in great Jewish centers of pre-Hitler Poland and Lithuania, in cities such as Vilna, Lublin, Volozhin and Zhitomer. So renowned were some of these *yeshivot* and so creative the Jewish scholarship which flowered around them that Jews called Vilna and other such great Jewish centers "sacred" to Jewish learning. Many young men over the generations considered it a rare privilege to be able to study at these great *yeshivot*. Their parents often sacrificed everything for the honor of having their sons become great "lights in Israel"—distinguished rabbis and Jewish scholars. But other young men —rather, boys who for one reason or another were unhappy at having to forsake their youth, their homes, their families and friends—and especially free spirits

like Bialik—rebelled at the harsh, lonely, joyless life of the academies.

Here are some excerpts from Bialik's poem. They describe the life of *ha-matmid* (the dedicated student), but one characteristic is missing: the familiar study-chant used by generations of Talmud students to accompany their learning. Bialik did not insert the music here, but any one of his contemporaries who read his Hebrew poem, upon reaching the talmudic passage quoted by Bialik, would very likely have broken into a chant similar to the one you'll find below. (The English translation of the poem, *Ha-Matmid*, is by Maurice Samuel.)

And when thou goest forth alone, at nightfall,
Wandering in one of these, the sacred cities,
When heaven above is quick with breaking stars,
And earth beneath with whispering spirit-winds,
Thine ear will catch the murmur of a voice,
Thine eye will catch the twinkle of a light
Set in a window, and a human form—
A shadow trembling, swaying back and forth,
A voice, an agony, that lifts and falls,
And comes toward thee upon the waves of silence.
Mark well the swaying shadow and the voice:
It is a *Matmid* in his prison-house,
A prisoner, self-guarded, self condemned,
Self-sacrificed to study of the Law. . .

In the *Yeshivah* is a holy silence
Which he, the holy youth, is first to break;
For there, in the dark corner, wait for him—
Faithful companions since the day he came—
Three friends: his stand, his candle, and his Talmud.
As if the moments could not move too swiftly
That lie between him and his trusted friends,
He hastens to his place and takes his stand,
And like a pillar stays from morn till night.
Still standing he will eat his midday crust,
Still standing he will half out-watch the night.
Granite is yielding clay compared with him,
A Jewish boy unto the Torah vowed.

Hoi o - mar Ra - ba, to - nu ra - bo-non

Thus Raba speaks, and thus our teachers taught.
(Backward and forward swaying he repeats,
With ceaseless sing-song the undying words.)

Oi, oi, omar Ra - ba,

o - mar Ab - ba - - ye

Not *he*, then, knows the bitterness that rings
In the dark Talmud-melody, a sound
That clutches at the heart and sunders it.

Not *he*, but one that in the silent night
Or in the quiet dusk before the dawn,
The old *Yeshivah* passing, stands a while
And through the window hears the lonely voice
Pouring sweet bitterness and bitter sweetness
Upon his muffled spirit. Only *he*
Can know the burning anguish of the chant,
The pain, the glory of the Talmud-song.

There are corners of the world where you can still
hear this study-melody. Most of the East European
academies of which Bialik wrote were destroyed in the
holocaust, but many exist elsewhere—in the Williams-
burg section of New York City, for example; in the
Meah Shearim quarter of Jerusalem where Orthodox
Jews retain many of the forms of East Europe; in the
Jewish sections of Mexico City, Buenos Aires and
other cities. In all these places, one will find students
of the Talmud, some old men, others young, like
Bialik's *matmid* standing at their high reading desks,
swaying and chanting aloud in study. Here is a fragment from the Talmud as it might sound:

Ex. 33   *Amar Rabbi Elazar*   TALMUD CHANT

A - mar Ra - bi El' - a - zar, a - mar Ra - bi Ha - ni - nah

Tal - mi - dey ha - kha - mim mar - bim sha - lom ba - o - lam

She - ne - e - mar ve - khol ba - na - yikh li - mu - dey a - do - nai

ve - rav sha - lom ba - na - yikh. Al tik - ra ba - na - yikh

e - la bo - na - yikh.

The translation of this chant appears on p. 73, top.

Meierke, Mein Zun
(Meierke, My Son)

YIDDISH FOLK SONG

Mei - er - ke mein zun, O Mei - er - ke mein zun, O
Mei - er - ke my son, O Mei - er - ke my son, O

Mei - er - ke mein zun. Tzu veisst du far ve - men du shtayst? Tzu
Mei - er - ke my son. Do you know be - fore whom you stand? Do

veisst du far ve - men du shtayst? Lif - ney me - lekh mal -
you know be - fore whom you stand? Be - fore the king of

khey ha - m'lo - - khim, ta - ten - yu, lif - ney me - lekh mal -
Kings of Kings, fa - ther dear, before the King of

khey ha - m'lo - - khim, ta - ten - yu, lif - ney me - lekh mal -
Kings of Kings fa - ther dear, be - fore the King, of

khey ha - m'lo - - khim, ta - ten - yu ta - ten yu.
Kings of Kings fa - ther dear fa - ther dear.

Thus said Rabbi Elazar, "Thus said Rabbi Haninah: 'Students who study with the wise increase the peace of the world, as it is said: And all thy children shall be taught by the Lord and great shall be the peace of thy children.' Do not read 'thy children' but read it 'thy builders.'"

(This last line is a play on words. The word for "thy children" in Hebrew is *banayikh*. The word for "thy builders" is *bonayikh*.)

The habit of swaying and chanting to accompany study goes back a long way in Jewish history. A fourteenth-century Jewish scholar, Profiat Duran, living in the south of France, wrote that the practice was necessary in order to help the student memorize the text he was studying. The custom is found in many widely separated Jewish communities—among Yemenite Jews, for example, and among the Jews of Morocco. The study melody of the Yemenites is exactly like the setting of Psalm 92 quoted in Chapter Four (Ex. 2). The Moroccan melody is different. The chant which has found its way into Jewish folklore is the sing-song of the East European *matmid*. The swaying of the body, the characteristic gesture of the talmudic thumb—the downward dig and the upward pointing motion of the thumb used in talmudic argumentation—the question-and-answer of the Talmud text are all present in a famous Yiddish folk song, a dialogue between a father and his son. Father asks his son three questions. Each answer, in turn, is a quotation from a traditional prayer. (See Ex. 34 on p. 72.)

2. Meierke, my son,
   Do you know who you are?
   I am one who is poor in good deeds, father dear!

3. Meierke, my son,
   What are you going to ask of Him in your prayers?
   Sons, and life, and sustenance, father dear!

If you want to fit these words of the second and third stanzas to the melody, don't strain for a note-for-note match, but treat the song as a free chant. Guitar chords have been suggested for this version. Use a constant unrhythmic strumming with no beat. Those seeking a piano accompaniment would do well to look up the interesting arrangement of this folk song by Maurice Ravel. It is one of a group of three Jewish songs the French composer arranged for voice and piano, the

other two being *Kaddish* (see Chapter Ten, p. 55) and *The Eternal Question* (in Yiddish, *Die Alte Kasheh*).‡

A somewhat more cheerful version of the study mode lives on in the chant which many generations of Jewish children have learned for the Four Questions, the *Mah Nishtanah* asked at the Passover *seder*. The text of the questions is taken from the Mishnah. The traditional melody, in this case, is in the major mode:

Ex. 35   *Mah Nishtanah*   TRADITIONAL

Mah nish-ta-nah ha-lai-lah ha-zeh mi-kol ha-ley-lot? She-be-khol ha-ley-lot a-nu okh-lin ha-metz u-ma-tzah ha-lay-lah ha-zeh ku-lo ma-tzah.

But it is a long way from the cheerful *Mah Nishtanah*, chanted at the joyous Passover *seder* in the warmth of the family circle, to the bleak and lonely study chant of the *matmid*. A classic Yiddish song, with words by the noted Yiddish poet, Abraham Raisin, captures the same dark atmosphere described by Bialik.

What Is the Meaning?

A. Raisin

Melody by A. Raisin

Ah, the

rain, what is its mean - ing, or the wind a - round me
roof is old and leak - ing. Mud - dy riv - u - lets in -

sweep - ing? On the win - dow - pane the rain - drops sound to
form me that we're get - ting near to win - ter, And I

me like bit - ter weep - ing. And the

have no cloak to warm me. What's the

mean - ing of the can - dle And what sig - ni - fies its

sput - ter As the wax drips on my tab - le and it

waves its fi - nal flut - ter? Thus I sink here, at my

study like a dark and wea - ry mourn - er, Like the

can - dle I am melt - ing in the si - lent east - ern cor - ner.

2. And the clock, what is its meaning,
   Its monotonous tick-tocking?
   With its face of faded yellow,
   With its bell, the hours mocking?
   How mechanical its workings,
   Without life, and without feeling!
   Comes the hour, and willy-nilly
   Once again I hear its pealing.

3. And my life, what is its meaning?
   Like the clock, what can it tell me?
   In my youth I wilt and wither,
   Toward old age the hours impel me.
   I "eat days" and tears I swallow,
   I sleep cold beneath the rafter,
   Giving up the goods of this world
   Waiting for some good hereafter.

(The expression "eat days" is a literal translation of the Yiddish *essen teg*. It refers to one of the harsher aspects of the life of the *yeshivah* student. Far from home, with little or no money, he would be quar-tered for meals in the household of some Jewish family in the community. He might even have to take his meals in different homes on different days. Frequently he went hungry. The townspeople themselves had little food to spare. Even though they considered it a worthy deed—a *mitzvah*—to feed a potential scholar, their hospitality may occasionally have been a little grudging. The poor student would often have to swallow some humiliation along with his meager fare.)

It is possible to savor the study method of the *yeshivah* student without the anguish, of course, and without the intensive learning. Select a passage from the *Ethics of the Fathers* and study it aloud, with the chant and even the swaying. You can use the major form found in the *Mah Nishtanah* (Ex. 35) or the minor form of *Amar Rabbi Elazar* (Ex. 33). Select another passage, and apply the Yemenite study chant (Ex. 2) to it. None of these chants is inherently sad or glad. The mood will be determined by the manner in which it is performed.

Thirteen
THE VOICE
OF THE PROPHET

SOME young American Jewish boys are being trained for the *Bar Mitzvah* ceremony. They are learning to chant the cantillation of the prophetic books according to the ancient musical accents. Since each one will mark his thirteenth birthday on a different date, each will be reading a different prophetic portion (*Haftarah*) on the Sabbath he will become *Bar Mitzvah*. One boy may be preparing to chant a narrative passage from the story of David and Jonathan (*I Samuel 20: 35*): "And it came to pass in the morning, that Jonathan went out into the field at the time appointed with David, and a little lad with him." A second will be

Jeremiah, by Michelangelo (1475–1564)

studying the tender reminder of God's great love for Israel in the passage from *Jeremiah 2: 2*: "Go and cry in the ears of Jerusalem, saying: Thus saith the Lord, I remember for thee the affection of thy youth, the love of thine espousals; how thou wentest after Me in the wilderness, in a land that was not sown." A third may be required to chant the fearful prophecy of doom and destruction from *Isaiah 29: 1–2*: "Ah, Ariel, Ariel, the city where David encamped! / Add ye year to year, / Let the feasts come round! / Then will I distress Ariel, / And there shall be mourning and moaning; / And she shall be unto Me as a hearth of God." Exs. 37, 38 and 39 show how those three portions will be chanted.

All three portions sound very similar despite the difference in the meaning of the words. Of course, the individual reader may put something of his own feeling into the chant by singing slowly or rapidly, loudly or softly, or by pausing to emphasize a particular word. But the melodic line in the three is essentially the same.

Try playing any one of the melodies on a violin. Or, better still, ask several violinists to play in unison. It will be difficult to keep the players together because there is no "beat" to hold them together. Let someone pronounce the words softly, and let the instruments follow the irregular rhythm of the words themselves. Now play the melody again, this time putting a sharp in front of every *F*. This is now a frequently heard variant—that is, a slightly different version of the prophetic cantillation. Play it slowly. Play it very fast.

Now listen to the opening bars of the second movement of Leonard Berstein's *Symphony No. 1 (Jeremiah)* in Ex. 40.‡ Does it sound familiar? Its key is different from the key in which the examples here have been written, but essentially it is a straightforward statement of the traditional Ashkenazic cantillation of *Nevi-im,* (Prophets).

I Samuel 20: 35

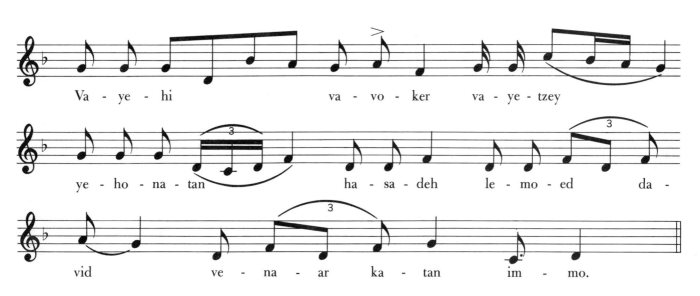

Va - ye - hi va - vo - ker va - ye - tzey ye - ho - na - tan ha - sa - deh le - mo - ed da - vid ve - na - ar ka - tan im - mo.

Ex. 38

Jeremiah 2: 2

Ha - lokh ve - ka - ra - ta be - oz - ney ye - ru - sha - la - yim le' - mor koh a - mar a - do - nai, za - khar - ti lakh he - sed ne - u - ra - yikh a - ha - vat ke - lu - lo - ta - yikh lekh - tekh ah' - rai ba - mid - bar be - e - retz lo ze - ru - ah.

Ex. 39   *Isaiah 29: 1-2*

Hoi a - ri - el a - ri - el   kir - yat ha - nah   da - vid.

Se - fu sha - nah   al sha - nah,   ha - gim yin - ko - fu

va - ha - tzi - ko - ti   la - a - ri - el   ve - ha - ye - tah   ta - a - ni -

yah   va - a - ni - yah   ve - ha - ye - tah   li ka - a - ri - el

Listen to Bernstein's entire second movement. Fragments of the chant appear again and again, twisted and stretched out, its odd rhythms creating the effect of restlessness and turmoil which the composer had in mind.

Ex. 40
Theme, 2nd movement
VIVACE CON BRIO

(♪ = ♪ Beat 8 in 3)

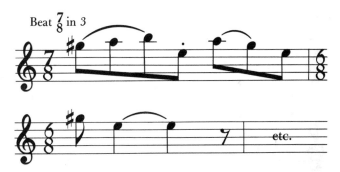

The same accents, applied to the same words in the same passage of Jeremiah just quoted, have an entirely different musical interpretation in the Sephardic cantillation. Ex. 41 is *Jeremiah 2: 2* in the chant used by the Spanish and Portuguese Jews.

Many passages from the writings of the prophets have become part of the prayer service itself. Sometimes a single verse is quoted, sometimes several verses in succession. In these instances, the prophetic words are not chanted according to the cantillation accents. Sometimes they are chanted in prayer modes —in *nusah.* Or sometimes they are set to melodies by composers. For instance, in the traditional synagogue, part of the text of the Torah service (after the scrolls have been removed from the open ark), is the verse: "For out of Zion shall come forth the Law, and the

Ex. 41   *Jeremiah 2: 2*   SEPHARDIC CANTILLATION

Ha - lokh   ve - ka - ra - ta

be - oz - ney   ye - ru - sha - la - yim   le' - mor

koh a - mar a - do - nai,   za - khar - ti lakh

he - sed ne - u - ra - yikh,   a - ha - vat   ke - lu - lo - ta - yikh

lekh - tekh ah' - rai   ba - mid - bar   be - e ___ retz lo ze - ru - ah.

word of God from Jerusalem" *(Isaiah 2: 3)*. This verse occurs originally in the midst of Isaiah's magnificent prophecy of the great day of peace in the "end of days." A century ago the verse was set to music for cantor and choir by Solomon Sulzer, one of the first Western-trained musicians to write music in the style of his contemporaries. Sulzer himself was a cantor whose sweet voice brought countless visitors to his synagogue in Vienna. He was a friend and admirer of the great composer Franz Schubert whose style of melody and even of harmony he was prone to imitate. His melody for the Isaiah verse is typical of that style. It has become so widespread and universally familiar that many people think it is traditional and are deeply dismayed if any other tune is substituted for it in the service. (Ex. 42)

An example of a more extensive prophetic text incorporated into the prayer service is a series of three verses quoted in the *Musaf* (additional) service of *Rosh Hashanah*. All three refer to God's remembering the people of Israel with love. The first is the same verse

Ex. 42   *Ki Mi-Tziyon*   MELODY BY S. SULZER

Ki   mi - tzi - yon   te - tzey   to -

rah,   ki   mi - tzi - yon   te - tzey

to - rah   u - de - var   a - do -

nai   mi - ru - sha - la - - yim.

(*Jeremiah 2: 2*) which appears earlier in this chapter in Ex. 38. The second (*Ezekiel 16: 60*) reads, "I will remember My covenant with thee in the days of thy youth, and I will establish unto thee an everlasting covenant." The final verse *(Jeremiah 31: 20)* speaks of Israel ("called Ephraim") as a beloved child rather than as a bride: "Is Ephraim a darling son unto Me? Is he a child that is dandled? For as often as I speak of him, I do earnestly remember him still; therefore my heart yearneth for him, I will surely have compassion upon him, saith the Lord."

This section of the liturgy is traditionally chanted by the *hazan* according to the *nusah* of *Rosh Hashanah*. It is frequently sung by cantor and choir in a setting composed by Lewandowski, only a few years after Sulzer wrote his *Ki Mi-Tziyon*. Just as Sulzer was much influenced by Schubert, so Lewandowski was an ardent disciple of his own contemporary, Mendelssohn.

Lewandowski's popular setting of the prophetic verses of remembrance has many features of a movement of an oratorio of the nineteenth century similar to the works of Mendelssohn. He opens with a recitative for cantor: "And by thy servants the prophets it is written: Go and cry in the ears of Jerusalem, saying, Thus saith the Lord." Now the choir sings the first of the three verses beginning with the words, "I remember." The upper voice carries the tender, crooning minor melody. The other three voices simply accompany the melody, moving along in the same rhythmic pattern and forming a series of soft, easy harmonies. The second verse is introduced by the cantor with the chanted words "And it is said." Now the music, with the melody still carried by the sopranos, moves into a major key (the "relative major," for those who wish to use the technical term). The recollection of the covenant has a sterner tone. There is a declamatory quality in this second part of the piece even though the chords remain simple and soft. When Part II ends, we have another transitional snatch of recitative by the cantor, "And it is said," and then the choir resumes with the same melody as that of Part I, the original minor melody now bearing the text of the last of the three verses. After the words, "I do earnestly remember him," the choir stops; the cantor sings a brief outcry, "Therefore my heart yearns for him!" Then the choir sings a short *coda* changing from the minor into the (parallel) major, "I shall surely have compassion upon him, saith the Lord."

This composition is admirably suited for performance by amateur choral groups. The cantor's recitatives can be sung easily by a nonprofessional soloist even of moderate ability. Indeed, since the melody of the whole piece is consistently sung by the upper voice, the piece can be a unison song, or a solo song, with the harmonies supplied by an accompanying piano. (Ex. 43)

The books in the *Nevi-im* (Prophets) section of the Hebrew Bible have found their way into music in the world outside the synagogue. Since the prophetic writings are Holy Scripture for the Christians as well as the Jews, they are chanted in the church, and many non-Jewish composers have set them to very beautiful music. Cantatas and oratorios have been written on narrative and poetic passages taken from *Nevi-im*, beginning with the *Book of Judges* all the way through what we call the books of the "Minor Prophets," with texts in Latin, German and French. Many of these works are performed more frequently in the concert hall than in the church.

Such compositions are too numerous even to be listed in this book. One oratorio, however, is especially interesting to us in the context of this chapter because it seems to epitomize the classic concept of the "prophet." Felix Mendelssohn's famous *Elijah*, based on the narrative in *I Kings 17–20*, shows us the prophet Elijah in characteristic moments of anger, despair, gentleness and hope. Read the original narrative. Then listen to a recording with the score in front of you.‡ You will be able, even with only a little experience in reading music, to follow the score and also to sing along with the recorded music, taking the voice part in which you are most comfortable—soprano, alto, tenor or bass. Sing along with the soloists as well, if you wish. This kind of activity is not performance before an audience. It is, however, an enjoyable way to enter into the spirit of Mendelssohn's work and of the biblical story.

With Mendelssohn's music, we are still in the nineteenth century. A twentieth-century score will be considerably more difficult to read. Today's composers write melodies that are jagged in contrast with the smooth-flowing tunes of the period known as the Romantic Era. Modern composers have broken away from the even, regular rhythm and from the strictly symmetrical form which were so evident in Lewandowski's short piece and in Mendelssohn's larger and more important work.

Ve-al Yedey Avadekha

L. Lewandowski

Ve - al   ye - dey   a - va - de - kha han' - vi -

im ka - tuv _____ le' - mor,   ha -

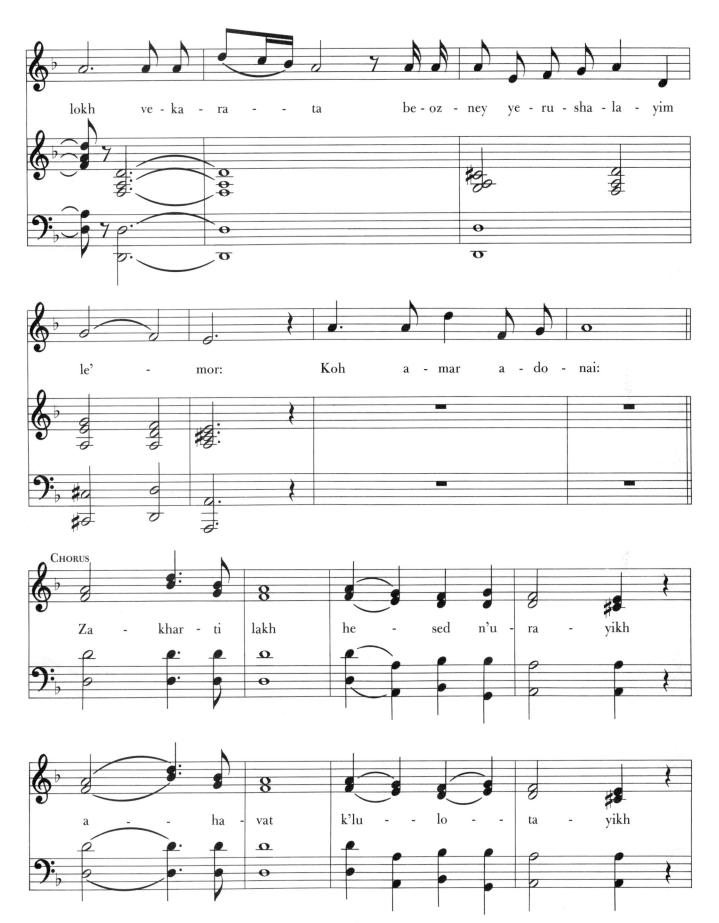

lokh ve-ka-ra----ta be-oz-ney ye-ru-sha-la-yim

le'----mor: Koh a-mar a-do-nai:

Zakharti lakh he-sed n'u-ra-yikh

a-ha-vat k'lu-lo-ta-yikh

85

Despite the difficulties, students would find it worthwhile to read through Robert Starer's cantata, *Ariel,* based on excerpts from Isaiah.‡ From the very first notes of the instrumental accompaniment, the harshness of Isaiah's prophecy "Woe to Ariel!" becomes apparent. (This is the passage quoted above in Ex. 39 in a slightly different translation.) The dissonances of the opening bars warn of destruction.

Ex. 44   Opening bars

Ariel

ROBERT STARER

Starer's *Ariel* has six movements. It proceeds from dread anticipation to bitterness in describing the corrupt ways of the people of Judah. Lament, hope and thanksgiving are expressed in subsequent movements, leading to a joyous finale: "Break forth in joy, sing together, for the Lord hath comforted His people. He hath redeemed Jerusalem" (*Isaiah 52: 9*).

The feeling in this last movement suggests a *hora* in the land of Israel. And that is not strange. The composer, now living and working in the United States, lived for many years in Israel and absorbed much of the spirit of the youth there. It was not unusual for the young people to dance their jubilant circle dance to the words of the prophets. Their choice of texts, quite naturally, focuses on those which speak of the great return and the rebuilding of the homeland. The *Mayim* song (see Chapter Eleven) is one example of this kind of dance. Another is the *Ki Mi-Tziyon* composed by Emanuel Amiran with the same text as the excerpt by Sulzer in Ex. 42. This may be sung in Amiran's own arrangement for two voices quoted below or in the arrangement by Max Helfman.‡

Ex. 45   *Ki Mi-Tziyon*   E. Amiran

87

tzey to - rah   u - de-var   a - do - nai   u - de-var   a - do - nai

rah   u - de-var   a - do - nai   u - de-var   a - do - nai

u - de-var   a - do - nai   mi - ru - sha - la - yim   ho

u - de-var   a - do - nai   ye - ru - sha - la - yim   ya - ho

ho   ho ho   ya - ho

ya - ho   ho

ya - ho   ki mi-tzi - yon   ho te - tzey to - rah

ho   ya - ho   ya - ho

Fourteen
LOUD SONG OF JOY

THE BIBLE is filled with moments of high joy, triumph and thanksgiving. And the Psalmist tells us how such moments are to be celebrated: "Clap your hands, all people! Shout to God with loud songs of joy!" (*Psalm 47: 2*). That isn't the subdued, genteel kind of sound some people tend to regard as religious song! The composer, Leonard Bernstein, recaptured the biblical explosion of joy in the opening movement of his *Chichester Psalms.*‡ "Awake, psaltery and harp! I will rouse the dawn," sings his chorus in great dissonant chords, the voices executing dazzling leaps and the orchestra providing a great spate of "noise." Then the whole ensemble swings into a syncopated, jazzy, dance-like setting of Psalm 100: "Make a joyful noise unto the Lord, all ye lands!" Some of the excitement of this movement comes from its uneven rhythm—seven beats to the measure, *i.e.*, four beats and then three beats in each measure.

Try to count the rhythm: *one* two three four, *one* two three. If you are with friends, or in a class, let half the group clap every beat and the other half clap just the *one* (accented) beat. Do it fast. Do you feel the breathless quality? Now listen to Bernstein's music. Follow the Hebrew text, if possible, in the Bible itself or in the transliteration below.

The Exodus, from an old Haggadah

You can feel some of the excitement of "shouting to God with loud songs of joy" by way of a folk song. Yemenite Jews have a song (Ex. 46) they sing in the same exuberant spirit. The text comes from two psalms: "The Lord is my strength and song, He is my salvation!" (*Psalm 118: 14*) and "The Lord is strong and mighty, mighty in battle!" (*Psalm 24: 8*, slightly altered). The first part of this song has a rhythm of seven counts—in this case, three plus four.

Psalm 108: 2

Urah ha-nevel ve-khinnor!
A-irah shahar.

Awake, psaltery and harp!
I will rouse the dawn.

Psalm 100

Hariyu la'donai kol ha-aretz
Ivdu et Adonai be-simhah
Bo-u lefanav bir'nanah
De-u ki Adonai hu Elohim.
Hu asanu velo anahnu.
Amo ve-tzon mar'ito
Bo-u she-arav be-todah
Hatzerotav bit'hilah.
Hodu lo, barekhu Shemo
Ki tov Adonai, le-olam hasdo
Ve-al dor va-dor emunato.

Make a joyful noise unto the Lord, all ye lands!
Serve the Lord with gladness;
Come before His presence with singing.
Know ye that the Lord He is God;
It is He that hath made us and not we ourselves.
We are His people and the sheep of His pasture.
Enter into His gates with thanksgiving
And into His courts with praise;
Be thankful unto Him, and bless His name.
For the Lord is good, His mercy is everlasting;
And His truth endureth unto all generations.

Count it: *one* two three, *one* two three four. This is not fast like the Bernstein rhythm. Count it at a marching speed. Let half your class clap out every beat, the other half clap only the accented beats. Now a guitarist might play an E minor chord in double time (eighth notes). A second person might tap the beat (quarter notes) on a tambourine. Add a drum (a simple frame drum or an Israeli clay drum) which should be struck only on the strong beats. There follows a suggested score of the Yemenite song for voice, percussion, guitar and two recorders. Any one or more elements can be used in combination, or invent new combinations. Repeat the song over and over and over, each time slightly faster than before, adding instruments each time 'round. The ending is up to you; it can conclude either on a high climax or as a receding sound as though the singers and players were moving off into the distance. How will you achieve that latter effect?

We quoted Psalm 118: 14 as the source of the first line of the Yemenite song. But even the Psalmist himself was quoting when he composed his poem. He took the verse from a still older song, one of the oldest in Jewish history—the song Moses and the children of Israel sang after they had crossed the Red Sea. It is found in the *Book of Exodus,* Chapter 15, and is known as "The Song of the Sea" or "The Song of Moses" or, in Hebrew, simply as *Shirah,* "Song." The Sabbath on which *Exodus 15* is read in the synagogue as part of the regular cycle of Torah readings is called the Sabbath of the Song, *Shabbat Shirah.* (The chapter is also chanted in a special Torah reading on the seventh day of Passover.) As the *ba-al keriyah* (reader) starts to chant it, traditional congregations will rise and join him in singing the closing words of certain verses. The chant is based on the cantillation accents, but it differs somewhat from the regular Torah chant described in Chapter Six. The verse endings (cadences) have an especially triumphant sound. A few selected verses from the *Song* follow. (Ex. 47) The

version here is written to be played entirely on the black keys of the piano. It is in the pentatonic or five-tone scale.

That last verse "Who is like unto Thee—" has found its way into the prayer book and is sung by the cantor and choir, or the congregation, during Sabbath and festival prayer services. Over the centuries it has been set to a wide variety of tunes and to more elaborate compositions. One of the finest versions was composed by the late Ernest Bloch in his great Sabbath Morning Service *(Avodat ha-Kodesh)* for solo, chorus and orchestra.[‡] Bloch's *Mi Khamokhah* weaves in some of the ancient cantillation chant. Listen to the recording of the service. In the *Mi Khamokhah* you will hear some of the high triumphant spirit of *The Song of the Sea.*

Sephardic Jews chant the *Song* on every Sabbath eve. Their tune is not based on the cantillation signs but rather is a metrical lyrical melody. (Ex. 48)

This melody became a kind of theme of rejoicing and thanksgiving in the Sephardic tradition. There is a hymn to that melody in Judaeo-Spanish, the vernacular of the Sephardim, called *Bendigamos.* Appropriately, on Passover, when the exodus from Egypt is being celebrated, Sephardic Jews chant the joyous Psalm 118 to practically the same tune. (Ex. 49)

Any mention of *The Song of the Sea* automatically recalls the composer, George Frederick Handel, whose famous oratorio, *Israel in Egypt,* provides a monumental setting for the song. Handel built each single verse into an entire composition, calling on his singers, sometimes in chorus, sometimes as soloists or duettists, to weave long ornamental melodies, stressing the meaning and importance of every word. Look up Handel's magnificent oratorio, and listen especially to the entire second half which is devoted solely to *The Song of the Sea.* As you listen, follow the English text of the Bible. You will be listening to a master composer's interpretation of a great biblical song of joy.

Ex. 46   *Ozi Ve-zimerat Yah*   YEMENITE FOLK SONG

2ND RECORDER

O - zi   ve - zi - me - rat   yah   va - y' hi   li   li - shu - ah,   O -

zi ve - zi - me - rat yah va - y'- hi li li - shu - ah. E -

zuz ve - gi - bor yah, gi - bor mil' - ha - mah, E -

zuz ve - gi - bor yah, gi - bor mil' - ha - mah. O - etc.

1ST
RECORDER

2ND
RECORDER

TAMBOURINE

92

93

TRIANGLE

94

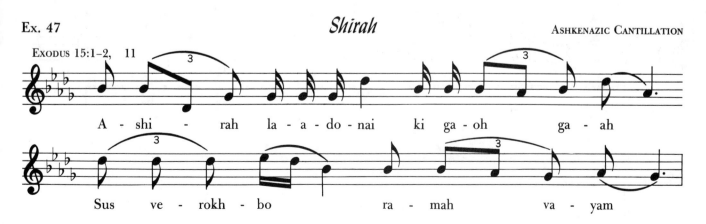

Ex. 47   *Shirah*   ASHKENAZIC CANTILLATION

EXODUS 15:1–2, 11

A - shi - rah la - a - do - nai   ki ga - oh   ga - ah

Sus   ve - rokh - bo   ra - mah   va - yam

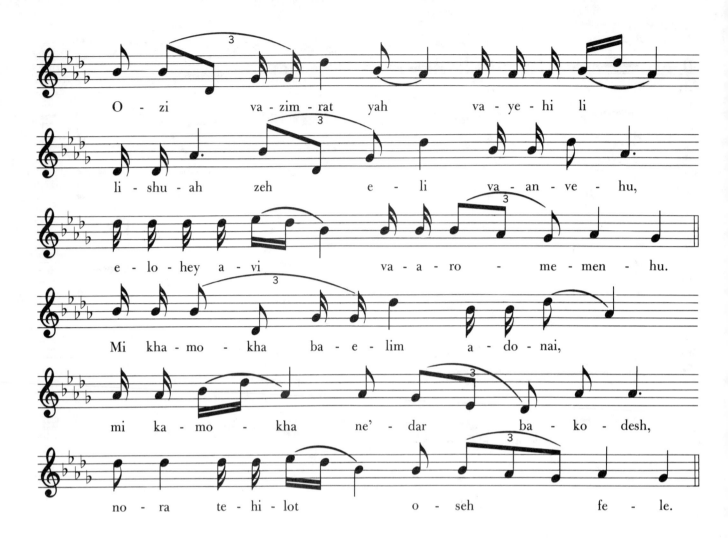

O - zi va - zim - rat yah va - ye - hi li
li - shu - ah zeh e - li va - an - ve - hu,
e - lo - hey a - vi va - a - ro - me - men - hu.
Mi kha - mo - kha ba - e - lim a - do - nai,
mi ka - mo - kha ne' - dar ba - ko - desh,
no - ra te - hi - lot o - seh fe - le.

I will sing unto the Lord, for He is highly exalted;
The horse and his rider hath He thrown into the sea.
The Lord is my strength and song,

And He is become my salvation;
This is my God, and I will glorify Him;
My father's God, and I will exalt Him.

Who is like unto Thee, O Lord, among the mighty?
Who is like unto Thee, glorious in holiness,
Fearful in praises, doing wonders?

Ex. 48   *Shirah*   TRADITIONAL SEPHARDIC CHANT

EXODUS 15:1

Az ya - shir Mo - sheh u - ve - ney yis - ra -

el et ha - shi - rah ha - zot la' - do - nai

va - yo - me - ru le - mor: a - shi - rah la - do - nai

ki ga - oh ga - ah sus ve -

rokh - bo ra - mah va - yam.

Ex. 49   *Psalm 118: 5-6*   TRADITIONAL
SEPHARDIC CHANT

Min ha - me - tzar ka - ra - ti

yah a - na - ni

ba - mer - hav - yah, a - do - nai

li lo i - ra

mah ya - a seh li a - dam.

Out of my straits I called upon the Lord;   The Lord is for me, I will not fear;
He answered me with great enlargement   What can man do unto me?

Fifteen

SONG OF LAMENT

JUST as the Bible records outbursts of sublime joy, so too it records episodes of infinite tragedy, suffering and sorrow. At times the suffering is personal; and, at other times, the suffering engulfs the entire people of Israel.

One of the most poignant examples of personal grief is that moment when Joseph's brothers bring his cloak—the blood-stained cloak of many colors—to their old father, Jacob. Joseph was the son of Jacob's beloved Rachel, and, of all his sons, Joseph received the greatest measure of the father's love and attention. Jacob's anguish at that terrible moment is described in *Genesis 37: 34–35* in these words: "And Jacob rent his garments and put sackcloth upon his loins and mourned for his son many days. And all his sons and all his daughters rose up to comfort him; but he refused to be comforted, and he said: 'Nay, but I will go down to the grave to my son mourning.' And his father wept for him."

King David suffered deep sorrow throughout his life for tragedies befalling those who were closest to

---

Tisha B'Av, mourning at the Western Wall in our own day

him. The death of his beloved friend, Jonathan, and of his king, Saul, evoked from David one of the most eloquent threnodies known to man:

Thy beauty, O Israel, upon thy high places is slain!
How are the mighty fallen!
Tell it not in Gath,
Publish it not in the streets of Ashkelon;
Lest the daughters of the Philistines rejoice,
Lest the daughters of the uncircumcised triumph.
Ye mountains of Gilboa,
Let there be no dew nor rain upon you,
Neither fields of choice fruits, . . .

(II Samuel 1: 19–26)

And years later when David is approaching old age, his son Absalom launches a rebellion against his father's throne and life. David has no choice but to send troops to quell the rebellion, in the course of which Absalom is trapped and killed. David's grief upon learning of the young man's death is too powerful for language. All the broken father can say is, "O my son Absalom, my son, my son, Absalom! would I had died for thee, O Absalom, my son, my son!"

These episodes of personal grief have inspired many composers—Jewish and non-Jewish—to turn to musical expression. Jacob's experience, with some additional text, was written into a four-part choral piece early in the sixteenth century by a German composer, Ludwig Senfl. The group called the New York Pro Musica has recorded Senfl's German piece, and if you can find the recordings you should listen to this interesting example of Renaissance music.‡

David's magnificent dirge has been given a very dramatic musical setting by the modern Swiss composer, Arthur Honegger, in his oratorio *Le Roi David*.‡ The passage entitled *Lament for Gilboa* is introduced by two solo female voices: "Gilboa, Gilboa!" Then the orchestra takes up a monotonous funereal rhythm, all the women's voices join the wailing and the rest of the text is spoken above the music. This lament is only one of many beautiful passages in Honegger's oratorio. The entire work has been recorded. Listen to it, and follow the text if you can.

The same threnody has been set, in its original Hebrew *(Ha-tzevi Yisrael)*, by another contemporary composer, Stefan Wolpe. He is a far more radical composer than Honegger. His song for voice and piano is highly dissonant, its melodic line much more difficult than Honegger's. The Honegger selection is sorrowful, Wolpe's is bitter. This is a good example of how the same text can be interpreted in widely varying music.

Wolpe's song has been recorded.‡ Only a highly trained musician can sing it. A moderately trained person, however, could very effectively sing David Diamond's song, *David Mourns for Absalom.*‡ Diamond, a contemporary American composer, has written a simple and moving piece which starts with the brief narration "David the King was grieved and much moved . . ." and goes on to the dirge itself. This would be a fine solo piece to include in a concert of Jewish music.

Any group might sing the old English round based on the Absalom passage. It is not a very easy round, and thus it would be advisable to sing it through several times as a unison song before proceeding. Then, softly and carefully, sing it as a round.

Ex. 50

O Absalom

C. KING

Tisha B'Av, from an old woodcut

ra - ba - ti am ha - ye -tah

ke - al - ma - nah. Ra - ba - ti

va - go - yim

sa - ra - ti ba - me - di -not

ha - ye - tah la - mas

Laments for the Jewish people, for Jerusalem and for the land of Israel occur far more frequently in the Bible than the laments of personal sorrow. One entire biblical book, *Lamentations,* is of course the most famous of all expressions of sorrow. In Hebrew the book is called simply *Eykhah* after the opening words: *Eykhah yashevah vadad ha-ir rabati am* (How doth the city sit solitary, that was full of people). The book is chanted in the synagogue on *Tisha B'Av,* the ninth day of the Hebrew month of *Av* (at the end of July or the beginning of August) which is traditionally observed as the anniversary of the destruction of both the First and Second Temples in Jerusalem and the exile of the people from their land. It is chanted according to the *ta-amey neginah.* In the Ashkenazic synagogue *Eykhah* sounds like this:

Turn back to your recording of Bernstein's *Jeremiah* symphony. The last movement is based entirely on the text and the Ashkenazic cantillation of *Eykhah.* It is sung in Hebrew, but non-Hebraists can follow the English text.‡

Most biblical cantillations are not expressive of feeling. However, both the Ashkenazic and the Sephardic cantillations of *Eykhah* do seem to carry a feeling of lament. This is how the book is chanted in Sephardic synagogues:

Ex. 51   *Lamentations 1:1*   ASHKENAZIC CANTILLATION

Ex. 52   *Lamentations 1:1*   SEPHARDIC CANTILLATION

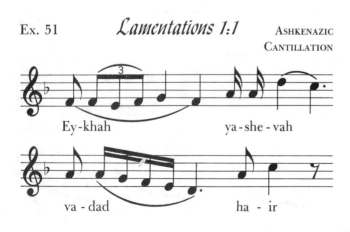

Ey-khah ya - she - vah

va - dad ha - ir

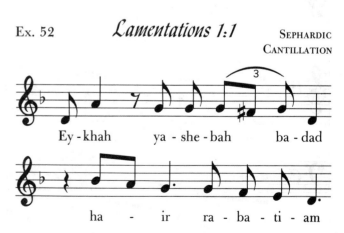

Ey - khah ya - she - bah ba - dad

ha - ir ra - ba - ti - am

100

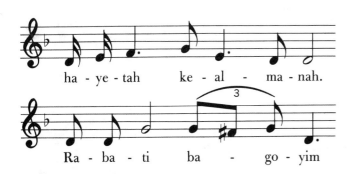

More than a thousand years after the destruction of the Second Temple a whole group of new laments were written which, like the *Book of Lamentations,* are also sung on *Tisha B'Av.* The laments *(kinot* in Hebrew; the singular is *kinah)* are poems with meter and rhyme. The earliest were written in Spain as the brilliant Jewish "Golden Age" began to dim in the shadow of the Inquisition. Premonitions of disasters to come struck the hearts of many poets and singers. They sang their *kinot* in the style of the music which

they heard in the courts and in the market places. Following is one which was probably borrowed directly from the song of a troubadour of northern Spain. Its text comes from the *Book of Lamentations;* the verses are merely rearranged to provide a meter and rhyme scheme. (Ex. 53)

A second *kinah,* also from the ritual of the Spanish and Portuguese synagogue, while it still bears some resemblance to troubadour song, is more original in both text and melody. (Ex. 54)

Eykh Navi Shudad

Ex. 53

SEPHARDIC KINAH

na - dad, ha - ir ⎯⎯⎯⎯⎯ ra - ba - ti am ey -

kha ya - she - bah ba-dad ba - dad ke - al -

ma - - - nah ha - ye - tah

ne - e - ma - nah.　　La - - khen　　e - sa ki - nah　be - yom

zeh　　be - khol　sha - - nah.

Ex. 54　　　　　*Borey Ad Anah*　　　　　SEPHARDIC KINAH
　　　　　(O Creator, How Long?)

Bo - - rey　ad
O　　Cre - a - - tor, how

a - nah yo - na - te-kha bim' - su - dah
long shall Thy dove be cap - tive and torn,

tokh pakh ha - mo - kesh a - ni - yah um' -
In the net of the fowl - er all de - so - late and for -

ru - dah. U - b'li ba - ne - ha
lorn, And with-out her child - ren,

bi   a - bi   a - bi   a - bi   yo - she

she   -   bet   gal - mu   -   dah,   tzo   e   -   ket   "A -
sits   a - lone   to mourn,   to   cry   a - loud   "A -

bi"   -   tzo   e   -   ket   "A - bi!"
bi"   to   cry   a - loud   "A - bi!"

The Ashkenazic Jews also sing *kinot*. The best-known of them, however, seems to have, oddly enough, a Spanish ancestry. It has been compared to a song found in an old manuscript which was sung by Christian pilgrims to the great monastery of Compostela in northern Spain. Some itinerant Jew may very possibly have encountered the pilgrims in his travels and brought the melody home to Germany.

Ancient tortures, Spanish Inquisition, by Picart

Ex. 55   *Eli Tziyon*   Ashkenazic Kinah

E - li Tzi - yon ve - a - - re - ha ke - mo i -

shah be tzi - - re - ha, ve - khiv' - tu - lah ha -

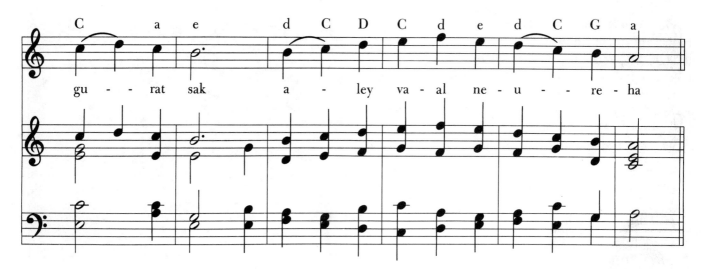

[I sing of] Zion among her cities
Like a woman in birth-pangs,
And like a maiden girt in sackcloth
In mourning for the husband of her youth.

Though they are not called *kinot,* new laments have appeared in the twentieth century. The concentration camps, the prison ghettos, the death marches of the Nazi era—all are bitterly recalled in songs which, unlike their medieval predecessors, are not religious in tone. Nor are they sung in the Hebrew of the Bible or the prayer book. The laments of the holocaust were sung in the language of the folk, in Yiddish. Like some of the *kinot,* many have melodies that echo strains in popular songs of their Christian neighbors.

The following song, a survivor of the Vilna Ghetto, is a bitter travesty of an older Yiddish folk song, a gay, carefree wedding song. In its new form it becomes a dance of death, a veritable *"valse macabre."*

Ex. 56   *Dance of Death*   FOLK, VILNA GHETTO

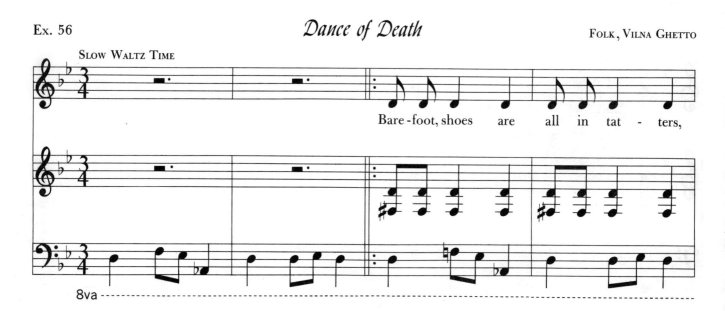

Woe is me and moan - ing ! Col - lars ripped, our

throats are freez - ing, bare - ly strength for groan - ing !

Dance, dance, dance ! It's one, two, three, you

know. Freeze, you bit-ter breez - es, from Si-

be - ri - a you blow.

8va- -

Yellow permits, pink permits
  Permits polychrome;
When, my sweetheart, will they let me
  Take you to our home?
Dance to the permits,
  Green and blue and red.
If you have a yellow ticket,
  Surely we shall wed.

Bread by the centimeter,
  Kindling by the splinter,
This is what the *Judenrat**
  Provides us for the winter,
Dance this waltz,
  One and two and three!
If you have a yellow ticket,
  You must marry me.

* The Jewish council appointed by the Nazis to administer the affairs of the
ghetto.

The tragedy of the holocaust has found its expression in art music as well as in the songs of the folk. The Israeli composer Odeon Partos wrote a composition for viola and orchestra called *Yizkor*.[‡] This title is the first Hebrew word of the traditional memorial service for the dead and serves as the traditional name of that service. Partos, himself, is an accomplished violist and writes for the virtuoso performer on that instrument, in contemporary style. However, this piece is replete with moving allusions to traditional melody. While there are no such allusions in Arnold Schoenberg's *A Survivor from Warsaw*,[‡] his short composition by that name is, in its way, a powerful memorial to the terrible days of the Warsaw Ghetto uprising. Schoenberg wrote his own text for the narrator (in *sprechstimme*), the tale of near-death and escape through the sewers. The orchestra and chorus, background to the narrative, culminate with a hair-raising outcry of the ancient Hebrew words *Shema Yisrael*. . . .

A third piece which is quite different from either of those is a composition called *A Mitzvah for the Dead* by the American composer Michael Sahl.[‡] It is in the idiom of the 1960's, being written for violin and tape recorder. Somewhat in the spirit of the *Dance of Death* (Ex. 56) it is built on references to waltzes, Polish dances, sentimental ballads, all of them twisted and distorted by tape recording. It concludes with a lengthy set of brilliant variations on the nostalgic song, *The Last Rose of Summer*. The composer explains his title thus: "The sense in which this piece is a *Mitzvah* for the dead is that it is an attempt . . . to write the kind of music that might have gratified them had they heard it." (From the record jacket.)

Two drawings, in memory of the Warsaw Ghetto revolt, by Maurice Mindjinsky

111

Sixteen

DO NOT MOURN!

Do not mourn, do not weep on such a day!
Off, and back to work, away! Away!
 Plowman, push your plow,
 Sower, sow your seed,
 A thousandfold toil!
 A thousandfold build!
Ye shall plant, ye shall dig,
Gather stones, raise a wall,
Build a road smooth and straight
For the day of freedom, the day of light.

This day's pain paves the way
For redemption next day.
 Blood of those who fell
 Cries—ah! hear it well!—
 "Back to work, be brave!
 Save yourselves, and save!"

(From the Hebrew of David Shimoni, 1886–1956)

LAMENTS and dirges are not the only types of song that emerge in times of overwhelming disaster or terrible trial. When hope is not altogether crushed, when faith is strong or when the human spirit rises up in defiance, another variety of expression may at times be heard—songs of protest, of courage and of faith. The whole world now knows *We Shall Overcome, If I Had a Hammer, We Shall Not Be Moved,* songs associated with the American Civil Rights movement. They initiated the most recent group in a long line expressing the indomitable will of man to challenge tyranny, injustice or enslavement.

Resistance to tyranny swept up many men in many nations at the end of the eighteenth century. To the strains of *Yankee Doodle, Buttermilk Hill* and *Boston Tea Party,* American colonials fought a revolution and won against great odds. Across the Atlantic in France, the passion of the people for *"Liberté, Egalité, Fraternité"* surged up with tremendous force to the accompaniment of Rouget de Lisle's stirring *Marseillaise.* Eastward across Europe, in the Austria ruled by an absolute empress, the great musical genius Mozart—under the guise of telling a charming fairy tale—sang of his dream for a free and peaceful world to the aristocratic opera patrons of Vienna. (Listen to Sarastro's noble aria "Within These Holy Halls" from *The Magic Flute.*)

Revolt in the Warsaw Ghetto, by Mindjinsky

Farther East still, in the remote and backward Russian Ukraine, in a small town light-years away from any currents of progress in the world of that time, there lived another singer of protest. The town was Berditchev; the singer–an unlikely rebel, uninformed about the tides of revolution, about firebrands like Tom Paine or about Mozart, Haydn and Beethoven, his contemporaries—was the saintly rabbi of Berditchev, Levi Yitzhak.

Hundreds of stories and legends have come down about the piety and gentleness of Levi Yitzhak, one of the early hasidic leaders (1740–1809) and among the greatest of all the hasidic masters. Yet this same rabbi and teacher had no moment of hesitation in challenging the Ruler of the Universe! Levi Yitzhak had a cause and a case: the Jewish people suffering under oppression, persecution and injustice. Like some defense attorney who pleads with all his fervor for justice for an innocent and much-abused client, Levi Yitzhak argued before the highest court of all. And carried away by the enormity of the just grievances he was presenting, Levi Yitzhak passed the point of pleading. He demanded, actually *demanded,* that the Judge of all mankind Himself do justice! Perhaps he was using the famous precedent of the patriarch Abraham, who dared to argue with God on behalf of Sodom and Gomorrah, when he placed the Judge on trial!‡

How did the saintly Levi Yitzhak first come to voice his now-classic song of protest-complaint-challenge? It was his habit during religious services to stand on the altar before his people, sunk in thought and prayer. Then he would start to speak to them, slowly, meditatively; then gradually his speech became a chant, the chant of the synagogue, sometimes *nusah,* sometimes the study chant. As he became more and more absorbed in his message, he would break into real song, fervent and intense. Perhaps this was the way Levi Yitzhak launched into his passionate argument with God.*

As a song of protest as well as of sanctification, Levi Yitzhak's remarkable outpouring is in a class by itself. From a musical point of view, it is a free chant without any meter and can be sung only by a soloist. Several well-known opera singers, cantors and folk singers have recorded the song effectively in the original

* The transliterations in this song indicate the Ashkenazic pronunciation, which is what Rabbi Levi Yitzhak would have used.

Synagogue at Berditchev

Yiddish. Listen, and follow the translation. After a few playings, the Yiddish will be understandable. And listen, too, for the musical themes which Levi Yitzhak wove into his song, themes out of the *nusah,* so familiar to his congregation. His song begins with a fragment of the penitential chant of the High Holy Days. Look at the music over the first appearance of the words "of Berditchev." This is the cadence and *Amen* theme of the three Pilgrim festivals:

(Note that this *Amen* is the motive out of which Bernstein built the first movement of his *Jeremiah* symphony and which he reiterates at the end of his third movement with great force.)

Rabbi Levi Yitzhak's chant (Ex. 57) reaches a climax with a recital of the opening words of the *Kaddish* on the *nusah* of *Ne-ilah,* the closing theme of *Yom Kippur.* (See Ex. 28 in Chapter Ten.)

The song of Levi Yitzhak is a uniquely personal statement expressing the forceful character, conviction and faith of the hasidic rabbi. It is a courageous statement—certainly, only a very few men would dare fling up the challenge as directly as he did. Hearing him sing it must have amazed his congregation and filled them with new strength and hope. But, yet, this was *his* song, and what could *they* sing as a group to keep up *their* courage, voice *their* protest, assert *their* feelings and aspirations?

A century after the death of Levi Yitzhak, new kinds of songs began to be heard. To be sure, they expressed

The Kaddish of Rabbi Levi Yitzhok

Good morn - ing Lord, Mas - ter of the u - ni - verse!

I, Le - vi Yitz - hok son of So - roh of Ber - di - tchev,

I come to you with a *din to - roh* for your peo - ple Is - ra - el.

What do you want of your peo - ple Is - ra - el? What do you

de - mand of your peo - ple Is - ra - el? For ev' - ry - where I

look it says, "Speak un - to the child - ren of Is - ra - el," and

ev' - ry oth - er verse reads, "Say un - to the child - ren of Is - ra - el,"

and o - ver and o - ver it says, "Com - mand the child - ren of Is - ra - el!"

Fa - ther sweet Fa - ther in hea - ven, how ma - ny na - tions are

there in the world? Per - sians, Ba - by - lo - ni - ans, E - do -

mites! The Eng - lish, what do they say? That their king is the

ru - ler. The Prus - sians, what do they say? That their king shall

reign su - preme. The Rus - sians, what do they say? That the

Czar is the al - might - y Em - per - or. And I, Le - vi

Yitz - hok son of So - roh of Ber - di - tchev, what do I

say? "There is one King who sits on a high and ex - alt - ed

throne," and I, Le - vi Yitz - hok son of So - roh of Ber - di - tchev, say

"Yis - ga - dal ve - yis - ka - dash she - mey ra - bo, Mag - ni - fied and

Sanc - ti - fied is on - ly Thy Name!" And I, Le - vi

Yitz - hok son of So - roh of Ber - di - tchev, say "I shall not budge from this point, from this stand I shall not be moved, and let there be an end to our suf - fer - ing! Oh, yis - ga - dal ve - yis - ka - dash _____ she - mey ra - bo!"

daring and courage and even, at times, a certain amount of protest. But they were radically different in spirit, tone and purpose from those the Jewish people had been singing for some 1,800 years. Now, at the dawn of the twentieth century, the *halutzim,* the pioneers, were beginning to build a homeland in Palestine. They were determined to do it with their own hands, slowly, painfully, *dunam* by *dunam,* despite danger, disease, physical hardship and backbreaking labor. They needed songs to rouse their aching limbs to plow one more row, and yet another, past the point of normal endurance. Songs gave them new strength to wield the heavy pickaxes, lift the stubborn rocks, drain the marshlands, plant and sow and reap. And songs gave them solace and companionship in the long and lonely nightwatches against marauding neighbors.

The *halutzim* found their songs in themselves or out of their people's past. Sometimes they recalled old words and set them to new music or, at other times, they took old tunes and fashioned new words. For example, they borrowed texts from the Bible—*Mayim* and *Ki Mi-Tziyon,* songs discussed in earlier chapters, are two instances. They borrowed famous passages

from the Mishnah, including the well-known saying of Rabbi Hillel: "If I am not for myself, who will be for me? If I am for myself alone, what am I? And if not now, when?" (*Pirke Avot 1: 14*). Taking over the melody of a Russian folk song, the *halutzim* turned Hillel's teaching into a work song.

They were even able to find Hebrew texts from the dark days of the Inquisition in Spain, the very days when the first *kinot* were produced. The medieval Hebrew poet, Falaquera, wrote a pithy and succinct declaration of courage which was set to a marching melody by the *halutzim* of the 1930's. (Ex. 58)

But, of all the marching songs of the new generation, perhaps the most popular and cherished was *Tehezaknah* by Hayim Nahman Bialik. By the mid-1920's, the poet had left behind the dark and oppressive world of the *matmid* and had settled in the land. As the national poet of the people, Bialik wrote ringing poems to celebrate the spirit and the work of the pioneers. His powerful Hebrew phrases perfectly matched the strength and the vigor of the *halutzim.* His poem, *Tehezaknah,* was sung everywhere in the reborn land. Its melody is modelled on some spirited Russian revolutionary song. (Ex. 59)

Ex. 58

Im Ed Kemo Sela
(If Stone Walls)

FALAQUERA   In March time, with strong accents

FOLK SONG

GIRLS

Im ___ ed ke-mo se - la ke-mo pa-tish a - ni, ___
If stone walls should e'er en-com-pass me, a ham-mer I to bat-ter them,

BOYS

Im ed ke-mo se-la ho, ke-mo pa-tish a - ni ___
Stone walls en-com-pass me, ho, a ham-mer I to bat-ter them,

More soft and flowing

Va - a - ni ka-ma - yim im te-la-ah ra shef,
Like a flood of wa - ter I quench the flames of e - vil,

Va - a - ni ka-ma - yim im te-la-ah ra - shef,
Like a flood of wa - ter I quench the flames of e - vil,

Ka - ma-yim im te-la-ah ra - shef.
Like the wa - ter I quench the flames of e - vil.

Ka - ma-yim im te-la-ah ra - shef.
Like a flood of wa - ter I quench the flames of e - vil.

Start quietly and swell out

Li - bi be-vo-ah ye-he-zak, ve-hu ke-mo sa-har
My ___ heart will grow from might to ___ might, ___ as the moon's pale

Li - bi ___ be-vo-ah ye-he-zak, ___ ve-hu ke-mo
My ___ heart ___ will grow from might to ___ might, ___ as the moon's pale

117

me - o - ro ye - he - zak ba - na - shef. zak ba - na - shef.
light grows stron-ger in the dark - en - ing night. in the dark -'ning night.

me - o - ro ye - he - zak ba - na - shef. zak ba - na - shef.
light grows stron-ger in the dark -'ning night. in the dark -'ning night.

Tehezaknah
(Strengthen the Hands)

Ex. 59

H. N. Bialik

Translation by Alexander M. Dushkin

Folk Song

Te - he - zak - nah ye - dey kol a - he - nu ham' - ho - ne - nim
O strength - en the hands of our com - rades re - build - ing the

af - rot ar - tze - nu ba' - sher hem sham, Al yi - pol ru - ha-khem, a -
land of our fathers with the sweat of their brow. Toil - ers cour - a - geous

li - zim mit-ro-ne-nim, bo - u sh'hem e - had le - ez - rat ha - am, Al ez - rat ha - am.

Dream-ers of a - ges, shoul-der to shoul-der for Is - ra - el now. Is - ra - el now.

The long black night of the Hitler era, out of which we have heard the tortured *Dance of Death* (Ex. 56, in Chapter Fifteen), produced songs of faith and songs of defiance. Deeply religious believers went into the gas chambers with a declaration of abiding faith on their lips—faith that a better day was bound to come for this world. Using the Hebrew words from the *Thirteen Articles of Faith* written by the twelfth-century philosopher Moses Maimonides, they sang, "I believe with a perfect faith in the coming of the Messiah . . . Even though he linger, nevertheless, I believe!" Their song became the hymn of the death camps, an overwhelming declaration of a religious spirit which nothing—the hangmen, the tyrants, the torturers—could ever vanquish or destroy.

Ex. 60 is the song with no accompaniment, no harmonies, no dramatic embellishments to detract from its stark simplicity. At most, let a 'cellist play the melody an octave lower than it is written.

While the Six Million were caught up in the final agony of the extermination camps, small brigades of Jewish volunteers tried desperately to reach the captives. Some of these were young people who had managed to escape from the ghettos and to join up with partisan bands fighting behind the Nazi lines. Others came from Palestine—the sons and daughters of *halutzim*—who tried in a hundred different ways to penetrate what Hitler called "Fortress Europa" and to join the partisans there. Some landed on the beaches of Greece and Yugoslavia and made their way through the Nazi lines on foot; a few were dropped by parachute over the enemy lines. Many partisans lost their lives in the unequal struggle, among them one youth of twenty-three, Hirsh Glik, killed in 1943. While he lived and fought, Glik composed a thundering song of defiance, courage and, indeed, of faith. He wrote his song in his own native Yiddish, but before long it was taken up by all the partisan groups of Eastern Europe and made the official hymn of the partisans. It was translated into many languages. The Jewish fighters from Palestine sang it in Hebrew. Ex. 61 is the song in an English translation.‡

119

Ani Ma-amin

A - ni ma - a - min, a - ni ma - a - min, a - ni

ma - a - min, a - ni_____ ma -

a - min, be - e - mu - nah she - ley - mah,

be - e - mu - nah she - ley - mah, be - vi - at

ha - mo - shi - ah, be - vi - at ha - mo - shi - ah a - ni

ma - a - min, ve - af al pi she - yit - mah - mey - ah

im kol zot a - ni ma - a - min.

Ex. 61

Song of the Partisans

Hirsh Glik

Folk Song

O do not say "This path I tread shall be my last." Al-though the light of day by clouds is o-ver-cast, the dawn we've wait-ed for so long will yet ap-

121

pear and our foot-steps still will thun-der, "We are

here!" foot-steps still will thun-der, "We are here!"

2. From land of palm tree, and from land of ice and snow
   Through trial and terror, on our secret way we go,
   And every drop of blood we lose will join a stream
   Infusing courage to keep fighting for a dream.

3. Our folk shall soon behold the early morning light,
   The evil yesterdays will vanish with the night,
   But if the sun should rise too late for us to see
   Our song will yet be sung by people who are free.

4. The song was writ in blood and lead, it never dies,
   The song a bird of freedom carols as it flies,
   "Arise and sing with me," triumphantly it calls
   Amid an avalanche of crumbling ghetto walls.

5. So never say, this path I tread shall be my last . . .

Seventeen
SONG OF THE MYSTIC

They sing, sometimes hands and feet keeping time in accompaniment, and rapt with enthusiasm reproduce sometimes the lyrics of the procession, sometimes the halt, and...of the wheelings and counterwheelings of the choric dance.

COULD YOU have guessed that this description was written some 1,900 years ago by the Jewish philosopher Philo of Alexandria who observed the community of ascetic Jews called Therepeutae ("Worshippers of God") in their colony at Lake Mareotis near Alexandria? (Philo's comments appear in his work *De Vita Contemplativa*, On the Contemplative Life.) The Therepeutae were trying to lose themselves. They were trying to feel part of something beyond themselves, part of something greater than their own group. They hoped to make contact with something far beyond themselves and their comrades. They were mystics, trying to become one with Divinity.

Hasidim dance at the Western Wall in Jerusalem during their first visit after the Six Day War, June 1967

123

Throughout Jewish history there have been many such groups of mystics. Since they arose in different periods and under varying climates of thought, they naturally differed from one another in their conceptions of how best to achieve a true oneness with God. The earliest Jewish mystics imagined that heaven was made up of concentric spheres in the very center of which stood the throne of God. Fiery chariots of angels, *kheruvim* and *seraphim,* guarded the passages to the holy center. (It is possible that they took quite literally the graphic descriptions by the prophet Ezekiel of his visions in the first chapter of his book.) Their main preoccupation, then, was to find a way to penetrate through the spheres, to by-pass the demonic guardians and to reach to the very center.

As the centuries passed, new mystical sects arose. They sought a more elusive goal, a sense of union with a Divine Spirit or Force. They used new methods: first, magic formulas based on Hebrew letters and numbering systems; later, bouts of fasting and other forms of self-denial; still later, intensive performance of good deeds. But, interestingly enough, whatever their conception of Divinity and the method for making contact with it, they all made use of special songs and dances which, like those of the Therepeutae, would help them to lose themselves and lift them beyond their individual identities.

The oldest songs of the Jewish mystics still being sung anywhere in the world today are probably descended from thirteenth-century Spain. At that time a group of scholars and poets gathered around the sage, Rabbi Levi ben Gershom, known as Gersonides, in the Catalonian town of Gerona, to study the *Zohar,* the holy text of the Kabbalists, or mystics. Their purpose was to try and find the formula for reaching out to God. Among their numbers was a certain Abraham He-Hazan. Now in those days a *hazan,* you will recall, was a kind of wandering minstrel. Abraham must have heard the *cantigas,* or religious miracle songs, which were sung in the court of King Alphonso the Wise—songs about "Mother Mary" and the wonders which she performed. Abraham composed a song, a tender verse about the "Little Sister" which seems to be modelled on some of those *cantigas.* The "Little Sister" is a name for the people of Israel, taken from *The Song of Songs* in the Bible. (There will be more about *The Song of Songs* in the following chapter.) *Little Sister* (*Ahot Ketanah* in the original Hebrew) is used by Sephardic Jews as a *selihah,* a song of the penitential season ushering in the new year. Following is just one of the many melodies to which *Little Sister* is still sung.

Ahot Ketanah
(Little Sister)

Ex. 62

ABRAHAM HE-HAZAN

SEPHARDIC MELODY

A - hot ke-ta - nah te-fi - la - te - ha
Lit - tle sis - ter, oh hear her plea, her

or – khah ve – o – nah te – hi – lo – te – ha
prayers she or – ders all weep – ing to Thee,

El nah re – fa – nah le mah – lo – te – ha, tikh –
May all her wounds now heal – ed be, A –

leh sha – nah ve – kil – le – lo – te – ha. El na re – fa na le –
vert the stern de – cree. May all her wounds now

mah - lo - te - ha, tikh - leh sha - nah ve - kil - le - lo - te - ha.
heal - ed be. A - vert the stern de - cree.

2. Sweetest words she sings all her days,
   For unto Thee are fitting only songs of praise.
   Strangers rob her heritage, wilt Thou never see
      And avert the stern decree?

3. When will Thy daughter arise from the pit?
   The yoke of her imprisonment, shatter Thou it.
   With wonder at Thy miracles her eyes shall be lit.
      Avert the stern decree.

4. Rejoice, little sister, no long weep.
   The siege is ended, His covenant He doth keep.
   Up the road to Zion triumphantly sweep,
      Up roads now clear, up roads now free.
   May He avert the stern decree,
      May this new year blessed be.

(In Verse 4, the music is repeated from the 𝄋 for the last two lines.)

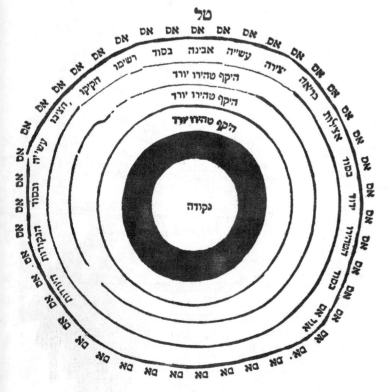

Kabbalist symbol, The Spheres, 1612

Some three hundred years later, a great mystical scholar and writer, Isaac Luria, led a band of disciples to settle in the town of Safed in northern Galilee. Perched high in the rolling hills overlooking deep valleys and outcroppings of wind-swept rock, Safed was an ideal setting for mystical contemplation. Under the influence of Luria's studies and kabbalistic writings, Safed became the center in the sixteenth century for Jewish mystical literature and poetry. Many of the kabbalist authors chose to convey their ideas in Aramaic, the language of the Talmud and the language used as the everyday spoken tongue of the Jews of Palestine and Babylonia during the Second Commonwealth. The Kabbalists even wrote songs in Aramaic, often fitting new words to existing popular tunes. As one example of the dark subject matter that preoccupied the Kabbalists, here is a translation of a poem in Aramaic written by the master Kabbalist himself, Isaac Luria. All kinds of angels, fiends, demons and devils inhabit his strange and menacing imaginary world:

Sons of the Palace

1. Sons of the palace who long for grace
   To see the glow of the Little Face,
   Sit at our table, a welcome guest.
   The King, in name, is in His place.

2. We pray you may be
   In our company,
   Where angels sing
   In magic ring.

3. These precious hours
   The feast is ours,
   When love holds sway
   Grief fades away.

4. Draw near to Me,
   My strength to see.
   Averted be
   The stern decree.

5. Then gather here
   And have no fear
   Of evil spell
   Or hound of Hell.

6. I, ancient of days
   In wondrous ways
   Bid you to feast,
   And vanish, beast!

7. Ye devils, flee,
   But leave us free,
   Quake, fiends, and cower
   Bereft of power.

8. They turn and flee, and deep in hole
   They bury themselves in dark *Sheol,*
   And we who gather, seeking grace
   Behold the glow of the Little Face.

(The "Little Face" refers to God. The various beasts are demons. *"Sheol"* is a deep pit, in biblical language. In this poem it is the equivalent of Hell.)

Of course, not all the poetry of Safed is as brooding and darkly kabbalistic as Luria's example. The beautiful song, *Lekhah Dodi,* which is sung at sundown on Fridays to welcome the Sabbath, was written in Safed during Luria's lifetime. Shelomo Alkabetz, the mystical poet, looked out at the setting sun over the hills of Galilee and imagined the Sabbath as a lovely bride, accompanied by a host of angels, coming toward the eagerly awaiting folk. Alkabetz fashioned his verses out of quotations from the Bible. Indeed, his very first words, *Lekhah Dodi,* are taken from *The Song of Songs.* There are many tunes for *Lekhah Dodi.* In European countries it was a favorite text for composers, especially from the eighteenth century on. Contemporary settings, too, are numerous. Two particularly interesting settings are: (1) a work by the Italian Jewish composer, Mario Castelnuovo-Tedesco, a graceful, melodious through-composed piece for solo and choir[‡] and (2) the composition of Darius Milhaud, the contempory French composer, as part of his *Sacred Service for Sabbath Eve,* a folk-like setting in the spirit of the composer's native Provence.[‡] Here is a setting

from the Middle East, from the part of the world where the poem itself was composed. This is a folk melody and may be many generations old. It seems to be closer to the type of tune to which Alkabetz himself might have sung his welcome to the Sabbath. Try to sing it in four parts.

Hasidim dance on Mt. Zion

Lekhah Dodi

Shelomo Alkabetz

Sephardic Melody

129

The tomb of Bar Yohai at Meron

year 135. A strange elusive soul who disappeared for months on end in the wilderness of the Jordan River to search out his heart in solitude, Bar Yohai was a particular favorite of the mystics and Kabbalists who ascribed to him the authorship of their basic text, the *Zohar.* Accordingly, on *Lag Ba-Omer,* the thirty-third day after the beginning of Passover, mystics would gather (and still do) at Meron to light great bonfires and to dance and sing all night and into the following day. Among their songs are praises of their hero: "Bar Yohai, you are indeed blessed, you have been anointed above all your comrades!" Ex. 64 is a Middle-Eastern song to Bar Yohai.

Come, my beloved, to greet the bride. Let us welcome the Sabbath. . . . Come in peace, thou, crowning glory of thy husband, come in happiness and rejoicing, in the midst of the faithful of the chosen people, come, O bride, come O bride! Come, my beloved . . .

The mysticism of Safed spread to Jewish communities elsewhere in the Middle East. One such community was in Yemen. As a Jewish minority in a Muslim society, they were always "second-class citizens" and subjected to oppressive and humiliating treatment. Mysticism, which offered a prospect of rising above the physical and material aspects of life and of dwelling in a spiritual realm, had a great appeal for suffering Jews. Since their real world was so ugly and harsh, mysticism seemed to open a door toward a higher world of Divine love and solace. Yemenite poets took over some favorite kabbalistic images and wove them into songs. Their melodies resembled those of their Arab neighbors. Long, unmetrical rhapsodic introductions would lead into strong, dance-like, metrical tunes which were accompanied by handclapping or the beat of drums. Ex. 65 is a mystical Yemenite song.

Under the impetus of the kabbalistic movement in Safed, a new festival arose in the nearby village of Meron. According to tradition, Meron was the burial place of Rabbi Simeon Bar Yohai, a scholar who was a contemporary of Rabbi Akiba and Bar Kokhba, the last Jewish rebels against the Roman Empire in the

Ex. 64

Bar Yohai

FOLK SONG

Bar Yo-hai, nim-shah-ta, ash-re - kha, she - men tov me - ha-ve-re - kha.

Im Ninalu

Ex. 65

YEMENITE MELODY

If the doors of princes are closed to me, the doors of Heaven are not closed. The living God will lift us on the wings of *kheruvim*. All of us shall rise on the strength of His spirit.

Wars, earthquakes and plagues ended the period of Jewish mystical literary and philosophic creativity in Safed and the Middle East in the eighteenth century. But mysticism was by no means dead. Varieties of mysticism had swept over European Jewry for centuries. The variety most familiar to Jews today is called Hasidism. This movement began in the Ukraine early in the eighteenth century under the leadership of a simple pious Jew, Israel ben Eliezer, who was called the *Ba-al Shem Tov,* "Master of the Divine Name." Hundreds of legends have grown up about the Ba-al Shem Tov, making of him a great saint with the ability to perform miracles. Among his teachings was the principle that to achieve *devekut* (linking one's soul to the Divinity) one had to practice intense concentration, deep sincerity and great fervor and joy in prayer. He took over many of the ideas of the Safed mystics and even some of their songs. His followers, called *Hasidim,* sang the kabbalistic poem of Isaac Luria in a setting of their own. This melody like other hasidic tunes is probably borrowed partly from the folk song of the countryside, partly from gypsy songs and partly from local drinking songs. But the melody is touched with a fervor that makes it new and original. The song is sung at the third meal of the Sabbath, the *seudah shelishit,* just before sundown. Notice how the tight rhyme and meter of the Aramaic poem are broken into an alternating meditation and dance. Sometimes the words are dropped altogether, and wordless melodies—or melodies with meaningless syllables like *bim, bam, bam*—carry the mood of deep religious feeling. A *Hasid* would sing these syllables with his eyes closed—rhythmically and with great intensity.

Beney Heykholo
(Sons of the Palace)

Ex. 66

132

me - he - zey ziv diz' - er an - pin
see the glow of the lit - tle face,

ye - hon ho - khoh be - hai ta - ko de - vey_____ mal - ko_____
sit at our ta-ble, a wel-come guest, the King, in _____ name, is _____

bim bam bim bam bim bam bam, be - gi - lu - fin, bim bam bam.
the King, in name, is in His place,

Bim bam bim bam bim bam, bim ba-bim bam bam etc.

Tzvu lah - do b'nai va - do
We pray you may be in our compa - ny.

The *Hasid's* feeling of nearness to God has already been illustrated by Rabbi Levi Yitzhak's famous appeal for justice. That is only one of his two widely-known songs. The second is more typically the song of a mystic searching for God and finding Him everywhere. This song is called a *dudele,* which means literally a "little tune." Perhaps it even meant, originally, a song for a *dudelsack,* a German bagpipe. But the title is also a play on *"Du,"* the Yiddish word for "Thou." Levi Yitzhak sings his song in Hebrew and translates into Yiddish as he goes along. "Master of the Universe," he begins, "I will sing You a *dudele.* Where can I find Thee, and where can I not find Thee? If things go well, it is Thou. If things go ill—ah, it is Thou. Thou alone, ever Thou." Thus far, his melody has emerged directly out of the chant which he would have used for his study. (See Ex. 33, Chapter Twelve.) But now Levi Yitzhak breaks into a typical hasidic dance tune: "East—Thou, West—Thou, North—Thou, South—Thou," etc. This part of the song needs movement: at first, perhaps, just the snapping of fingers, then a more vigorous clapping of hands; now, a gesture to fit the directions indicated by the words, a restrained dance step: step, together, step, together; or step, bend the knees, step, knee-bend. But the dance comes to an end, and Levi Yitzhak adds a rather startling conclusion, or *coda*. Slowly, majestically, in the major mode, he sings: "Thou, Thou," and then he returns to the minor: "Wherever I look, wherever I turn, Thou."

Ex. 67

Dudele

LEVI YITZHAK OF BERDITCHEV

bo - no shel o - lom ich vell dir a du - de - le zing - en,
I'll sing you a du - de - le, hark - en!

Du du du du du. A - yey em - tzo - e - kho, ve - a - yey

lo em - tzo - e - kho? Vu vell ich dich yoh ge - fin - nen un
Where shall I sure - ly find Thee, and

vu vell ich dich nit ge - fin - nen? Du du du du du Az
where shall I fail to find Thee? For

vu ich gay iz doch du un vu ich shtay iz doch du
where I stray, there art Thou, and where I stay, there art Thou,

Rak du, nor du, vi - der du, o - ber du
Rak, Thou, only Thou, e - ver Thou, al - ways Thou,

du   du   du   du   du.   'siz
                                                                         when

e - mi - tzen   gut,   du,   ve - ho - li - loh shlecht,   oy,   du!
all   goes   well, Thou!   And when things go   wrong,   ah - Thou!

Oy du du du du du du,   du du du du du du du!

139

du   du   du   du du du   du!   Sho-
In

ma - yim   du,   e - retz   du,   ma' - loh   du,   ma   toh   du,
hea - ven Thou, on earth   art Thou, a - bove art Thou, be - low   art Thou

du   du   du   du   du du du du   du,   du!

Miz - rah du,   ma' - rov du,   tzo - fon du,   do - rom du,
East art Thou, West art Thou,   North art Thou,   South art Thou,

du   du   du   du du du   du!   Oy

du,   du,   du,   du,   du   du du du   du!

141

Vu ich vend zich, vu ich ker zich, du! Du!
Here and there and ev' - ry - where art Thou! Thou!

The great-grandson of the Ba-al Shem Tov, the great hasidic leader named Nahman of Bratzlav, also handed down some unusual songs. The Bratzlaver, as he was called, loved song and dance and felt that they were indispensable to joyous religious feeling. "Song is the soul of the universe," he said. "The throne of God breathes music; even the four letters, *Yod, He, Vav, He,* that spell the name of God are four musical notes." Here is one of his own songs. His words are taken from the opening of Psalm 42: "As the hart panteth after the waterbrooks, so panteth my soul after Thee, O God." His song, too, starts slowly, meditatively and then breaks into dance rhythm. Sing it with great fervor as his *Hasidim* undoubtedly did. A solo takes the lead, the group sings the responses and the refrain.

Ka-ayil Ta-arog

Ex. 68

MELODY ATTRIBUTED TO
NAHMAN OF BRATZLAV

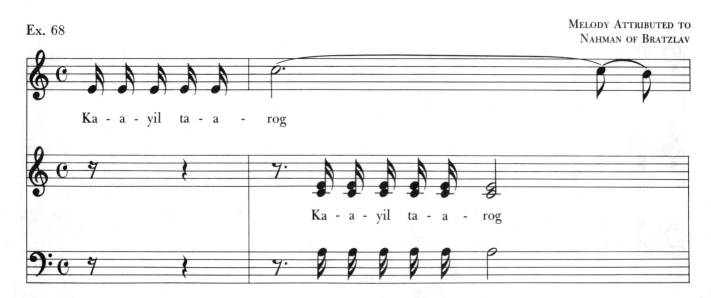

Ka - a - yil ta - a - rog

Ka - a - yil ta - a - rog

The Hasidic movement split into various sects after the death of the Ba-al Shem. Rabbi Schneour Zalman of the town of Lyady in White Russia founded a sect called *Habad.* (The word *habad* is made up of initial letters of three Hebrew words, *hokhmah, binah, da-at,* meaning wisdom, understanding and knowledge.) The songs of the *Habad Hasidim* had to adhere to a definite form in order to fulfill their purpose, which was to transport one's soul along the approach to joy—or, in kabbalistic language, along the "Corridor of the Palace." Schneour Zalman taught: "The song of the souls consists of tones only, dismantled of words."

The songs had to go through five stages: (1) a rhapsodic outpouring of the soul; (2) a somewhat livelier spiritual awakening; (3) intense concentration; (4) communion with God; and (5) a feeling of complete liberation from the physical as if one had no body at all, only spirit.

The fragments of melody which made up any of the *habad* songs may have had very worldly—possibly, even disreputable!—origins like those of Levi Yitzhak. But, in the new arrangement given them and in the manner in which they were sung, they became prayers without words. They are called *nigunim* (singular, *nigun*)—the Hebrew word for "melody." The *nigunim* were sung, like the little interludes in Isaac Luria's poem, to meaningless syllables, *dai-di-di-dai* or *ya-ba-bam*. In English print the syllables may look strange, and even funny, but, if you were to hear a true *Hasid* sing them with genuine hasidic fervor, they would no longer seem strange. The *dai-di-di-dais* would have a sharp, bright percussive effect. The

ya-ba-bams give the rich vibrating timbre of string instruments.

Ex. 69 is a *nigun* from the "court" of Schneour Zalman. The numbers indicate the stages of the "approach to joy."

The Hasidic movement continues to flourish in separate communities in various parts of the world. It is possible to visit a hasidic service in many of the

Ex. 69

The Rabbi's Nigun

large cities of the United States. On *Simhat Torah* (festival of the Rejoicing of the Torah, immediately following *Sukot*) particularly, the *Hasidim* sing text from the prayers, *nigunim* and dance-songs to which they dance, carrying the scrolls of the Torah. Some of their songs are old, handed down to them from previous generations. Others may have been created in our own time, but they are in the old style and still couched in the musical idiom of Eastern Europe.‡

The quality and spirit of Hasidism have been expressed through many wondrous tales, told and retold by writers with a poetic flair. One superb expression—like that of the *Hasidim* themselves, free from the bonds of language—is the *Ba-al Shem Suite* composed in 1923 by Ernest Bloch.‡ This suite for violin and piano has three movements, each of which

conveys the mood of a phase of hasidic ecstasy. The first is called *Vidui* (confession or contrition). The second, entitled simply *Nigun*, is a rhapsodic meditation. The third, *Simhat Torah*, is a joyous dance movement based on a popular Yiddish folk tune.

Some modern American composers have tried to reproduce the hasidic atmosphere through written services composed for cantor and choir. Among these works are a *Hasidic Service* by Isidore Freed; *Hasidic Sabbath* by Charles Davidson and *Shir LeShabbat* by Lazar Weiner.‡ These are all straightforward and relatively simple enough to be performed by an amateur choral group. In some sections they lend themselves to community singing. To get the true hasidic spirit, one cannot merely listen. You must sing, clap, snap your fingers and move as the *Hasidim* do.

Eighteen
SPRING
SONG

Behold the winter is past
The rain is over and gone,
The flowers appear on the earth,
The time of singing is come,
And the voice of the turtle dove is heard in the land.

(The Song of Songs 2: 11–12)

THESE are words out of one of the oldest collections of love songs in the world. The songs, in their original Hebrew, were very popular in the ancient land of Israel. In many of them, the lover seems to be King Solomon himself, that monarch of many wives; and thus it is not surprising that people thought he had written them. For reasons of authorship alone, the love poems might have been included in the Bible. But the sages who edited the Bible had still another idea. In their view, these were the songs of love between God and the people of Israel. They wrote them all down as "The Song of Songs which is Solomon's" *(Shir ha-Shirim asher li-Shelomo)*.

Because of this religious interpretation, *The Song of Songs* has been chanted as a religious rite in the synagogues of the world over the centuries. In the Sephardic synagogue, it is chanted on Sabbath eve; in the Ashkenazic synagogue, however, it is reserved for the Sabbath during the spring festival of Passover. The reader chants according to the accents, and the Ashkenazic version of the verses opening this chapter sounds like this:

var ha - ge - shem ha - laf

ha - lakh lo; Ha - ni - tza -

nim nir' - u va - a - retz

et ha - za - mir hi - gi - yah,

ve - kol ha - tor nish - ma be - ar - tze - nu.

The opening verses, which include the title of the poems, are sung this way:

From Shir ha-Shirim

ASHKENAZIC CANTILLATION

Ex. 70a

Ki hi - ney ha - s'tav a -

Ex. 70b

Shir ha - shi - rim a - sher li - sh'lo - moh

yi - sha - ke - ni   mi - ne - shi - kot   pi - hu

ki to - vim   do - de - kha mi - ya - yin.

As we learned in Chapter Six, the biblical accents have different musical meanings for different Jewish communities. Scholars of Jewish music have turned up cantillations from remote times and places. Reproduced (p. 148) is a page from a beautifully illuminated Bible discovered in the Cairo *Genizah*. It was copied by hand in the thirteenth century in Catalonia, the northernmost district of Spain. The page here shows the opening chapters of *The Song of Songs*. If you look closely at the scroll which winds around the flowery pole, you will see some musical notes in an old form of music writing or notation. The notes run from right to left over the Hebrew words which are taken from Verses 2 and 3 of *Shir ha-Shirim*. This fragment of music has been deciphered and written in modern notation by the Hungarian musical scholar, Bence Scabolczi. His transcription follows:

From Shir ha-Shirim

Ex. 71   CATALONIAN CANTILLATION

Yi - sha - ke - ni min' - shi - kot pi - hu

ki to - vim do - de - kha mi - ya - yin,

she - men tu - rak she - me - kha

al ken a - la - mot a - he - vu - kha.

The discovery and deciphering of that Catalonian chant has a parallel in yet another discovery. Early in the twentieth century, the composer and musical scholar, Lazare Saminsky, was travelling through the provinces of Russia, listening to the melodies of the Jews living in some of the more remote regions and writing them down. He found no manuscripts—only the living musical heritage that had been handed down over the generations by word of mouth. In an old synagogue in Tiflis, in Russian Georgia, Saminsky heard this chant for the *Shir ha-Shirim*. Notice how closely it resembles the Catalonian chant:

From Shir ha-Shirim

Ex. 72   GEORGIAN CANTILLATION

Yi - sha - ke - ni mi - ne - shi - kot pi - hu

ki   to - vim   do - de - kha

mi - ya - yin.

(By the way, Saminsky made a very fine arrangement of this for voice and piano. It is an effective solo for a musical program.)‡

Did some unhappy exile from fifteenth-century Spain carry that chant all the way from the Pyrenees to the Caucasus Mountains? No one knows and, unless some new and undreamed of discovery provides more clues, we shall probably never know how this tune travelled across the whole expanse of a continent.

For centuries the Jews sang the love songs from *Shir ha-Shirim* only in the synagogue and only in cantillation. But, in recent decades, the songs have made a comeback in the State of Israel, as real-life love songs. Choice passages have been set to new, folk-like melodies, and most of the songs are used for folk dancing. One of the most graceful and pleasing is the couple dance set to several verses by the Israeli composer,

Sara Levi. The arrangement given here is intended for three equal voices, preferably female. It can also be played by three recorders—two sopranos and an alto. The alto part must be played an octave higher than it is written here.

Ex. 73

El Ginat Egoz

S. of S. 6: 11; 7: 12–13; 4: 16

MELODY, SARA LEVI

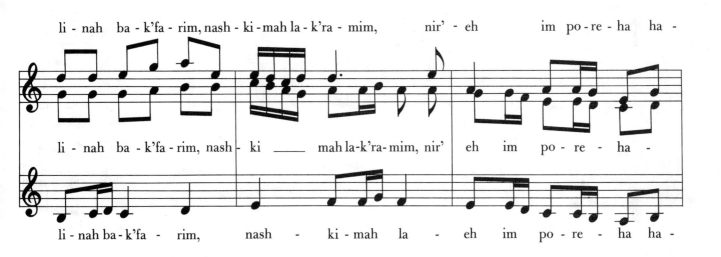

151

I went down into the garden of nut trees
To look at the green plants of the valley,
To see whether the vine budded,
And the pomegranates were in flower . . .

Come, my beloved, let us go forth into the field;
Let us lodge in the villages.
Let us get up early to the vineyards;
Let us see whether the vine hath budded,
Whether the vine-blossom hath budded . . .

Awake, O north wind;
And come, thou south;
Blow upon my garden,
That the spices thereof may flow out.
Let my beloved come into his garden,
And eat his precious fruits.

(Note that the second stanza of this song, "Come, my beloved," is the source from which Alkabetz drew the opening words of his Sabbath song, *Lekhah Dodi,* Ex. 63 in Chapter Seventeen.)

That is only one of the many contemporary Israeli settings for portions of *The Song of Songs.* Popular Israeli folk singers have made a number of recordings of the songs, and perhaps you have even done folk-dancing to the tunes. But comparatively few persons have the opportunity to hear them sung at a *kibbutz seder.* The people of Israel have kept up the tradition of linking the *Shir ha-Shirim* with the *Hag ha-Aviv* (Festival of Spring, another name for Passover). And no wonder, for the Israeli springtime is enchantingly beautiful and a perfect setting for *The Song of Songs.* The air is fragrant with orange blossoms and narcissus, the fields are brilliant with poppies and daisies. The songs express far more than ordinary love songs: they rehearse the love between the folk and the land of Israel, and they celebrate the reunion between the two long-separated lovers. "Let my beloved come into his garden, let him inhale the fragrance of its spices" (*Song of Songs 4: 16*).

The famous passage beginning "Lo, the winter is past . . ." (*2: 11–12*) is sung the following way, in two voices, at a *kibbutz seder.*

Ex. 74

Hiney ha-Stav Avar

S. OF S. 2: 11–12

YIZHAR YARON (POPPER)

laf ha - laf ha - lakh lo, hi - ney ha - s'tav a - var.

s'tav a - var, hi - ney ha - s'tav a - var.

SOLO

Ha - ni - tza - nim nir' - u va - a - retz, et ha - za - mir hi -

gi - ya, ve - kol ha - tor nish - ma be - ar - tze - nu, nish -

ma, nish - ma be - ar - tze - nu. *D.C. (chorus) al Fine*

154

Nineteen
SONG
OF LOVE

During the centuries when *The Song of Songs* was treated as a religious poem and confined to chant in the synagogue, Jewish boys and girls sang their own varieties of love and courtship songs. They did not sing in Hebrew—that language was reserved over all those centuries as the Holy Tongue, *Leshon ha-Kodesh*. It was considered a sacrilege to use Hebrew for ordinary everyday life; it was the language of Holy Scriptures, prayer and scholarship. Thus, wherever Jews lived, they sang their love songs in their own vernaculars—that is, in the many languages they spoke.

For example, in the distant region of Bokhara, once a part of the Persian empire, now a province of the Soviet Union, Jews spoke a dialect of Persian mixed with Hebrew called Judaeo-Persian. They sang love songs not only in their special dialect but also in the musical idiom, very strange to our ears, of their own countryside. You can hear their songs, and those of other remote Jewish communities, in some of the ethnic records which are now available.‡

Listen, too, to the love songs of the Jewish Yemenite girls, sung in Judaeo-Arabic, with melodies very much like those of the Arabs of Yemen. And seek out an example of the *romanza* of the Moroccan Jew with its accompaniment of the *'ud,* the ancient Arabic instrument which was the ancestor of our European lute (*al-'ud*), and with its strong flavor of *flamenco*. For Westerners accustomed to tempered tuning, these songs are difficult to catch and to sing. However, you would have no trouble with the Judaeo-Spanish (Ladino) *romanzas* which have been preserved since the exile from Spain. These songs are still sung in Turkey and Greece and until very recently in Egypt, Syria and Iraq.‡ Their Western character is immediately recognizable. As a matter of fact, they will remind you of French folk songs and of the songs of the Provençal troubadours which have been recorded in the past few years.

In an unusual book, *Farewell to Salonica,* describing the life of a Jewish family in that Greek city before World War I, Leon Sciaky provides a vivid scenario to show how the *romanzas* brightened his childhood. He recalls his visits as a boy to the home of his grandmother and great-aunt—happy, exciting occasions always featuring exotic goodies to eat, fascinating family tales (particularly tales of great feasting) to drink in and *romanzas* to listen to—those softly crooned

romanzas that had been brought, the boy was told, "from Spain by our *hidalgo* forefathers centuries ago." He tells how he would beg for another and yet another of the old songs, marvelling at the strange, romantic, mysterious world opened up to his youthful imagination—the queens and the noblemen, the kings and the pages, the sailors aboard ships hoisting sails of smooth silk, the sinister figures weaving dark and fearful webs of court intrigues. Even as a little boy who could scarcely understand the meaning of the words, the author nevertheless was struck by a feeling of deep longing aroused by the *romanzas*—nostalgia for an ancestral past he had never himself experienced at first hand.

Some of the *romanzas* are long and elaborate. Among them, there are tunes with the Arabic flavor of Andalusian songs. Touches of melody as well as vocabulary from the local Turkish surroundings have

crept into many other *romanzas*. Ex. 75 is a comparatively simple folk song in Ladino which probably came from northern Spain and which has some of the character of the well-known French song, *Au clair de la lune*. It is a dialogue between a suitor and his sweetheart.

Jews living in the villages of Eastern Europe produced many love songs in Yiddish. Some are exact duplicates or the equivalents of foreign songs. For example, most people know "Lazy Mary, Will You Get Up?"—the old English folk song in which mother cannot persuade Mary to get up even with offers of goodies and pretty clothes. Only when she promises "a nice young man with rosy cheeks" does Mary at last reply, "Yes, mother, I will get up!" The French have their equivalent of that dialogue in "*Maman, si veux-tu un bouquet.*" Ex. 76 is a Yiddish form of the same sentiment.

Galanica

Ex. 75

LADINO FOLK SONG

Av - rix mi ga - la - ni - ca que ya v'a ma - na - cer, Av-
O-pen up the door, my dear-est one, the day will soon be here,

ri no vos av - ro mi lin - do a - mor. La
dare not o-pen the door to you, though you are ve - ry dear, I

no - che yo no dur - mo pen - san - do en vos, La
can - not sleep a wink all night for think - ing a - bout you! I

no - che yo no dur - mo pen - san - do en vos.
can - not sleep a wink all night. I think a - bout you too.

2. *Mi padre 'sta meldando* } 2
   Mos oyera.
Amaltalde la luzezica
   Si se dormira
Amaltalde la luzezica
   Si s'echara.

3. *Mi madre 'sta cuziendo* } 2
   Mos oyera.
Pedrelde la algujica
   Si se dormira
Pedrelde la algujica
   Si s'echara.

4. *Mi hermano 'sta'scriviendo* } 2
   Mos oyera.
Pedrelde la pendolica
   Si se dormira
Pedrelde la pendolica
   Si s'echara.

2. My father's up and reading } 2
   And he is sure to hear,
Put out the light, my dearest one,
   And he will go to sleep,
Put out the light, my dearest one,
   His slumber will be deep.

3. My mother's up and sewing } 2
   And she is sure to hear,
Then hide her needle, dearest one,
   And she will go to sleep,
Then hide her needle, dearest one,
   Her slumber will be deep.

4. My brother's up and writing } 2
   And he is sure to hear,
Then take away the ink, my dear,
   And he will go to sleep,
Then take away the ink, my dear,
   His slumber will be deep.

Yomeh, Yomeh

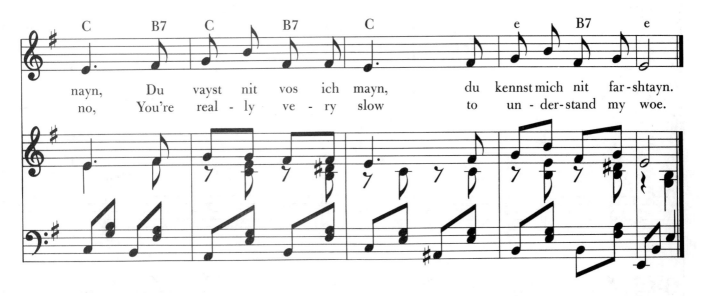

nayn, Du vayst nit vos ich mayn, du kennst mich nit far-shtayn.
no, You're real - ly ve - ry slow to un - der-stand my woe.

2. *Yomeh, Yomeh, zing mir a lideleh,*
   Vos dos maydeleh vill.
   Dos maydeleh vill a por shichelech
   hoben,
   Darf men gayn dem shuster zogen,
   Nayn, . . .

3. *Yomeh, Yomeh, zing mir a lideleh,*
   Vos dos maydeleh vill.
   Dos maydeleh vill a klaydeleh hoben,
   Darf men gayn dem schneider zogen,
   Nayn, . . .

4. *Yomeh, Yomeh, zing mir a lideleh,*
   Vos dos maydeleh vill.
   Dos maydeleh vill a chossendel hoben,
   Darf men gayn dem shadchen zogen,
   Yo, mamenyu, yo,
   Du vaysst shoin vos ich mayn,
   Du kennst mich shoin farshtayn.

2. Yomeh, Yomeh, sing me a little tune,
   What does the little maid wish?
   The little maid wants new shoes,
      don't worry,
   To the cobbler we must hurry.
      No, mama dear, . . .

3. Yomeh, Yomeh, sing me a little tune,
   What does the little maid wish?
   The little maid wants a new dress,
      don't worry,
   To the tailor we must hurry.
      No, mama dear, . . .

4. Yomeh, Yomeh, sing me a little tune,
   What does the little maid wish?
   The little maid wants a bridegroom,
      don't worry,
   To the matchmaker we must hurry.
      Yes, mama dear, yes,
      You've understood my distress,
      You'll bring me happiness!

Folk songs of all kinds are rich sources of information about the life and hopes of the people who produce them. The Yiddish love and courtship songs are no exceptions.‡ For example, here is a dialogue between a matchmaker (*shadchen*) and a young girl in a *shtetl*. The matchmaker offers the young girl a choice of bridegrooms. Does she want a tailor, a cobbler, a jeweler? "No," she says. "My father was not a tailor, a cobbler, a jeweler." Does she want a scholar? "Ah, yes," she says, "I am a scholar's daughter, and I'll gladly wed a scholar." From this lively Yiddish song we get clear understanding of exactly who was the true aristocrat, the person held in the highest esteem in the *shtetl. Everywhere* Jews lived, it was the scholar.

Vozhe Villst Du?
(What Would You Like?)

Ex. 77

YIDDISH FOLK SONG

Vos - zhe villst du, vos - zhe villst du, a schnei - der far a
What would you like, oh what would you like, to be a tail - or's

mann, a schnei - der far a mann? A schnei - der far a
wife, to be a tail - or's wife? I will not

mann vill ich nit, A schnei - der's toch - ter
be a tail - or's wife, my fath er did n't lead a

160

bin ich nit! Zitz ich oif - 'n shtayn shtil - ler - heyt un vayn,
tail - or's life. I sit on a stone! Here I weep and moan!

Al - le may - de - lach hob - en has - se - neh, nor ich bleib al - layn!
All the oth - er girls have their hus - bands, I am all a - lone!

Al - le may - de - lach hob - en has - se - neh, nor ich bleib al - layn!
All the oth - er girls have their hus - bands, I am all a - lone!

2. *Vozhe villst du*
   Vozhe villst du
   A shuster far a mann?
   A shuster far a mann?
     A shuster far a mann
     Vill ich nit, . . .

3. *Vozhe villst du*
   Vozhe villst du
   A balagoleh far a mann?
   A balagoleh far a mann?
     A balagoleh far a mann
     Vill ich nit, . . .

4. *Vozhe villst du*
   Vozhe villst du
   A lerner far a mann?
   A lerner far a mann?
     A lerner far a mann
     Vill ich yo,
     A lerners tochter
     Bin ich yo,
     Zitz ich oif'n dach
     Den gantzen tog un lach,
     Alle maydelach hoben chasseneh,
     Ich bin bei zei gleich.

2. What would you like
   Oh, what would you like?
   To be a cobbler's wife?
   To be a cobbler's wife?
     I will not be a cobbler's wife, . . .

3. What would you like
   Oh, what would you like?
   To be a teamster's wife?
   To be a teamster's wife?
     I will not be a teamster's wife, . . .

4. What would you like
   Oh, what would you like?
   To be a scholar's wife?
   To be a scholar's wife?
     I'd gladly be a scholar's wife,
     My father led a scholar's life!
     To the roof I run,
     And laugh out in the sun,
     All the other girls have their
       husbands,
     I'll have the very best one.

Some of these Yiddish songs are quite old, and others, we know, appeared only towards the end of the nineteenth century. Jews by the thousands began to leave the *shtetl.* Young men in particular fled the *shtetl* —some to escape the ordeal of military constriction (forced service in the Czar's army was for a period of twenty-five years!), others to seek their fortune in far lands, particularly in America. It is not surprising, therefore, that we have many sad Yiddish songs of abandoned maidens. Ex. 78 is a song of one girl who would not stay behind but insisted on joining her beloved.

All the pictures in this chapter depict courtship, Yemenite style. The Inbal Dance Theatre bases its performances on the traditional movement and dance of the Jews of Yemen

Her Nor Du Shayn Maydele
(Listen to Me, Pretty One)

YIDDISH FOLK SONG

al - le gas - sen un vell shrei - en "Vesh tzu vash - en," a-
streets I'll wan - der, cry - ing, "Give your clothes to laun - der," if

bi mit dir tzu - zam - men zein, a - bi mit dir tzu - zam - men zein.
on - ly I can be with you, if on - ly I can be with you.

2. *Her nor du shayn maydeleh,*
   Her nor du fein maydeleh,
   Vos vestu essen in aza veiten land?
   Vos vestu essen in aza veiten land?
   Broit un saltz vell ich essen,
   Tatteh un mamme vell ich fargesson,
   Abi mit dir tzuzammen zein,
   Abi mit dir tzuzammen zein.

3. *Her nor du shayn maydeleh,*
   Her nor du fein maydeleh,
   Avu vestu shlofen in aza veiten land?
   Avu vestu shlofen in aza veiten land?
   Ich bin noch a yungeh froi,
   Ich ken shlofen oif a bintel shtroi,
   Abi mit dir tzuzammen zein,
   Abi mit dir tzuzammen zein.

2. Listen to me, pretty one,
   Listen well, my sweetest one,
   What will you eat in that
     strange and far-off land?
   Bread and salt! I will not
     bother,
   I'll forget mother and father,
   So long as I can be with you,
   So long as I can be with you.

3. Listen to me, pretty one,
   Listen well, my sweetest one,
   Where will you sleep in that
     strange and far-off land?
   I'm still young, there'll be
     no weeping,
   If in a haystack I'll be
     sleeping,
   So long as I can be with you,
   So long as I can be with you.

Toward the end of the nineteenth century, the Hebrew language had a rebirth. European Jewish writers began to use it as a living language for the expression of ideas, poetry, literature and daily communication. Yiddish works, including Yiddish love poetry, were translated into Hebrew. The great Bialik wrote many beautiful Hebrew poems in folk style, which were set to popular melodies very much like those of the Yiddish songs quoted above. These were sung everywhere—especially the love songs among them—by young Hebraists. Perhaps the best-known of Bialik's "folk poems" (*Shirey Am*) is *'Twixt Tigris and Euphrates.*

Another moment in the Inbal courtship dance. The organizer and director of the Inbal Dance Theatre of Israel is Sara Levi

Ben Nehar Prat
('Twixt Tigris and Euphrates)

Ex. 79

H. N. BIALIK
TRANSLATED BY MAURICE SAMUEL

FOLK MELODY

Ben   n'har   Prat   un'har Hi-de-kel,   Al   ha-
On   the   hill   there blooms   a   palm,   'twixt

har   mi-ta-mer de-kel.   U-va-de-kel
Tig-ris   and Eu-phra-tes old,   And   a-mong   the

165

2. *Tzipor zahav, ufi hugi,*
   Tze-i u-vakshi li ben zugi,
   U-va-asher timtza-ihu
   Kifti oto va-havi-ihu.

2. Bird of gold, go forth and find me
   Him whose bride I am to be:
   Search and circle till thou find him,
   Bind him, bring him, bird to me.

In modern Israel, Hebrew, of course, is the national language. And, as in all modern countries, new popular love songs appear daily. Some are successful, others not. With radio, television and recordings, popular songs of the West travel quickly to Israel; and, at times, some of their popular songs reach the West. Perhaps the only difference between their popular songs today and those in America is the Hebrew lyrics.

Twenty

LOVE SONG
TO QUEEN SABBATH

For love of thee my chalice I raise,
Welcome, O Sabbath, beloved of days.

How sweet it is, between day and night
To glimpse Sabbath's face, aglow with light.
Bring apples and dainties for her delight,
Sing out her praise, sing roundelays,
Welcome, O Sabbath, beloved of days.

Love songs I sing, Sabbath, my bride,
Love songs to thee, my joy and my pride.
Come to the feast, the door's open wide,
Let the lights blaze, with love I gaze,
Welcome, O Sabbath, beloved of days.

(From a poem by Yehudah Halevi)

SAILORS sing of their love for the sea, cowboys for their horses, American pioneers for the great prairie, workmen for their tools—the list is endless. For the Jewish people, the Sabbath has always been an object of love; it is a time for rest and renewal, an island of peace in a stormy week, the respite from the toil and pain of everyday living, the foretaste of the long Sabbath-to-come when all eternity will be peace and healing. And since the Sabbath holds such blessing for Jews, it is easy to understand how this beloved concept became transformed, in the imagination of the poets and the people, into a radiant princess, a queen and a dazzling bride.

As the *jongleurs* and troubadours of medieval Europe went about singing their eloquent love songs to "Lady Mary," Jewish poets began to pour out their love for the *Shabbat*. They wrote their poems in the Holy Tongue, in Hebrew, because their beloved was holy; and they used strict meter and rhyme. Perhaps, on occasion, they set their Hebrew poems to familiar melodies of the countryside. The mystics of Safed, as we have already seen, expressed their love for the Sabbath sometimes in Aramaic.

Certain of these Hebrew and Aramaic poems have been incorporated into the complete editions of the traditional prayer book in conjunction with the grace after meals. They are not synagogue songs. They are the Jewish equivalent of Christian carols—that is, home songs intended to be sung by families—and these Jewish songs are sung around the festive Sabbath table. Since there have been countless Jewish families singing them to melodies of their own choosing or even of their own devising, we have a large variety of tunes for these Sabbath poems handed down by family tradition.

These Sabbath "table songs" have a special Hebrew name: *zemirot*, meaning "tunes" or "songs." (The singular is *zemer*.) Generally the melodies reflect the tunes sung by people in a given locality, that is, by the neighbors of the Jewish families. And, while many individual families have their own traditional *zemirot*, they have never hesitated to share them with members of their Jewish community or with visitors who carried the tunes back to their own homes and families. If your family has its own traditional *zemirot*, you should cherish them and keep them alive for the next generation. But, if your family's *zemirot* have been lost, perhaps you may want to institute a new custom in

Greeting the Sabbath

your home, which can become your Jewish legacy to your children and grandchildren. Some examples of *zemirot* from various Jewish communities will follow. Try singing them to enrich your own family tradition or to launch a tradition of your own.

The old prayer books which contain the *zemirot* prescribe a specific order in which they are to be sung. Some are sung at the Friday evening family meal, others at the noonday meal on the Sabbath and still others at the third meal, the *seudah shelishit*. The first *zemer* of the repertory is sung almost everywhere in a chant which derives from the *nusah* of the evening service on Friday night. The synagogue chant for *Va-yekhulu* (Ex. 8, in Chapter Six) is an example of that *nusah*. The following version of that first *zemer*, almost a free chant, is a variant. Its text is made up of a large number of four-line strophes, each of which has a single rhyme and ends with a biblical quotation.

Everyone who hallows the Sabbath as is its due, who guards the Sabbath zealously from any desecration, his reward shall be in keeping with his deeds, "every man with his own camp and every man with his own standard" *(Numbers 1: 52)*.

Those who seek the Lord, seed of His loving Abraham, who delay departure from the Sabbath and hasten to enter into it, who guard it and protect it, "this is the day . . . we will rejoice and be glad on it" *(Psalms 118: 24)*.

A modern chalice

Ex. 80

Kol Mekadesh Shevi-i

ASHKENAZIC MELODY

CHORUS — Rhythm not too strict

Kol me - ka - desh she - vi - i ka - ra - ui_____ lo, Kol sho - mer shab - bat ka-
Dor 'shey a - do nai ze - ra av - ra - ham o - ha - vo, ha - me - a - ha - rim la tzet min ha - shab

a tempo

dat me - hal - le - lo,_____ Se - kha - ro_____ har - bey me-
bat um' - ma - ha - rim la - vo, Se - me - him le - shom - ro

broadly

od al pi fo - o - lo, Ish al ma - ne - hu ve - ish al dig - lo.
v'la - a - rov e - ru - vo, Zeh ha yom na - gi - lah ve - nis - me - hah vo.

broadly

169

That first *zemer, Kol Mekadesh Shevi-i,* is one of the most difficult to sing because of its recitative-like character. By way of contrast, here is a song in triple meter—fairly unusual for *zemirot*—which was transmitted by a Jewish family in England. This is a Western melody. It suggests a lute accompaniment but, since few people own lutes, try playing broken chords on an autoharp or even a guitar.

Blessing the Sabbath candles

Yom Zeh Le-Yisrael
(To Israel This Day)

ENGLISH MELODY

Yom zeh le-yis-ra-el o-rah ve-sim-hah, Shab-
To Is-ra-el this day brings rest and re-lease, O

bat me-nu-hah, Shab-bat me-nu-hah. Tzi-
Sab-bath of peace, O Sab-bath of peace. God

170

bat me-nu – hah, Shab – bat me-nu – hah! Yom *al Fine*
Sab – bath of peace, O Sab – bath of peace. To

2. *Hemdat ha-levavot le-umah shevurah*
Lin'fashot nikh'avot neshamah yeterah.
Minefesh metzerah yasir anahah
Shabbat menuhah, Shabbat menuhah.

Yom zeh leyisrael, . . .

2. Beloved to the hearts of a people sorely grieved,
An added soul to them of hope and joy bereaved,
When thou comest, of sorrow and sigh they are relieved,
O Sabbath of peace, O Sabbath of peace.

To Israel this day. . . .

We turn for a moment to a *zemer* which is not a love song to the Sabbath but, rather, a song of thanksgiving for the Sabbath meal, namely *Tzur Mishelo Akhalnu*. This melody, a good example of environmental influence, was carried to America in the mid-nineteenth century by a Jewish Bohemian family and strongly resembles a German folk song. It shares this resemblance with certain melodies from another group of table songs—those included in the traditional Passover *Haggadah*. The well-known and beloved *Adir Hu* and *Had Gadya* which are sung at the conclusion of the *Pesah seder* have their origin in medieval Germany and are among the oldest Jewish songs still in popular usage. This *Tzur Mishelo* melody is in a 6/8 meter which appears almost exclusively in Western versions of the *zemirot*.

Tzur Mishelo

Ex. 82

BOHEMIAN MELODY

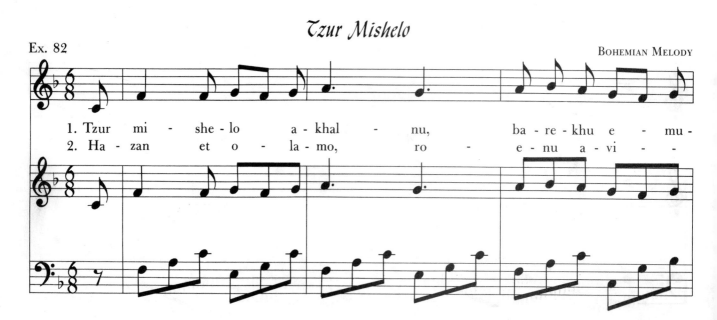

1. Tzur mi – she-lo a – khal – nu, ba – re-khu e – mu –
2. Ha – zan et o – la-mo, ro – e-nu a – vi –

va - nu ve - ho - tar - nu kid - var a - do - nai.
mar - nu ve - a - ni - nu, en ka - dosh ka - a - do - nai.

DS Tzur

Rock from whose store we have eaten
Bless Him, my faithful companions.
Eaten have we and left over—
This was the word of the Lord.

Feeding His world like a shepherd—
Father, whose bread we have eaten,

Father, whose wine we have drunken.
Now to His Name we are singing,
Praising Him loud with our voices,
Saying and singing forever:
    Holy is none like the Lord. Rock, . . .

(Trans. Nina Salomon)

From the ghettos of Eastern Europe comes this popular melody for a song sung at the Sabbath noonday meal. Notice its similarity to some hasidic *nigunim* and to some Yiddish folk songs in earlier chapters.

Yom Zeh Mekhubad
(This Is the Day)

Ex. 83

EAST EUROPEAN MELODY

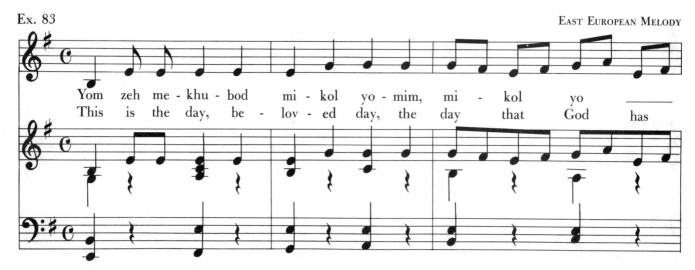

Yom zeh me - khu - bod mi - kol yo - mim, mi - kol yo ____
This is the day, be - lov - ed day, the day that God has

mim, ki vo sho-vas tzur o-lo-mim, tzur o-lo - - - -
blessed, This is the day He chose to rest, the day He chose to

mim.
rest.

Fine

Shey-shes yo-mim ta-'seh me-lakh-te-kho,
Six long days you ply your trade, for

Yom ha-sh'vi-i le-lo-he-kho, Shab-bos, Shab-bos lo -
in six days the world was made, but greet the sev-enth

ta - a seh bo m'lo khoh ki kol o - soh she - shes yo - min. *DC al Fine*
proud and un - a - fraid, the day God chose to rest.

An entirely different flavor is found in the songs of the Middle Eastern communities. Following is an- other song for the Sabbath noonday meal, written down by Idelsohn from the singing of Yemenite Jews.

Deror Yikra
(Liberty Proclaim)

Ex. 84

YEMENITE MELODY

D'ror yi - ke - ra le - ven im bat, ve -
Li - ber - ty pro - claim to each girl and boy!

yin - tzor - khem ke - mo ba -
Guard them with love, that no - one their ho - nor may des -

176

vat, ke - mo ba - - - vat. Ne - im shi - me -
troy, their ho - nor may des - troy. The gold of their good

khem ve - lo yush - bat, she - vu
name shall suf - fer no al - loy, and

ve - nu - hu be - yom Shab - -
no fear of shame shall mar their Sab - bath

bat,   be - yom   Shab   -   bat.
joy,   shall mar their Sab - bath   joy.

It is customary in many families to add other songs than the traditional *zemirot* to their singing at the Sabbath table. Hasidic *nigunim*, with their joyous sense of religious devotion, are great favorites. But there are many new songs which have been composed for the Sabbath. They are not necessarily table songs. Some are hymns to be sung in the synagogue, and examples can be found in the various collections of such hymns. Other Sabbath songs are for singing at all different kinds of festive gatherings. One such type of gathering has now achieved the status of a tradition practically everywhere. It is the *Oneg Shabbat,* initiated in the early decades of the twentieth century by the poet Bialik in the city of Tel Aviv. At first in his own home, later in a building constructed for the purpose (it was called the *Bet Am*), he introduced the custom of assembling to hear readings from Hebrew literature, to listen to discourses on matters of general interest and to sing Sabbath songs, old and new. Many of the new Sabbath songs composed in Israel express a renewed feeling for nature—the sea and the sky, the fields and the woods.

But of course modern Israeli composers are also finding inspiration for new Sabbath music in the rich treasury of the past. For example, the beautiful love poem to the Sabbath Bride by Yehudah Halevi at the opening of this chapter does not have any traditional melody. The Israeli composer, Yitzhak Edel, has set it to music for mixed chorus. The opening section of Edel's work presented in Ex. 85 can easily be sung by a school chorus.

The Blessing of the Candles, painting by Isidor Kaufmann

Shalom, Yom ha-Shevi-i

Yehudah Halevi

Yitzhak Edel

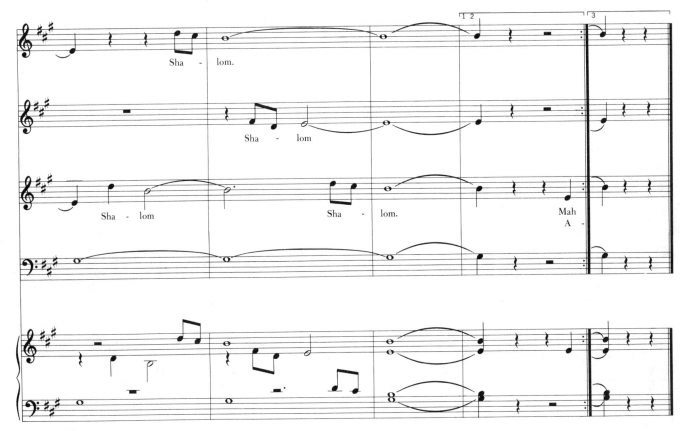

The departure of the Sabbath at sundown is also accompanied by ceremony and song. The ritual of *Havdalah,* the separation between the Sabbath and weekday, between holy and profane, is performed with a cup of wine, a candle made of twisted strands, the fragrance of spices and with chant. But the sorrowful mood which is inevitable in all farewells to a beloved is expressed in its own repertory of song. Following is a song with a text in the same classical meter and rhyme scheme as the *zemirot.*

Be-motza-ey Yom Menuhah
(Sing Farewell to Sabbath Day)

Ex. 86   ASHKENAZIC MELODY

181

nas ya - gon va - a - na - hah mi - seh ni - da - hah. Ye -
For E - li - jah now we pray, Oh, may he not de - lay. Oh,

hi nah sha - vu - a zeh ha - ba a - le - nu le - to - vah
help us face the com - ing week ____, free from sor - row ____, strong and gay,

li - shu - ah ul' - ne - ha - mah le - yis - ra - el a - me - kha.
Add - ing strength to Is - ra - el with each suc - ceed - ing day.

182

This song includes a prayer for the coming of Elijah. It does, indeed, refer to the same prophet Elijah of the *Book of Kings,* the central character of Mendelssohn's oratorio. But the poet did not have in mind the fiery, angry biblical personality. That tempestuous Elijah became transmuted in the minds of the folk into a very different personality. Based on a verse at the end of the *Book of Malakhi,* Elijah was to be the one who would announce the coming of the Messiah in the end of days. Over the long centuries of persecution and hardship, while the Jewish people hoped and prayed for speedy deliverance, the folk imagination began to see Elijah as a kindly rescuer. Legends grew up around him as a worker of good deeds, and even magic, who, single-handedly and in many disguises, could vanquish evil-doers and heap blessings upon the poor. This was the Elijah whom the folk expected to come riding up one day, heralding the coming of the longed-for Messiah. Today when we sing of Elijah, he is no longer that legendary figure; we think of him as symbolic of the hope for a Messianic age, a time of justice and peace for all mankind, a sort of universal Sabbath. As each Sabbath departs, and we must once again face the coming week of work and turmoil and hardship, we sing longingly a familiar song.

Elijah heralds the Messiah, from an old prayer book

Eliyahu ha-Navi

EAST EUROPEAN FOLK SONG

Ex. 87

E - li - ya - hu ha - na - vi, E - li - ya - hu ha - tish - bi,

E - li - ya - hu E - li - ya - hu, E - li - ya - hu ha - gil' - a -

di. Bim' - he - rah ya - vo, ya - vo e - le - nu im mo - shi -

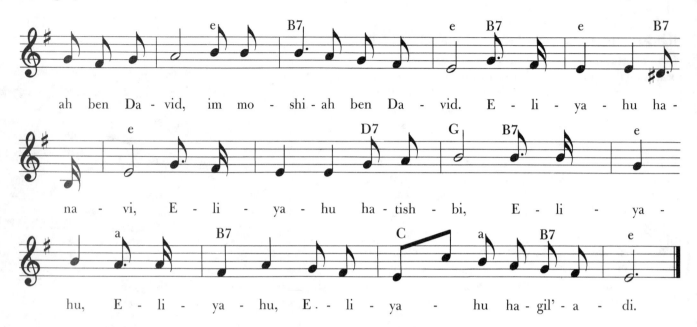

ah ben Da - vid, im mo - shi - ah ben Da - vid. E - li - ya - hu ha -

na - vi, E - li - ya - hu ha - tish - bi, E - li - ya -

hu, E - li - ya - hu, E - li - ya - hu ha - gil' - a - di.

Eliyahu songs are not quite as numerous as *zemirot,* but we do find them in almost every Jewish community around the world and, like the Sabbath songs, their melodies are cast in the idiom of the locality of each community. Here is a song of hasidic origin. It has many features in common with the songs of Levi

Yitzhak of Berditchev. It is part Hebrew and part Yiddish. It begins—recitative—in a prayer mode and winds up with a jolly dance tune. Think of it as a dialogue between a hasidic *rebbe* and his followers and sing it that way, alternating between solo and chorus.

Yovo Adir
(A Day Will Come)

Ex. 88   HASIDIC SONG

Yo - vo a - dir ve - yi - g'a - le - nu, yo - vo e - li - yo - hu vi -
A day will come, oh, let our voic - es ring, E - li - jah will be here, Good

185

ven vet er ku - men.
When will he be here?

Sha, nit shrei'n, er vet shoin ku - men!
Hush, don't cry, He'll soon be here!

Ven - zhe, ven - zhe vet dos zein?
When, oh when will that day be?

Bim - he - roh ve - yo - me -
In our own time and speed - i -

nu. Un vos far a tog vet dos zein?
ly. And what kind of day will that be?

Yom gi - loh, yom ri - noh, yom - di - tzoh, yom hed - voh
Day of glad - ness, day of sing - ing, day of danc - ing and re - joic - ing

Gi - loh, ri - noh, di - tzoh, hed - voh, Hal - le - lu - yah!
Glad - ness, sing - ing and re - joic - ing, Hal - le - lu - yah!

Yom gi - loh, yom ri - noh, yom di - tzoh, yom hed - voh
Day of glad - ness, day of sing - ing, day of danc - ing and re - joic - ing,

Gi - loh ri - noh
Glad - ness, sing - ing,

Gi - loh, ri - noh, di - tzoh - hed - voh, Hal - le - lu - yoh!
Glad - ness, sing - ing and re - joic - ing, hal - le - lu - yoh!

Di - tzoh, hed - voh, hal - le - lu - yoh!
danc - ing and re - joic - ing, hal - le - lu - yoh!

Just as *Yavo Adir* is characteristically East European in melodic style, so is our next song typical of Sephardic popular song. In this song, the text refers to the ancient tradition that Elijah was a direct descendant of Aaron, the High Priest, who was the brother of Moses. It also speaks of the people of Israel as *Yeshurun,* a name given to the folk in a number of biblical passages.

E-erokh Mahalal Nivi
(I Will Raise My Harp)

Ex. 89

EASTERN SEPHARDIC SONG

E - e - rokh ma - ha - lal ni -
I will raise my harp in

vi   li - fe - ney   e - lo - hey   a - vi _____

song,   Lord,   and   praise Thee   all   day   long   in

li - khe - vod   hem - dat   le -   va -   vi,   E - li - ya - hu

thanks   for   him   be - lov -   ed   to   me,   E - li - ya - hu

ha -   na -   vi,   li - khe - vod   hem - dat   le -

ha -   na -   vi,   I   sing   of   him   be -   lov -

va - vi,   E - li - ya - hu   ha - na - vi.
ed to me,   E - li - ya - hu   ha - na - vi.

2. *Nata ha-el bi-shurun*
Havatzelet ha-sharon
Ish migeza aharon
Ha-tishbi ha-gil'adi
Likhevod hemdat levavi
Eliyahu ha-navi.

2. The Lord planted in Yeshurun
Lovely lily of Sharon,
Man descended of Aharon,
Tishbite he, Gileadite he,
I sing of him beloved to me,
Eliyahu ha-navi.

The same melody, with its odd syncopated opening, is used by the Eastern Sephardim for the medieval poem which follows immediately upon the recitation of the *Havdalah: Ha-Mavdil.* The refrain, "I sing of him beloved to me, *Eliyahu ha-navi*," is retained and appended to each of the rather doggerel strophes of the poem. The poem has innumerable settings; this chapter ends with a lively old German melody.

Ha-Mavdil

Ex. 90

GERMAN JEWISH MELODY

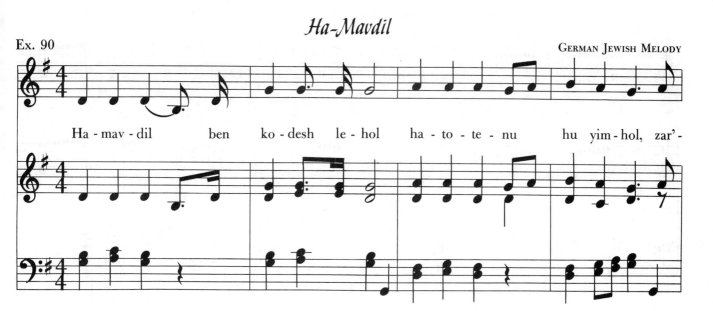

Ha - mav - dil   ben   ko - desh   le - hol   ha - to - te - nu   hu yim - hol, zar' -

e - nu ve-khas-pe - nu yar-beh ka - hol ve - kha-ko-kha-vim ba-lai-lah,

Yom pa-nah ke - tzel to - mer, ek - ra la-el a - lai go - mer

A - mar sho-mer, a-tah bo-ker ve - gam lai - lah.

May He who sets the holy and profane
Apart, blot out our sins before His sight,
And make our numbers as the sand again,
    And as the stars of night.

The day declineth like the palm-tree's shade,
I call on God who leadeth me aright.
The morning cometh—thus the watchman said—
    Although it now be night.

(Trans. Alice Lucas)

UPPER LEFT: Chair of Elijah, in the synagogue in Rome

LOWER LEFT: For the Havdalah ceremony—spice box, candle and chalice

BELOW: Havdalah ceremony in West Germany

Twenty-One
RITES
OF PASSAGE

BIRTH, puberty, marriage, death: since time immemorial the Jews, like all peoples, have evolved religious ceremonials to mark these significant milestones in life. As in the case of Jewish worship, these rites of passage vary in details from region to region and traditional melodies, which are almost sure to accompany them, vary also.

Any male born to Jewish parents is "a child of the covenant" and thus Judaism has no need for any ritual to initiate the infant into the faith. Birth as such is

Circumcision ceremony, Holland, 18th century

Ketubah (marriage certificate) from Italy, 18th century

not marked by any rites but, eight days after the birth of a baby boy, the Jews observe the very ancient and mandatory ceremonial of *Berit Milah,* "the covenant of circumcision," given as a divine commandment to Abraham in *Genesis 17: 9–12.* This ritual has been surrounded by special festivities over the ages. In Oriental and Eastern Sephardic communities they are conducted in the synagogue itself, where a special "chair of Elijah" is always ready for seating the person who holds the baby. Also, among the Sephardic and Eastern Jews, poetry and song were created to enhance the feelings of thanksgiving, joy and hope of the occasion. Following is an Eastern Sephardic hymn to welcome and bless the new son. The sentiment of this blessing is characteristic of Jewish prayers everywhere. The strict meter and rhyme in which it is cast, however, resemble the form of the Hebrew poetry of medieval Spain.

Hymn for the Berit Milah

Ex. 91

Eastern Sephardic Song

Girls' Voices

Ye - hi sha - lom be - he - le - nu
May peace reign in all our ranks, wher - e - ver we dwell

Men's Voices

Ye - hi sha - lom be - he - le -
May peace reign in all our ranks, wher - e - ver we

Ve - shal - vah be - yis - ra - el
Peace and se - re - ni - ty for all Is - ra - el.

nu. ve - shal - vah be - yis - ra - el
dwell. Peace and se - re - ni - ty for all Is - ra - el

be - si - man tov ben ba _ la -
Un - der a luck - y star came this son to hus - band and

be - si - man tov ben
Un - der a luck - y star came this

nu. Be - ya - mav ya -
wife. Ah, may the re - deem - er come

ba _ la - nu. Be - ya -
son to hus - band and wife. Ah, may the re -

195

be - ya - mav ya -
Ah, may the re - deem - er come to us

vo _____ go - el.
come to us dur - ing his life.

vo - go - el.

That hymn is still part of the living heritage of the descendants of Jewish exiles from medieval Spain. Another song, quite different in character from the example we've just seen, survives for our enjoyment only in the pages of old, out-of-print volumes. An eighteenth-century prayer book of the Jews of the Provence, the *seder ha-konteres* (daily rituals), contains a poem written half in Hebrew, half in the old Provençal language. The Provençal words are printed in Hebrew letters. For the melody to which this poem was sung, one has to turn to a nineteenth-century volume which contains the musical liturgy of the Jews of the comtat Venaissin. That is a small region in the Provence where thriving, even prosperous, Jewish communities once flourished in the towns of Avignon, Carpentras, Cavaillon and L'Isle. The original Jewish communities have been dispersed for many decades, but their charming synagogues may still be visited, and the volumes containing their traditions are stored in libraries. Here is a brief excerpt from the long and rather repetitive hymn of that lost community:

Eftah Sefatai

Ex. 92   PROVENÇAL SONG

Ef - tah se - fa - tai be - ri -

nah Can - ta - rem dé - man

a - di - na Ve - o - deh

na le - el el yon

Dés - sur tam - bou - rin

éi viou - lon

I will open my lips in joy,
Tomorrow at supper we'll sing.

I will sing praises unto the Lord,
Both on the drum and on the violin.

The French writer, Armand Lunel, tells us that the favorite instrumental accompaniment to all sorts of celebrations in the Provence of the Middle Ages was provided by a little "fipple-flute," a violin and a small drum or tambourine. Very likely there was just such a three-piece ensemble in attendance at the *Berit Milah* where this hymn was sung.‡

In the same prayer book where that song appears, one may find the libretto of a complete cantata intended for performance at a *Berit Milah*. The music for this cantata has only recently been discovered in an Amsterdam synagogue and identified by Israel Alder. It was written in the early eighteenth century by a certain M. Saladin (believed to be a fairly well-known composer in the area and a non-Jew), presumably commissioned by a wealthy Jew from the town of Carpentras. The cantata is composed in the prevailing style of the French Baroque for solo singers, string orchestra and chorus. It opens with an instrumental prelude. Solos, duets and choral pieces are interspersed with long instrumental selections called *ritornellos*, among them popular dance forms of the period: a *bourrée*, a *rigaudon* and a *gavotte*.‡ One can readily imagine the family and friends of the baby's parents, gathered at the ceremony in all their finery, solemnly celebrating the religious ritual, and then partaking of wine and refreshments and proceeding to dance the formal and elegant dances.

While it is true that song and dance and even instrumental music were almost always included in the celebrations of Ashkenazic Jews, they were not, except for the prayers of the ritual itself, dignified by being printed in the sacred volumes of prayer. We shall read more about such music in a later chapter.

The second major rite of passage in the life of a young Jew takes place thirteen years after the *Berit Milah* when he becomes *Bar Mitzvah,* a "son of the commandment." At thirteen, the Jewish boy is ushered into adulthood at a ritual in the synagogue, during which he is accorded the adult privilege and honor of being called up to the Torah. (In our own day, this privilege has been extended to the girl, who becomes *Bat Mitzvah.*) If he is especially proficient, he may lead the whole service (in a traditional synagogue). In many instances, he may be prepared to chant the Torah portion of the week. But the most prevalent assignment for the average *Bar Mitzvah* is the chanting of the blessings which precede and follow the chanting of his section of the Torah portion—usually the last several verses called the *Maftir*—then the blessing preceding the prophetic portion (*Haftarah*) which he learns to chant and the blessing following the prophetic portion.

Exs. 93a, b, c and d are the Ashkenazic chants for the blessings which the *Bar* or *Bat Mitzvah* must learn, in addition to the cantillation according to the biblical accents.

Bar Mitzvah, painting by Moritz Daniel Oppenheim

Blessing before the Torah Portion

ASHKENAZIC CHANT

Blessing after the Torah Portion

Ex. 93b

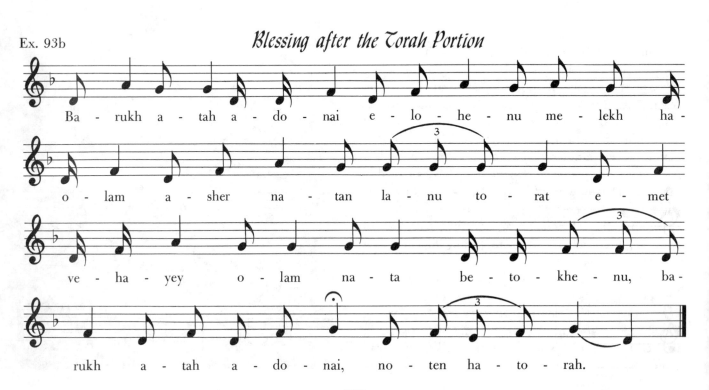

200

Blessing before the Haftarah

(Sung according to the accents in the prophetic cantillation)

Ex. 93c

ASHKENAZIC CHANT

Ba - rukh a - tah a - do - nai e - lo - he - nu me -
lekh ha - o - lam a - sher ba - har be - ne - vi -
im _____ to - vim ve - ra - tzah be - div - re - hem
ha - ne - e - ma - nim be - e - met, ba - rukh a - tah _____
_____ a - do - nai _____ ha - bo - her ba - to -
rah u - ve - Mo - sheh av - do u - ve - yis - ra - el _____
_____ a - mo u - vi - ne - vi - ey ha - e - met va - tze - dek.

201

Ex. 93d

Blessing after the Haftarah

ASHKENAZIC CHANT

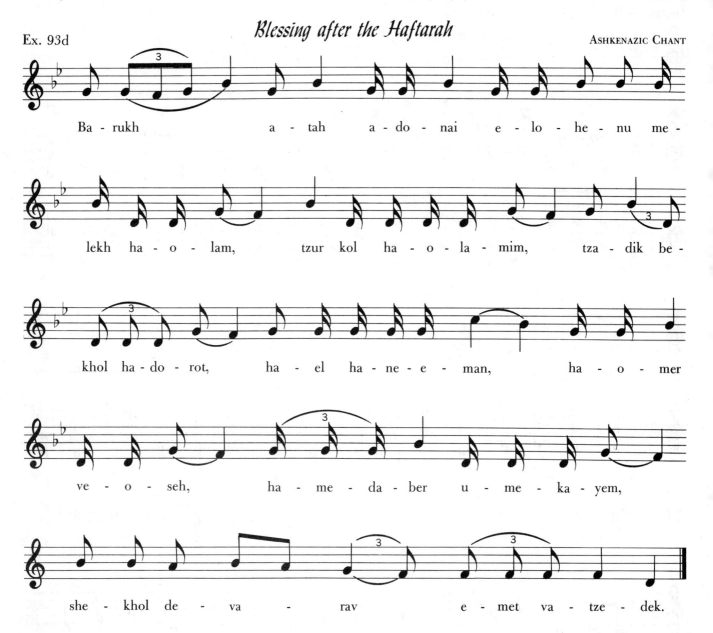

Ba - rukh   a - tah   a - do - nai   e - lo - he - nu   me -

lekh   ha - o - lam,   tzur   kol   ha - o - la - mim,   tza - dik   be -

khol   ha - do - rot,   ha - el   ha - ne - e - man,   ha - o - mer

ve - o - seh,   ha - me - da - ber   u - me - ka - yem,

she - khol   de - va - rav   e - met   va - tze - dek.

The third ritual of passage, Confirmation, is comparatively recent in Jewish life and, like the *Bat Mitzvah*—another modern innovation—the ritual affects girls as well as boys. It was not until the rise of Reform Judaism in nineteenth-century Germany that girls began to share in the religious ceremonial of the synagogue. The Confirmation service allows participation by both girls and boys of fifteen or sixteen. The singing of hymns very often accompanies the service. When Reform Judaism first introduced this practice in Germany, the hymns were sung in German; later, when the Reform movement spread to America, hymns were sung in English. One of the favorite Reform hymns for Confirmation services is "Father, See Thy Suppliant Children." Like other early hymns of the Reform service, this one is markedly influenced by the music of the neighboring Protestant churches.

Ex. 94

Father, See Thy Suppliant Children

ADAPTED BY MALCOLM H. STERN

MRS. S. E. MUNN

Fa - ther, see Thy sup - pli - ant child - ren

trem - bling stand be - fore Thy throne, To con - firm the vow of Si - nai,

"We will serve the Lord a - lone!" Now that we have stud - ied Thy To - rah

From the *Union Songster*. Central Conference of American Rabbis, N.Y., 1960.

may its laws e - ter - nal - ly guide our thoughts and

thus make our ac - tions be ac - cep - ta - ble un - to Thee. Thou shalt

love___ the Lord, thy Fa - ther, with thy heart and

soul and might. Let Him on - ly be thy

Guar - dian to guide thy foot - steps by day and by night.

As we reach the con - fir - ma - tion of our faith in

Is - ra - el's past, May the mes - sage of this ser - vice be the trea - sure we hold fast. Fa - ther, hear the vow we of - fer of our loy - al - ty to Thee; _____

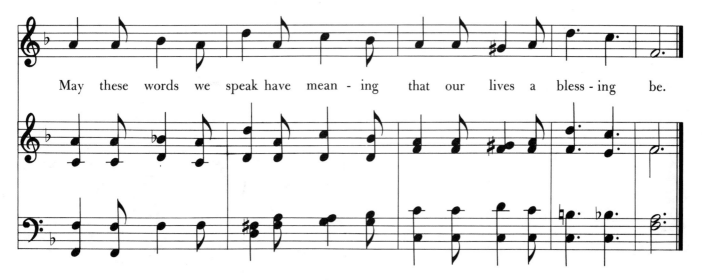

May these words we speak have mean-ing that our lives a bless-ing be.

Since the 1932 revision of the *Union Hymnal,* there has been a growing trend in the Reform synagogue to introduce melodies more closely related to the Jewish tradition. Today, the *Union Songster* (1960) furnishes several additional songs for the Confirmation service, which takes place on *Shavuot.* These all have melodies which are derived from synagogue chant—*nusah* and cantillation. One of the songs, "Could We with Ink," is a translation by the English Jewish writer, Israel Zangwill, of a medieval poem from the traditional *Shavuot* service, set to its original chant. The first word of that poem—which is written in Aramaic—is *"Akdamut,"* and hence the chant is known as the *Akdamut* melody. The bare, unadorned chant follows.

Ex. 95

This chant has been adapted in tradition to the recitation of the *Kiddush,* the sanctification prayer over wine, on the three Pilgrim festivals, *Pesah, Shavuot* and *Sukot.*

Ex. 96 is a little-known hymn, a song of the young initiates into the Jewish religious community in southwest France. The first stanza is in French, the second in Hebrew, taken from Psalm 118. Do you recognize the melody? It is derived from the Sephardic *Song of the Sea* quoted in Ex. 48 (Chapter Fourteen). The Jewish community in and around Bayonne, France, consists primarily of descendants of refugees from Portugal and Spain in the early sixteenth century. Their melodies closely resemble those of other Sephardic communities but, since they have been French-speaking for over three centuries, some of their songs are in the language of the people—French— as in the case of this hymn.

In the past several decades the Confirmation service has frequently become an occasion for presenting a musico-dramatic work in which each confirmand can participate. The custom was initiated on *Shavuot* of 1942 with the performance of *What Is Torah?* by the Confirmation class of the Society for the Advancement of Judaism in New York. This was a sort of folk cantata, a genre made popular at the time by John Latouche and Earl Robinson with their *Ballad for Americans.* It was intended as both a summary of the year's studies and as a vehicle for a variety of traditional and folk melodies which were not part of the ordinary school repertory.

Since that time such cantatas have proliferated. The reader might try his own hand at devising one based on almost any chapter in this book. The style, at the time of this writing, would necessarily be different from that of the forties. Guitar and percussion accompaniment and perhaps original verses instead of straight narrative would lend a more contemporary flavor to the project.‡

Bénissez-nous

Bé - nis - sez nous Dieu de lu - miè - re é - loi -

gnez de nous les mal - heurs, Et sur no - tre fa - mille en - tiè - re é - ten -

dez vos sain - tes fa - veurs. Ho - du la' - do - nai ki

tob   ki   le - o - lam   has   -   do,   ho - du

la' - do - nai   ki   tob   ki   le - o - lam   has - do.

Bless us, O God of light,
Remove from us all misfortune,
And upon all our family
Shed Thy holy protection.

Oh, give thanks unto the Lord, for He is good
And His kindness endureth forever.

The fourth rite of passage in the lifetime of a Jew is
marriage, a joyous and deeply religious ceremonial
throughout Jewish history. The traditional Jewish
wedding ceremony features the chanting of seven
beautiful blessings. Their melodies may vary even
within any one given community. There are cantors
who improvise long and elaborate chants, even introducing extraneous dance-like tunes in the blessings
when they reach such words as *gilah, rinah, ditzah,
hedvah* (joy, mirth, singing, happiness) or the lovely
passage, *Kol sason, vekol simhah, kol hatan vekol
kallah* (The sound of joy, the sound of happiness, the

Wedding procession, Germany, about 1700

voice of the groom and the voice of the bride). However, each Jewish locality has its fundamental chant, like a *nusah* of the synagogue. In a traditional wedding ceremony, the guests will sing the responses ("Blessed

be He, and blessed be His Name. Amen") just as they do in a synagogue service. Following is an example of basic, unadorned chant for the Ashkenazic *Shevah Berakhot* (Seven Blessings).

Ex. 97

BLESSINGS 1–3

ASHKENAZIC CHANT

Wedding Blessings

butz ba - ne - ha be - to - kha be - sim - hah, Ba - rukh a - tah a - do

nai, me - sa - me - ah Tzi - yon be - va - ne - hah. A - men.

Blessing 6

Sa - me - ah te - sa - mah re - im ha - a - hu - vim ke - sa -

me - ah ye - tzir - kha be - gan e - den mi - ke - dem, ba - rukh a - tah a - do -

Blessing 7

nai, me - sa - me - ah ha - tan ve - kha - lah. A - men. Ba - rukh a -

tah a - do - nai, e - lo - he - nu me - lekh ha - o - lam, a - sher ba -

ra sa - son ve - sim - hah, ha - tan ve - kha - lah, gi - lah, ri -

nah, di - tzah ve - hed - vah, a - ha - vah ve - ah - vah ve - sha - lom

ve - re - ut. Me - he - rah* a - do - nai yi - sha - ma be - a -

211

rey ye - hu - dah u - ve - hu - tzot ye - ru - sha - la - yim kol sa - son ve -

kol sim - hah, kol ha - tan ve - kol ka - lah, kol mitz - ha -

lot ha - ta - nim me - hu - pa - tam u - ne - a - rim mi - mish - tey ne - gi - na -

tam. Ba - rukh a - tah a - do - nai me - sa - me - ah ha - tan im ha - ka - lah. A - men.

1. Blessed art Thou, O Lord, our God, King of the universe, who dost create the fruit of the vine.

2. Blessed . . . in whose glory all things are created.

3. Blessed . . . who dost create man.

4. Blessed . . . who dost create man in His image, and endow him with eternal life, blessed art Thou, O Lord, Creator of man.

5. The barren one shall rejoice and be glad, when her children are gathered unto her with happiness; blessed art Thou, O Lord, who dost make Zion happy with her children.

6. Thou shalt gladden the beloved pair, as Thy creatures were glad in the Garden of Eden of old. Blessed art Thou, O Lord, who dost gladden bridegroom and bride.

7. Blessed art Thou, O Lord, our God, King of the universe, who didst create happiness and joy, bride and groom, gladness, singing, celebration and delight, love and fellowship, peace and friendship. Soon,* O Lord, may there be heard in the cities of Judah and the streets of Jerusalem, the sound of happiness and joy, the sound of bride and groom, the voice of the bridal pair from their wedding canopy and of youths from their feasts. Blessed art Thou, O Lord, who dost gladden bridegroom and bride.

*Since the establishment of the State of Israel, the sound of rejoicing of bridegroom and bride may already be heard in the "cities of Judah and the streets of Jerusalem." Many rabbis, therefore, in officiating at marriage ceremonies, are now substituting the word *le-olam* (forever) for the word *meherah* (speedily, or soon) at this point in the blessings.

Wedding ceremony, Poland

212

In traditional families, the custom is still observed of reciting the *Shevah Berakhot* once again after the wedding feast, directly following the grace after meals. This is a survival from the older custom (also still observed in very Orthodox families, particularly in the East) of celebrating a marriage for seven days, with a festive meal each day followed each time by the Seven Blessings.

The Jews of Yemen developed their own special customs for the days of wedding festivity. As we have already seen, the Yemenite Jews were at one time profoundly influenced by the mystics of Safed. Certain deep mystical approaches were adopted by the Yemenites even in their marriage rituals. They came to regard every wedding as a symbol of the love between God and Israel—the same love they saw expressed in the poetry of *The Song of Songs*. Thus, at every wedding they enacted this little drama: God and Israel are betrothed (reread the passage from *Jeremiah* quoted in Chapter Thirteen); Israel (the bride) sins and is sent away into exile; she repents and begs forgiveness; God grants forgiveness, takes her back into His own house (or palace, or garden) amid great rejoicing and a jubilant procession. Each "act" in this folk play has its own selection of songs—long poems of many stanzas, some in Hebrew, some in Arabic—which are sung by pairs of male singers who read the words out of books to the accompaniment of drumbeat and dancing. (This music and dancing are the exclusive prerogatives of the men; the women have their own songs and dances, which are not part of the religious ceremony, and which are performed in Arabic.)

One of these Yemenite creations—a joyous reconciliation song—is presented below. The text, by an unknown poet, is comprised of many stanzas, some in Hebrew, some in Arabic. Each stanza follows a strict pattern, which was learned by the Jewish poets from their Arabic neighbors. Called the "girdle form," it begins with a quatrain of rhyming lines—fairly long—followed by three shorter lines in a new meter and rhyme scheme; and it concludes with a couplet in the same meter and rhyme scheme of the quatrain. (The translation following the song attempts to demonstrate the pattern.) The melody begins with a free, unrhythmical chant in the style of the Arabic song of the region (see Ex. 62, Chapter Seven) and soon breaks into strong rhythmic melody sung by alternating pairs of singers.

Yemenite Wedding, a dance based on the traditional tribal marriage rites, as depicted by the Inbal dancers

You can sing it that way, too, omitting the piano accompaniment and improvising your own accompaniment of drumbeats and hand-clapping. This piano accompaniment was devised by Joel Engel in the mid-1920's. Engel, the Russian-born composer and music critic, is an interesting and important personality whom we shall meet in a later chapter.

This arrangement is, perhaps, more romantic than is warranted by the text or the folk melody. Nevertheless, it does provide a very pleasant recital piece which merits a place in a concert of Jewish music. It can be used, in addition, as a welcome innovation in an actual marriage ceremony. The introductory "recitative" can precede either the processional or the recessional which would then be accompanied by the more metrical section which begins at the top of page 216.

Ahavat Rayah

YEMENITE SONG
ARR. JOEL ENGEL

bi. Esh' - a - lah _____ tzu - ri _____
bi. Rak _____ be - se -

ve - ko - ni, esh - le - hah _____ ma - re -
khel ra' - yo - ni te - _____ he - meh ru -

pey le - o - ze - bi.
hi be - kir - bi.

4. Es - me-hah an - shah ye - go — ni, ye - go - ni!

E - e-mod shah - ri ve - ar - bi, ve - ar - bi!

Ki be - no - am heg — yo — ni, heg - yo - ni!

217

Esh - ke-hah u - li ve - otz - bi!

8va

8va

Es - me-hah, an-

8va

shah ye - go - ni

A - a-mod - shah - ri ve - ar -

Poco accelerando

Poco accelerando

218

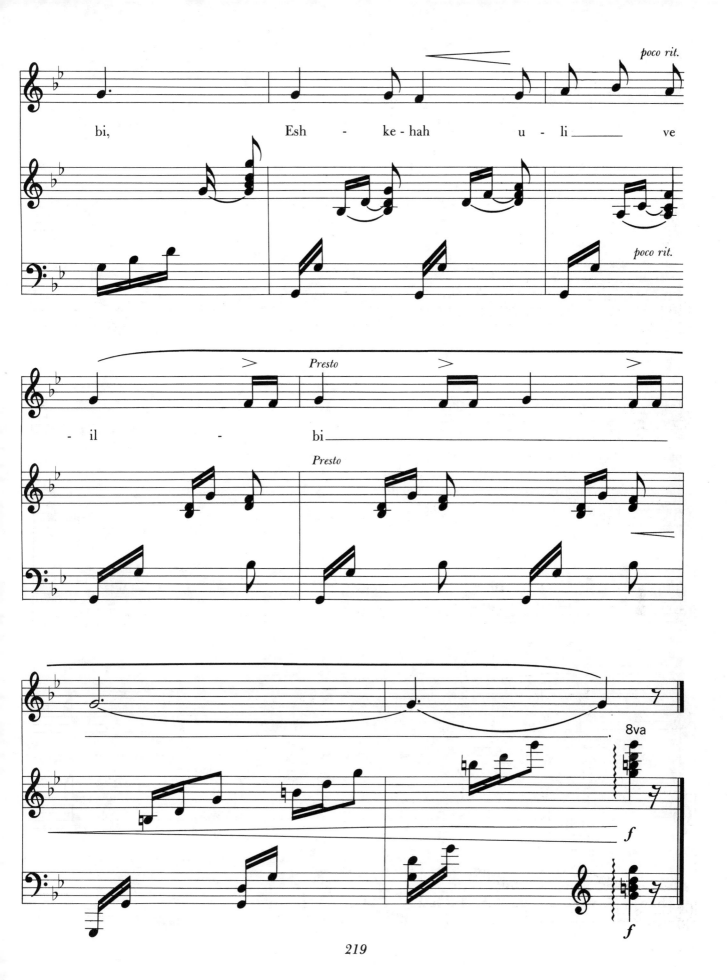

bi, Esh - ke - hah u - li _____ ve

- il - bi _____

219

For the love of a dear one I long, a delight to my soul
    she will be.
My Rock and my Maker I pray, for my sorrow send solace
    to me.
When I call, He will answer, I know, for my sword and
    my crossbow is He.
Meditation and song shall alone let the turmoil within me
    go free.
    I will walk a straight way
    'Midst the remnant who stay
    With devotion to pray.
With rejoicing I overcome grief, as morning and evening
    to Thee
In thanksgiving I utter sweet song, for my joy and my
    comfort is she.

For the final ritual of passage—death—Jewish tradition provides no elaborate requiems. The traditional Jewish funeral has no flowers, is extremely simple and has only the chant to accompany it. At the Ashkenazic service there might be the straightforward chanting of a psalm and of the special solemn prayer *El Maley Rahamim* (God, full of mercy) in a simple *nusah* which begins like this:

The Sephardic funeral ritual includes a special text which is chanted at the burial, when the mourners walk around the coffin seven times. The Jewish community of Bayonne, France, sings that text to this austere melody:

220

Have mercy on him, O living God, King of the universe, for in Thee is the source of life. May he ever walk in the land of the living, and may his spirit rest in the bond of life.

Sephardic funeral, 18th century

Twenty-Two
SING LE-HAYIM

THE RELIGIOUS rites are completed. The party is on! It could be the celebration of a *Berit Milah,* a *Bar Mitzvah,* an engagement, a wedding, a birthday or an anniversary. A guest raises his glass and cries, *"Le-hayim"* (To life), and the company, raising their glasses in turn, respond with enthusiasm. *"Le-hayim tovim uleshalom"* (To a good life and to peace). A family of hasidic background—always ready to burst into song—will toast all the principals around the table, addressing the formula to each one individually: *"Le-hayim* to the father—to the mother—to the groom—to the bride!" Here is the tune:

Le-Hayim!

Ex. 100   FOLK TUNE

Le - ha - yim   dem
                       dem

ma - mes   ve - g'n,   le -
ta - t'n's

ha - yim   to - vim

u - le - sho - lom!

This unquenchable appreciation of the gift of life —and hope for peace—overflowed the bounds of religious song and permeated a host of songs of everyday life. The great occasions and the lesser ones, the workdays and the leisure moments of the Jew, from infancy to old age, are all reflected in a large treasury of songs. The bulk of these are folk songs—that is, songs by unknown composers long gone, which have been circulated by word of mouth and very often changed by singers from place to place, either unconsciously or consciously, to suit local circumstances or personal whims. A far smaller number are "art songs"—that is, songs written down in their final form by their composers, usually with an integrally related instrumental accompaniment which cannot be omitted or altered and which carry the composers' names.

Each such song—folk or art—is a vignette of Jewish life. We have been discovering some of these vignettes in earlier chapters of this book: the love songs, the laments and the resistance songs, all sung in the vernacular of the people wherever they dwelt. Text and melody together reveal a great deal about Jewish hopes, dreams and approaches to life.

For example, take the lullaby. Babies and lullabies are always associated together, but don't make the mistake of thinking that lullabies are necessarily baby songs! They are sung by adults to infants who may

Our Youngest Daughter's Married, figurines by Ryback

222

react to the lilt of the tune but who cannot possibly understand the words. Not long ago, a newspaper reported the lullaby a young suburban father sings to his baby: "Buy low, sell high," telling us in four words exactly what's on *his* mind! In the same way, the mother in the Jewish *shtetl* discloses her dreams for her child in this lullaby. She takes her melody from a fragment of synagogue chant, the *nusah* which is called *Ahavah Rabbah* after the prayer which begins with those words, "Great love." (It contains the "augmented second" step, which is found in many songs of the Near and Middle East, that is, the step from F to G sharp in Ex. 101.

There are folk lullabies in Yiddish, in Ladino and in all the languages that Jews have spoken. In addition, there are many composed lullabies with words in various languages. For instance, there is an art song called *Viglied* (Cradle Song) by the composer Lazar Weiner, a very sophisticated setting of a Yiddish poem by Bella Schumiatcher.‡ This is a concert piece, requiring performance by a trained singer and a skilled pianist. It is "through-composed"—the music varies from stanza to stanza, with repetition enough to produce a nicely balanced form. Written in America in the 1930's, it is nevertheless a direct descendant of the music produced by the school of national Jewish

Under the Cradle

Ex. 101

YIDDISH FOLK SONG

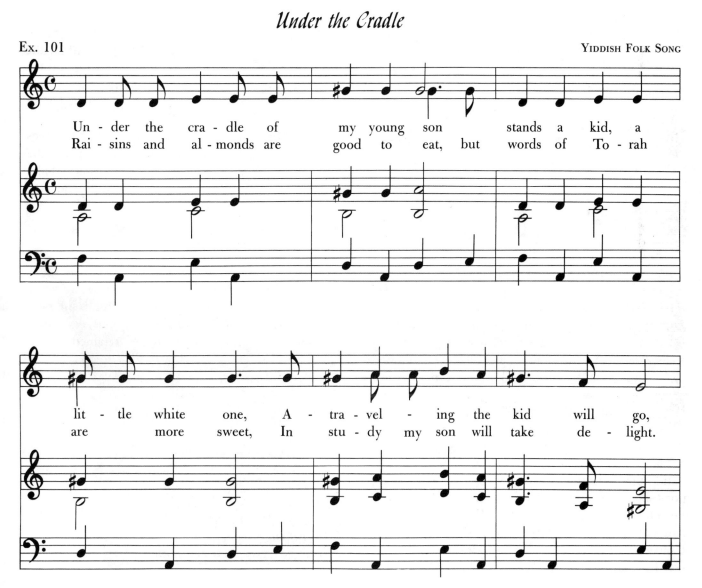

Un - der the cra - dle of my young son stands a kid, a
Rai - sins and al - monds are good to eat, but words of To - rah

lit - tle white one, A - tra - vel - ing the kid will go,
are more sweet, In stu - dy my son will take de - light.

223

bring - ing good - ies you love so. Rai - sins and al - monds are his
He'll be learn - ed, books he'll write. Pur - sue the To - rah

pride and joy, but To - rah is the pride of my lit - tle boy.
all your days, and fol - low in its right - eous ways.

composers of Russia in earlier decades. (They will be discussed in a later chapter.) Weiner, who is known for his fine liturgical music, immigrated to America from his native Kiev and throughout his life has been closely associated with the Yiddishist movement. His feeling for the Yiddish folk song of his own childhood and youth, together with his education in the musical techniques and style of the earlier twentieth century, helped to produce this tender lullaby, expressing the parent's vision of the future for his child: "Grow, my dear, to manhood strong, to field and toil do you belong."

At about the same time that Weiner was writing this lullaby in America, Saul Tchernichowsky, one of the great pioneers of modern Hebrew poetry, was writing a far different kind of lullaby in Palestine. The Hebrew poet was giving expression to the feelings of a young mother in a *kibbutz* during the time of the

Arab riots against the Jewish settlements in 1936. Here is a translation of his poem. The Hebrew refrain, *"Numah, num"* means "sleep, sleep." It has the same effect as "Lulla, lulla" in English lullabies, or *"Dodo"* in French songs and is therefore retained in the translation:

Lullaby

Lo, I have a child, a male,
Conceived to sound of jackals wail,
Given birth to sound of gun,
Halutzah and *halutz* son.
        Numah numah num.

Sleep and grow, be great and strong,
For the day ahead is long.
Every helping hand we crave,
Every heart that's stout and brave,
        Numah numah num.

Sleep, tonight I'll stay with you.
If you sleep, then I'll sleep too,
Weary (work is never done).
Sleep, beloved *halutz* son.
　　　Numah numah num.

Though you weep, you have no fear.
Only melody you hear,
Not the words with anguish filled,
"By a bullet he was killed."
　　　Numah numah num.

Grow up, as your cradle rocks
To wail of jackal, cry of fox,
To the rat-tat-tat of gun,
Halutzah and *halutz* son!
　　　Numah numah num.

　　　　　　　　(Saul Tchernichowsky)

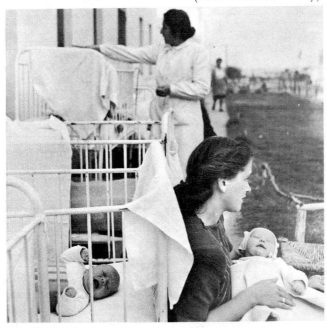

Kibbutz lullaby

Try to compose your own musical setting for Tchernichowsky's lullaby. It can be a very simple strophic song—the same melody for every stanza. Or you can make it a little more like an art song by casting it in a slightly more elaborate form—which we will describe simply as ABACA. That is, one melody to start with (first stanza), a contrasting melody for the second stanza, a return to the melody of the first stanza for stanza three, another new melody for stanza four and a return to the first melody for stanza five. Before you improvise your first melody, strum a rocking

lullaby rhythm on the E minor chord on your guitar. Now sing the first stanza. Shift to the key of G major for stanza two. Return to E minor for stanza three. Try B major for stanza four and return to E for the closing section. Of course, this is only one of the many possible ways to organize a song. You might wish to compose your own text, a lullaby of your own time and place, and set that to music. In any case, if you have never had a lesson in music theory or composition in your life, you will have at least as much technique at your disposal as did the composers of many of the best loved songs that have come down to us.

The songs were improvised, for the most part, by wandering entertainers called *badhanim,* who, in the Middle Ages, were able to juggle and perform acrobatics as well as to extemporize verses in the market place and at family celebrations. In later centuries, they dropped the more vigorous aspects of their clowning and restricted their talents for amusement to stories and songs. By the nineteenth century, there were entertainers who learned a little of the technique of music and were able to write down their songs. A new breed of "folk" composers grew up, whose songs continued to reflect the everyday life of their people. Among these composers was Mark Warschavsky, one of whose universally cherished songs gives us a vivid picture of the East European schoolboy in his *heder* (schoolroom). The children are huddled around a wood stove, while their *rebbe,* or teacher, teaches them the alphabet, the *alef-beis,* in the time-honored sing-song method of the *heder.* The children learned the first vowel sign, *komotz,* which in the Ashkenazic pronunciation has the sound "*aw,*" and then they applied the "*aw*" sound to each consonant of the alphabet: *komotz, alef, aw; komotz, beis, baw; komotz, gimel, gaw; komotz, daled, daw;* etc. Next they learned the second vowel, *pasah,* sounded as "*ah*": *pasah, alef, ah; pasah, beis, bah; pasah, gimel, gah;* etc. and similarly with the remaining vowels: *segol,* (*eh*), *tzerah* (*ay*), *hirik* (*ee*) and *shuruk* (*oo*). (Ex. 102)

In the heder

Oifen Pripitchik
(In the Little Stove)

Words and Melody by
Mark Warschavsky

Ex. 102

Oif - 'n pri - pi - tchik brennt a fei - e - rel un in shtub is
In the lit - tle stove fire is burn - ing, what a co - zy

heis,   Un der Reb - be le - rent klav - ne kin - der - lach
place!   Reb - be teach - ing, child - ren learn - ing

dem   a - lef beis.   Un der Reb - be le - rent
to read the a - lef beis.   Reb - be teach - ing

klay - ne kin - der lach dem a - lef beis. "Zeht - zhe kin - der - lach, ge -
child - ren learn - ing to read the a - lef beis. "Look here, child - ren,

denk - zhe tei - e - re, vos ihr le - rent doh, Zog - zhe noch a - mol un
think hard, lit - tle ones, read - ing has its law. Say it af - ter me, and

tak - ke noch a - mol, ko - metz a - lef aw. ko - metz a - lef aw!"
keep re - peat - ing it, ko - metz a - lef aw. ko - metz a - lef aw!"

Another song which dramatizes the scene in the *heder* is an art song (written in 1914) by the Russian composer Moses Milner. Milner, like Warschavsky, wrote both the words and the music of his song, but the result is a concert piece which requires a performer of skill and humor and which cannot be performed without its accompaniment.‡ (This song could be performed by two singers: one with a deep voice taking the part of the *rebbe* who is giving the little one his first lesson, the other singer, with a thin, high voice taking the part of the youngster who imitates the *rebbe* timidly, just a shade off key.)

The boy who sings the following folk song is older than the little fellow of Milner's song, and sadder. He has already mastered the *alef-beis* and has started to learn *Humash* (another name for the *Pentateuch* or the *Five Books of Moses*). His song gives a picture of the village—the same kind of scene painted so often by Marc Chagall. His melody, up to the refrain, is taken almost directly from the study chant. The refrain, with words from the first chapter of *Genesis,* is derived from the cantillation mode of the Torah.

Ex. 103

FOLK SONG

Zun - tik bin ich nit ge - ven in he - der, veil
Sun - day I did - n't go to he - der, For

zun - tik hob ich feint, az di zun sheint tzu
Sun - day my heart was pin - ing to see the sun shin - ing, not

zi - tz'n in fin - ster -'n he - der   un kvetch -'n die bank   ke - se - der
sit in the he - der so drear - y,   and bend over books till   I'm wear - y.

Ich bin ge - lo - fen biz ich bin ge - vo - r'n mid,   un ich hob ge - zung -'n
I   ran and ran un - til my feet   were sore,   and I sang a song   from

Yan - ke - le's lied. Oy!   vet mich der reb - be shmeis - s'n!   Di
days   of yore. Oh,   the Reb - be will give me a   beat - ing.   Oh!

hoit ... vet er mir in shtick-er tze - reis - s'n.
oh! the seat of my pants he'll be heat-ing!

"vay'- hi e - rev va - ye - hi vo - ker, yom e - hod."
"And it was eve - ning, and it was morn - ing of the first day."

2. Monday I didn't go to *heder*,
   For Monday my stomach rumbled.
   "Nothing to eat," it grumbled.
   My father ran out full of sorrow,
   My mother tried to beg, or to borrow.
   I sat and sat until my bottom was sore,
   And I sang a song of the days of yore.
     Oho! the Rebbe will give me a beating,
     O woe, the seat of my pants he'll be heating,
     "And it was evening, and it was morning, the second
        day."

3. Tuesday I didn't go to *heder*,
   For Tuesday the goat got smart.
   It tore the fence apart,
   Then over the bridge it went flying.
   We all chased it screaming and crying.
   We ran and ran till we could run no more,
   And I sang a song of the days of yore.
     Oho! the Rebbe will give me a beating,
     O woe, the seat of my pants he'll be heating,
     "And it was evening, and it was morning, the third
        day."

We have already met the older youth, the *yeshivah* student, and encountered some songs of love and courtship. Marriage, of course, is a time for great rejoicing not only for the happy couple but also for the loving parents who, under certain circumstances, can be pardoned an outburst of enormous relief at seeing their offspring wed at last. In another popular Yiddish song by Warschavsky, an East European mother kicks up her heels in glee after she has married off her youngest daughter. The song captures all the hilarity of the wedding, with its fiddlers and the dancers, and it's not hard to visualize the scene: the parents, the aunts and uncles and all the little cousins and the poor of the town—all of them rollicking in a joy-filled wedding hall. The bride's mother is at the center of the scene.

Die Mezhinkeh Oisgegeben
(My Youngest Daughter's Married)

WORDS AND MELODY BY
MARK WARSCHAVSKY

Ex. 104

Hech - er, bes - ser, di rod, di rod macht gres - ser
Loud - er, strong - er, the par - ty goes on long - er,

grois hot mir Gott ge - macht, glick hot er mir ge - bracht,
Let's make mer - ry all the night, shout and sing and dance with de - light,

Hul - yet kind - er a gan - tze nacht, di me me-
Now at last I have the right, my

zhin - ke ois - ge - ge - b'n, di me - zhin - ke ois - ge - ge - b'n.
young - est daught - er's mar - ried, my young - est daught - er's mar - ried!

2. Hey diddle, diddle, what's happened to the fiddle?
   Let it screech or let it scratch,
   Only get him playing with dispatch,
   I have no more eggs to hatch,
   My youngest daughter's married,
   My youngest daughter's married.

A somewhat different spirit is expressed in the following song which *Hasidim* often sing at their weddings. The bride sits on a throne-like chair. The guests— usually in two lines, one made up of men, the other of women—dance up to her and then back. Then individuals break out of line, dance up and then retreat, pantomiming welcome and praise. All clap hands and stamp feet, singing over and over: "How do you dance in honor of the bride—the bride so lovely and virtuous?" (Ex. 105)

Keytzad Merakedim

Ex. 105   HASIDIC SONG

Key - tzad me - ra - ke - dim,

key - tzad me - ra - ke - dim

Lif - ney ha - kal - loh?

Kal - loh no - oh va - ha - su -

doh, kal - loh no - oh

va - ha - su - doh.

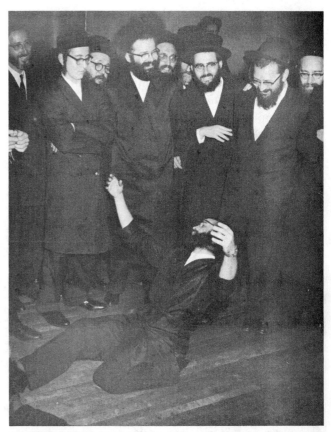

Hasidic wedding dance

The Sephardic Jews of the Middle East brought their wedding song with them from medieval Spain. It seems closer to the Arabic songs of their new environment than to the *kinot* which were quoted in Chapter Fifteen. However, it is possible that the song originated in southern Spain, where Jews and Arabs lived side by side, in that same Andalusia where even today traces of Moorish music are strong in flamenco song. The bride of this Sephardic wedding song is a poor girl, but undoubtedly the few *dineros* in her

dowry and also her small trousseau were furnished by the Jewish community and the guests who sing at her wedding.[‡] (Ex. 106)

One cannot write about Jewish wedding music without recalling the beautiful *Wedding Ode* that was composed at the very end of the sixteenth century by Salomone Rossi, sometimes called Salomone Ebreo (the Hebrew) of Mantua, Italy. Hebrew poets had been writing wedding odes since the Golden Age of the Jews in Spain. This composition by Rossi is a setting of such an ode by an unknown Italian Hebrew poet. The style of the music is that of the late Renaissance in Italy when the form of *chori spezzati* (split choruses) became popular. The ode requires two choruses of four voices each for performance. The second chorus sings an echo of the first at the end of each rhyming line. Singing it, or even only hearing it, calls up a picture of a prosperous Jewish family, garbed in the rich colors we know from Italian Renaissance paintings, presiding over an elaborate feast to which they have invited professional singers, conducted probably by the composer himself. One chorus would be at the front of the hall, the other would sing its echoes from the rear. The *Ode* would be only one part of the musical program. Their chief musician, Rossi, was a member of the sophisticated musical establishment at the court of the Duke of Mantua and a friend of the great composer Monteverdi. He would undoubtedly have brought other musicians to provide accompaniments for the courtly dances of the time—viols, recorders, harps, possibly a drum. The dances would be led by a popular Italian dancing master who was most likely to be a Jew out of their own ghetto. Surely, too, some of the music was background for the troupe of wedding jesters, acrobats and jugglers who were a necessary feature of any really splendid wedding party in a noble house.‡

Scalerica de Oro
(Staircase of Gold)

Ex. 106

LADINO FOLK SONG

Sca - le - ri - ca de o - ro, de o - ro y de mar - fil, pa - ra que su - va la no - via

Lit - tle stair - case of i - vo - ry, of i - vo - ry and of gold, where the love - ly bride as - cends for the

a dar ki - du - shin.   Sca - le - shin.   Ve - ni -
rite of ki - du - shin.   Lit - tle shin.   We all

mos a ver   ve - ni - mos a ver,   y
come to wit - ness, we all   come to watch,   to

go - zen y lo - gren, y   ten - gan mu - cho bien,   ve -
wish them both joy,   and to   bless them both with love.   We

ten - ga un ma - zal bue - no, que mos
wish her a ma - zal bue - no, But we

ten - ga un ma - zal bue - no. Ve -
wish her a ma - zal bue - no. We

237

Twenty-Three
SMILE WHEN YOU SING THAT!

SOME time around the year 1040, in the city of Saragossa, Spain, there lived a wealthy man named Moses, who committed an unforgivable *faux pas*. This Moses saw himself as a patron of young students and, in a great show of generosity and hospitality, invited them to dinner at his home. But the generosity ended at the threshold of his magnificent home for, when the thirsty and hungry students sat down at his table, they found, to their dismay, that Moses was stingy with his wine. In a land famed for fine vineyards and flowing with wine, Moses doled out his vintages in droplets; and, even worse, his servants diluted the tiny drops in giant beakers of plain, ordinary, tasteless,

Purim jesters, woodcut from the Minhagim Book, Amsterdam, 1662

everyday—water! In revenge for this affront to their dignity, this insult to Spanish wine, this breach of all the laws of hospitality and Jewish custom, the parched students invented an epithet for Moses which has clung to his name ever since: Moses the Miser.

How do we know about the parsimonious Moses? It seems that one of his student guests who had sat dry-tongued and fuming all evening was none other than Solomon Ibn Gabirol. Ibn Gabirol was later to write some of the most magnificent of all Jewish religious poetry; but, in his younger days, his poetic fancy could light upon lesser themes. The miserly Moses was the target of a set of derisive verses by Ibn Gabirol, which have immortalized his name—and his *faux pas*—over the ages.

But that is not the end of the story. Many centuries later, those verses were dusted off and set to a lively tune by some Russian Jewish students, and in recent years the song has been revived and "Orientalized" in Israel. Some mental gymnastics are necessary to understand some of the complex allusions in the verses, but we can all easily appreciate the root of the complaint of young Ibn Gabirol and his fellow students—too much water, not enough wine. The poet starts out in his opening two lines with a game of *gematria*, that is, the trick of finding hidden meanings in Hebrew words by adding up the numerical equivalents of the Hebrew letters. Each letter in the Hebrew alphabet stands for a number, *alef* = 1, *bet* = 2, *gimel* = 3, etc. The Hebrew word for "wine" is *yayin*, spelled *yod, yod, nun,* or $10 + 10 + 50$, adding up to a total of 70. The Hebrew word for "water" is *mayim*, spelled *mem* (40), *yod* (10), *mem* (40), adding up to 90. Thus the angry students, on the warpath for wine (70), are overcome by "90"—that is, by water. In the following translation, the word "rain" is substituted for water, partly in order to help the rhyme scheme but also because the form of the poem suggests that it may have been a parody on one of many rain prayers.

238

Song of Rain

Ex. 107

Solomon Ibn Gabirol

Folk Song

Sev - en - ty war - riors, sum of wine, Are o - ver - come by

ten times nine, To toast the host we must de - cline, Our

hearts are filled with pain, We sing a song of rain.

239

When wine ceas - es eye re - leas - es, When wine ceas - es

eye re - leas - es, When wine ceas - es eye re - leas - es

Floods of wa - ter - y rain, floods of wa - ter - y rain.

2. Finest wine can have no taste,
   And choicest dainties are a waste,
   When goblets not with wine are graced,
   But water dull and plain,
   Oh, sing a song of rain!
      When wine ceases, . . .

3. Like a frog I sit and croak.
   Of wine to drink there's barely a token.
   It's a drought, and that's no joke!
   We sing a sad refrain,
   We sing a song of rain.
      When wine ceases, . . .

The verses of that song are thought to be the oldest remains of a large collection of Jewish satiric poetry, humorous ballads and just plain fun songs written throughout the ages. Some 200 years after Ibn Gabirol, the Spanish Hebrew poet Al-Harizi went journeying to all parts of the Jewish world and wrote about his travels in a long poem made up of rhymed couplets with lines of unequal length,—a sort of thirteenth-century Ogden Nash. One of his stops was Babylonia, which, until the tenth century or so, had been a glorious center of Jewish learning. (Among other things, the first *hazanim* probably wrote and sang their religious poetry in Babylonia.) This is how Al-Harizi described what he found in the now-deteriorated Jewish community of Babylonia:

And in Babylon I beheld the singers,
Among them the glory of the Geonim no longer lingers,
For in proportion as their precepts are worthy,
So cloddish their poetry, and so earthy.
When we hear them, woe is us, we are undone!
They sound like frightened sheep, they bleat and run.
We sit and weep by the rivers of Babylon!

As for their favorite singer, Rabbi Yitzhak bar Israel,
    head of the Academy, some of his aren't too bad
    when spoken,
But most of them, when sung, sound like a pot that is
    broken,
Neither sweetness nor skill do they betoken.
His compositions in book form are given a haven,
A collection of songs and epistles so craven,
So cold, out of snow from Mount Hermon they seem to
    be graven.
As the desert manna that, for our sins, turned wormy
    and rotten,
So this gentleman's singing were better forgotten.

I couldn't choose the worst of them, for there are plenty
Would cause a shudder to the *cognoscenti*.
Ah, poetry in Babylon is stupefied and lying
In the bosom of stupidity, and dying.

And Rabbi Moshe ben Shashat of our land went to Baby-
    lonia to lead their folk and teach them.
Thinking some cure for their aches and pains could reach
    them.
No balm of Gilead could touch them where they ailed.
He would have healed Babylon, but failed.

It is fun to look for the many biblical allusions in that rather spiteful excerpt from a long and meandering poem. No one has ever set it to music, which is just as well!

The *badhanim* introduced many humorous and satiric songs which audiences took to their hearts and treated as folk songs forever after. The older ones have disappeared, but here is one—a song of pure non-sense—which has survived from the East European *shtetl*. Its silly Yiddish verses cannot be translated properly to fit the music. They say: "I have a pair of oxen that chop noodles; a pair of bears that sweep rooms; a pair of hens that gather kindling; a pair of dogs that make ink; a pair of little birds that bake bagels!" The cumulative form of the song (in each verse whenever a new pair of animals is mentioned, all the previous pairs are recalled until, in the end, the whole lot are listed) is in the best tradition of Jewish song. The Passover *Haggadah* has two such songs which provide a jolly end to the *seder: Ehad Mi Yodea* (Who Knows What "One" Stands For?) and *Had Gadya* (The Only Kid).

Hob Ich a Por Oksen

Ex. 108

YIDDISH FOLK SONG

Hob ich a por ok-sen ok-s'n vos zay bro-k'n

lok-sh'n lok-sh'n! Ay vun-der ib-er vun-der vos di ok-s'n

bro - k'n lok - sh'n, dos iz mir a vun - der, dos iz mir a vun - der. Hob ich a por be - r'n be - r'n Vos zay shti - ber ke - r'n, ke - r'n! Ay vun - der ib - er vun - der,

Vos di be - r'n shti - ber ke - r'n,
Vos di ok - s'n bro - k'n lok - sh'n,

Dos iz mir a vun - der, Dos iz mir a vun - der.

3. *Hob ich a por hener, hener,*
Vos zay kleiben shpener, shpener,
Ay vunder iber vunder,
Vos die hener kleiben shpener,
  Vos die beren shtiber keren,
   Vos die oksen broken lokshen,
Dos iz mir a vunder, dos iz mir a vunder!

4. *Hob ich a por hint, hint*
Vos zay machen tint, tint,
Ay vunder iber vunder,
Vos die hint machen tint,
  Vos die hener kleben shpener,
   Vos die beren shtiber keren,
    Vos die oksen broken lokshen,
Dos iz mir a vunder, dos iz mir a vunder!

5. *Hob ich a por feigelach, feigelach,*
Vos zay baken beigelach, beigelach,
Ay vunder iber vunder,
Vos die feigelach baken beigelach,
  Vos die hint machen tint,
   Vos die beren shtiber keren,
    Vos die oksen broken lokshen,
Dos iz mir a vunder, dos iz mir a vunder!

The majority of the *badhan* songs, however, are satiric, poking gentle fun (and sometimes not so gentle!) at notables and simple folk alike. Here is one of the best-loved of all Yiddish songs. It is sung by practically every Jewish singer—folk, operatic or cantorial—and is a sure-fire hit with any Yiddish-speaking audience. The song describes a visit by a cantor to a *shtetl* to conduct Sabbath services and then goes on to tell of the highly individual reactions of some of the village worthies, the tailor, the cobbler and the wagon-driver. The melody, of course, should be familiar: It is the Ashkenazic chant set to Psalm 92, the prayer mode or *nusah* of the Friday evening service. (See Ex. 5, Chapter Four.) Listen to one of the many recordings of the song. Follow the translation of the original Yiddish words.

Ex. 109

A Cantor for the Sabbath

YIDDISH FOLK SONG

To our town there came one day a vis-it-ing A can-tor for the Sab-bath, a can-tor for the Sab-bath. And there came to hear him three wor-thy ci-ti-zens, pil-lars of the con-gre-ga-tion. One was a tail-or, the se-cond a cob-bler, the third a wa-gon driv-er. Said the tail-or af-ter-ward, said the tail-or af-ter-ward, "Oh, oh! How that man *dav-ent*, how he sang the ser-vice! It sound-ed to me like the stab of the need-le, like the

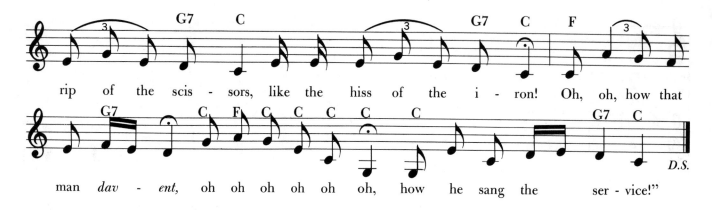

rip of the scis - sors, like the hiss of the i - ron! Oh, oh, how that

man *dav - ent,* oh oh oh oh oh oh, how he sang the ser - vice!"

2. Said the cobbler afterward,
   Said the cobbler afterward, "Oh, oh,
   How that man *davent,* how he sang the service,
   It sounded to me like the rap of the hammer,
   Like the punch of the awl, like the shine of the leather,
   Oh, oh, . . ."

3. Said the wagon-driver afterward,
   Said the wagon-driver afterward, "Oh, oh,
   How that man *davent,* how he sang the service,
   It sounded to me like the snap of the whip,
   Like the rearing of horses, like the yank of the reins,
   Oh, oh, . . ."

The song is not well-suited to group singing. Since it is actually a prayer chant, it has no meter. But here is an easier song, a spoof on a choir rehearsal. The cantor is teaching choir boys the hymn *Lekhah Dodi.*

Az Ich Vell Zingen "Lekhoh Dodi" (When I Begin with "Lekhoh Dodi")

Ex. 110

YIDDISH FOLK SONG

Az ich vell zing - 'n Le - khoh Do - di, zollt ihr zing - 'n
When I be - gin with Le - khoh Do - di, you must ans - wer

tchi - ri - bi - ri - bom. Az ich vell zing - 'n Lik - ras kal - loh
tchi - ri - bi - ri - bom. When I go on with Lik - ras kal - loh

zollt ihr zing - 'n tchi - ri - bi - ri - bom! Le - khoh Do - di
you must ans - wer tchi - ri - bi - ri - bom! Le - khoh Do - di

tchi - ri - bi - ri - bom, Lik - ras Kal - loh, tchi - ri - bi - ri - bom,

Le - khoh Do - di Lik - ras Kal - loh, tchi - ri - bi - ri - tchi - ri - bi - ri -

bom bom bom. Tchi - ri - bim Tchi - ri - bom, Tchi - ri - bim - bom - bim - bom

bi - bi - bom, Tchi - ri - bim Tchi - ri - bom, Tchi - ri - bim - bom - bim - bom

bi - bi - bom. Ai tchi - ri - bi - ri - bi - ri - bim - bom - bom, Ai tchi - ri - bi - ri - bi - ri

bim - bom - bom, Ai tchi - ri - bi - ri - bi - ri   bim - bom - bom, Ai tchi - ri - bi - ri - bi - ri bim - bom.

A favorite target for satire among certain Jews was the hasidic *rebbe* and his followers. The opponents of *Hasidism,* called *Mitnagedim,* were an appreciative audience for the *badhan* who would poke fun at the *"wonder-rebbe,"* the miracle-worker, and at the trusting disciples who sat in his "court" at his table. The *badhan* would borrow the hasidic musical style, introducing the *"bim bam,"* or the *"dei-di-di-dei"* or the

other syllables used so frequently in ecstatic songs. Here is a song about the follower of a *"wonder-rebbe"* who tries to convince a skeptical *Mitnaged* that his *rebbe's* miracles are more marvelous than the great inventions of the day (in this case, the nineteenth century). The audience undoubtedly joined the *badhan* in singing the refrain with great gusto and laughter.

247

Der Philosof
(The Philosopher)

Ex. 111

Yiddish Folk Song

Kum a - her, du phi - lo - sof, mit dein katz - ish -'n mo - ach'l,
Come o - ver here, phi - lo - so - pher, It's com-mon sense you're need - ing, At

Kum a - her tzum reb - b'n's tish, un lernt a bis - sel se - chel, Tchi - ri -
Reb - be's ta - ble sit a - while, his wis - dom to be heed - ing.

bim bom bom, tchi - ri - bim bom bom, tchi - ri - bim bom bim bom bom bom, Tchi - ri -

248

bim-bom bom, tchi-ri-bim bom bom, tchi-ri-bim bom bim bom bom bom!

2. A steam engine you figured out,
   Oh, aren't you full of notions!
   The *rebbe* spreads his tablecloth
   And flies right over oceans!

3. You figured out a gas balloon,
   And think you are a great one.
   The *rebbe* laughs, it's hardly worth
   The trouble to inflate one.

4. Do you know what the *rebbe* does,
   While he sits here and ponders?
   He flies to heaven in a flash,
   And dines amidst God's wonders!

Sometimes the satiric mood or style was so gentle that it quickly collapsed, leaving behind a song which was adopted everywhere as a folk song, its original intentions quite forgotten. One such song has the *rebbe* assuring his hungry *Hasidim* that somehow they would surely have *halot* (Sabbath loaves) and wine and fish in time for the Sabbath. (Ex. 112)

Satire and parody abound wherever Jewish life is vigorous. In Israel today, the best fun songs come from the army and the theater. The sergeant, the archeologist, the Egyptian soldier—all are topics for good-natured jibes. To understand these new songs, one really must know modern Hebrew and Israeli life for they are filled with "inside" jokes and thus are difficult to translate. But perhaps readers can pinpoint the foibles and absurdities of their own groups and, with gentle and affectionate laughter, expose them in song, in parody and in original verse and melody. And sing them with a smile!

Le-Koved Shabbes
(To Honor Shabbes)

Ex. 112

FOLK SONG

250

251

252

honor shab-bes, bom! To hon-or the ho - ly day, bim, bom!

ko-ved shab-bes, bam! Le - ko - ved dem hei - li-gen, bim, bam!

more slowly—fervently

Twenty-Four
SONG OF THE KLEZMER

THE BADHANIM, those purveyors of laughter and song, often attached themselves to troupes of musicians, players who travelled about seeking opportunities to furnish music for dancing and processions. The musicians were called *klezmorim* (plural of *klezmer*—a Yiddish word made up of two Hebrew words: *keley zemer*, meaning "musical instruments"). In a delightful little Hebrew book entitled *Ha-Klezmorim*, the Israeli 'cellist, composer and folklorist, Yehoiakin Stutchewsky, tells the story of these folk musicians, tracing their history back to the Middle Ages, comparing them to the instrumentalists of other Jewish communities, demonstrating with innumerable examples their important place in the literature, art and lore of East European Jewry and providing many illustrations of their tunes.[‡] One of his tales, purporting to be a true one, was told to him by the composer Joel Valbe, who

Klezmorim, drawing by Leonid Osipovitch Pasternak, Prague, 1901

migrated to Israel from a small town in Poland. Valbe had it from a certain Zaidel, who had it from his father, Yankel the Fiddler, to whom it actually happened:

It came to pass in Pitovska, in the province of Vholin, between Berditchev and Rovno. Pitovska was a tiny village which had no orchestra of its own. If music was needed for a wedding, or a Purim ball, the Jews of Pitovska had to call on the famous and accomplished troupe from the capital of the province, Zaslaw. This troupe, known as "The *Klezmorim* of Zaslaw," was kept very busy throughout the area, under the able leadership of Yankel the Fiddler.

Now it happened that the wealthy Polish nobleman, the Graf Potosky, a man of many holdings, had the main office of his extensive sugar factories in the village of Pitovska. He informed his chief overseer or *marschalik* that he planned to visit the main office just

Jewish musicians in Alsace, France, ca. 1700

in time for the first of May, when it was customary for the people to hold a great dance festival called a *mayovka*. The *marschalik*, eager to please his employer, decided to arrange an elaborate ball with lavish food and decorations and music for dancing. Casting about for musicians, he discovered that there were none at hand and, indeed, that the only players in the vicinity were the Jewish musicians of Zaslaw. Hastily he called on *klezmer* Yankel who came to the office for an interview.

"Next week," said the *marschalik*, "we're going to hold a fine aristocratic ball here in Pitovska. Many high-born guests will be coming from far and wide—even from the city of Warsaw. Can you arrange for a full orchestra to play for the dancing?"

"Assuredly, *Pan Marschalik*," replied Yankel. "It will be a pleasure."

"Good. You will be paid well for your services," said the overseer. "But you must meet one condition to be adequate for such an elegant affair: every musician must play from printed music. You, as conductor, will have to turn to face the dancers, and so you will have to play by heart. But, mind you, everyone else must read music!"

Poor Yankel. Neither he nor any musician in his troupe had the slightest notion of how to read music. They had none in their possession and had never laid eyes on any written music. Nevertheless, with the true bravado of a *klezmer*, he agreed and signed a contract which stipulated a good fat fee for himself and his players. Home he went, in a state of panic. But he sent out word to the men that they must come to rehearsal the very next day. All night he caressed the strings of his fiddle with his bow, trying to draw from the instrument some solution to the predicament. Came morning, he was ready to face his orchestra with aplomb. He told them about the lucrative engagement he had obtained for them, and they smiled with pleasure. He told them about the condition, and their faces fell. How could they possibly accept an engagement with such a condition?

"Don't worry," Yankel reassured them. "I have a plan. We must all go to the afternoon market and each of us buy a music stand. Then go home and pick a book—a *Humash*, a *Gemara*, a *siddur* (prayer book), a *mahzor* (holiday prayer book) or whatever other book you can lay your hands on. We'll bring the whole lot with us to the ball."

A band of klezmorim in Poland, 1927

Came the day of the ball. Two wagons conveyed "The *Klezmorim* of Zaslaw," together with their instruments, fiddle, trumpet, tuba, clarinet, flute, bass fiddle, drum and "tzimbel" (the European name for the dulcimer, an instrument of many strings played by hammers), together with a large bundle of music stands and a small library of bound volumes, to the great ballroom which belonged to the Graf Potosky. Each man proceeded to set up his stand and to place on it one or another of the religious tomes which he opened at random. Instruments were tuned and warmed up.

The ball opened up with a stately march. Bows glided across vibrating strings. The clarinetist, the flutist, the tuba player blew their very souls into their instruments. The drummer banged away with abandon. The "tzimbelist" manipulated his hammers with adroitness, keeping his eyes glued to the page of the tractate opened before him, worrying about the fine volume he had had to borrow from the sexton of his synagogue. They played with zest, slipping after a while from the $\frac{4}{4}$ rhythm of the march to the $\frac{3}{4}$ rhythm of the waltz, and from that into a mazurka, and then to a *krakovienne*. The dancers whirled past them, buoyed by the vigor of the music. Only one guest, a young noble from Warsaw, lingered a moment as he drew near to the musicians and wondered. He himself was a good amateur pianist who had studied long and practiced hard. But he had heard, back home, that these Jewish orchestras were made up of ignorant fellows who learned to play by ear from their fathers or their uncles or some other close relative and who never really learned to read notes. What were they doing with books of music in front of them?

When the pause came—the intermission when guests could amble over to the long tables of refreshments—our young city nobleman took himself in the direction of the musicians and looked over their shoulders to see their music. Such peculiar notation! "It must be some kind of magic or witchcraft," he muttered.

The *klezmorim* froze. Their ruse was about to be exposed! But Yankel the Fiddler didn't turn a hair. "This music is in a special kind of notation known only to Jewish musicians. It is our secret code which no one else can read."

His lordship was amazed, squinted once more at the mysterious characters in the books on the music stand, shrugged his shoulders and returned to his

Klezmorim, etching by Ryback, Paris, ca. 1940

companions. The bad moment was over. The *klezmorim* resumed their waltzes and mazurkas and *krakoviennes* and finished up the evening in glory, each with a fistful of coins—enough to tide him over until the next big Jewish wedding or Purim ball when his services would be in demand once more.

Even if this tale is apocryphal, it contains in a nutshell the full quality of the *klezmorim*. They were poor—in desperate need of opportunities to play. (In their own Jewish world, they were usually remunerated by coins contributed by the guests after each dance. The coins were put into a pot and shared by the whole group in true cooperative fashion.) They were untutored in the art and techniques of music but usually possessed a high degree of natural talent. (Many of the great Jewish violinists from Russia and other East European countries have a *klezmer* lurking somewhere in their family background.) And what is more, they were known to be not above a bit of chicanery when a situation required it.

The *klezmorim* resembled in many ways the gypsy musicians who used to roam throughout Europe, especially in Hungary and Roumania. In fact, there were occasions when Jewish and gypsy musicians joined forces to entertain in large non-Jewish gatherings like the grand ball in Pitovska. They had a good deal in common, too, with the country musicians—fiddlers, dulcimer players and others—who still play for square dances in rural sections of the United States and Canada. They exercised a great hold on the imagination of the folk and found their way into innumerable paintings, drawings, etchings, into poetry and story, into the very texts of dozens of folk songs. Beloved as they were, the *klezmorim* lost their audiences once a community became emancipated and its members were free to be exposed to the highly developed music of the Western world. Some *klezmorim* moved from country to country, retreating from the spread of the emancipation. Others went out into the sophisticated world of music, studied and became what we might call legitimate musicians. Still others, together with the *badhanim* who shared both their character and the vicissitudes of their lives, moved into the world of the theater. But that is another story.

It is interesting just to consider the titles the *klezmorim* gave to some of the melodies which have survived in the memories of older folk. Stutchewsky's book provides many examples, including: "Dance for a Rich Wedding," "Dance for an Orphan's Wedding," "A *Scherele* (scissors dance, a kind of square dance) for the Waitresses," "A Quarrel Dance," "A Reconciliation Dance," to name a few. Sometimes their music sobbed tears of joy for the lovers at last united in wedlock under the marriage canopy. At other times, it echoed and elaborated on prayer motives. Violinists, in particular, indulged in complex pyrotechnics, double stops, trills, long and difficult runs which drew gasps of admiration from the crowd.

Here is a tune which could have been played by a fiddler alone, or divided up to allow each instrument its turn, or played by all together. Drummer and bass, as in any modern combo, would keep the beat going. Clarinet or flute might fill in the rests with trills or runs. It is possible to improvise a typical *klezmer*

score for this *scherele*. And, finally, it would be easy to improvise a very simple square dance on the lines of the familiar American square dances.

Street Fiddler, painted in oil on canvas by Isaac Lichtenstein

257

A Scherele

VIOLIN OR RECORDER

KLEZMER TUNE

258

259

Twenty-Five
SONG OF THE THEATER

1.

Some of the world's best-known and loved music has come out of the theater. Consider only a few examples: operatic arias such as "Donna è mobile" from *Rigoletto,* or the "Toreador Song" from *Carmen;* overtures like Rossini's to *William Tell,* or Beethoven's *Leonore* overtures; incidental music for plays like Mendelssohn's for *A Midsummer Night's Dream,* or Grieg's for *Peer Gynt;* ballet music like Schubert's *Rosamunde,* or Rogers' *Carousel Waltz.* And then is a flood of highly popular hits from operettas, musical comedies and revues and films, songs like the *Merry Widow Waltz* and the theme from *Exodus.* Ever since the Middle Ages when the first miracle plays were performed with song and dance and procession, few composers, great or small, have been able to resist the temptation and the challenge of trying to write music for the theater.

Jewish communities since medieval times have had their own variety of theater to add zest and fresh vigor to their musical heritage. As with so much of that musical heritage, we no longer have the music from the old Jewish folk-comedies, the Purim plays that once were performed by mummers in the squares and market places of the ghettos or the extemporaneous farces provided by *badhanim* at entertainments for festive family gatherings. Nor do we have the songs which the earliest *badhanim* used to insert into their "acts," just as clever comedians today will often break into a satiric song. None of these early performers—the itinerant players, the jesters, the minstrels, the mummers, the musicians—knew how to write down their songs. Here and there librettos have been found, or we have discovered written accounts of plays, serious and frivolous, from the Middle Ages up to the nineteenth century, from all parts of Europe. With the coming of emancipation for Jews, the old, informal, improvised type of folk-comedies, as well as the *badhanim* who devised them and the *klezmorim* who accompanied them, began to disappear and in their place arose the beginnings of the Yiddish folk theater.

In the early days, there were very few regular Jewish theatrical troupes. We do know of one in the ghetto of Venice at the end of the sixteenth and the beginning of the seventeenth centuries. (This was at the same time that Salomone Rossi was living in Mantua and composing Hebrew synagogue music as well as Italian madrigals and instrumental trios.) The theater was directed by the same liberal and art-loving Rabbi Leon of Modena who encouraged Rossi to write choral music for the synagogue. Some bits and pieces of a Purim play in verse, with a few scraps of musical notation, have survived from that theater, but they are too small and fragmentary to permit us to reconstruct the original music. There are similar remnants of other musical plays; for instance, *Tragédie Provençale de la Reine Esther* was written and directed by the Rabbis

Purim players

Mordechée Astruc and Jacob de Lunel, presented in the open air in front of the *carrière* (ghetto gate) of Carpentras in southern France in the eighteenth century. This play had five acts, each of which ended with a song. Alas, none of the songs has survived.

Another Jewish theatrical troupe was organized in Germany in the seventeenth century by a certain Susskind of Offenbach and his wife Michaele. This group toured many Jewish communities throughout Europe and made music on the way.

These early plays were not performed in theaters. They were much more like an older form of European drama, played only by men, who wore masks and took women's parts when necessary, in market places, at ghetto gates, in the courts of synagogues and in buildings (particularly in Germany) called *Tanz-halle* (literally dance halls) where the folk gathered for all kinds of festivities. In addition to Purim plays (called *Purimspiel* in Central and Eastern Europe) which centered, of course, on Esther and Mordecai, Haman and King Ahasuerus, the plays and pantomimes were based on various famous Bible stories like the sacrifice of Isaac, the battle between David and Goliath, the triumph of Joseph and Jonah in Nineveh. The plays were not literal dramatizations of the Bible; the familiar tales usually formed a loose framework for buffoonery and satire. The traditional characters were merely "disguises" for some well-known local character, Jew or non-Jew, who was heartily disliked (Haman or Goliath) or greatly loved (Mordecai or David) by the folk. Everyone has engaged in this kind of play-making—at schools, clubs, summer camps, in take-offs on teachers, counselors, etc. And everyone has heard or participated in projects of writing skits based on popular musical comedies and inventing parodies on songs their audiences are sure to know. In this same way, the *badhanim* also leaned on the most familiar stories, and they wrote their parodies on whatever songs their audiences already knew and loved—synagogue chants, Sabbath *zemirot, klezmer* tunes, even the folk songs of their non-Jewish neighbors.

(Readers can stage their own *Purimspiel* or Bible play in the spirit of the old Jewish mummers, adding whatever songs are pertinent. A delightful *Purimspiel, The Megilla of Itzig Manger,* was produced on Broadway in 1969. This play by the fine modern Yiddish poet, the late Itzig Manger, was well received by the New York critics and earlier had been a great hit in Israel. For a charming account of how *The Story of*

Esther and *The Sale of Joseph* were actually performed in a Lithuanian village in the last century, read Shmarya Levin's autobiography, *Forward from Exile.*‡

By the second half of the nineteenth century, the *badhanim* began to acquire a veneer of pseudo-sophistication. They were now able to travel to the great cities of Europe, to attend the opera and the theater and to mingle with what used to be called grandly "the artistes." They learned some of the techniques of writing music, at least enough to write down the tunes of their songs. They had no hesitation about borrowing the melodies they heard on their travels and they frequently "improved" them by grafting on bits of synagogue chants or hasidic songs.

One of these latter-day transformed *badhanim* was Abraham Goldfaden, born in Roumania in 1840. As a young man he would entertain—whenever he had the luck and the opportunity—with a vulgar popular music routine. Later on, he moved to the large Russian city of Odessa and founded the first Yiddish musical theater. Goldfaden did everything: wrote the books, the lyrics, the music and directed the productions. After a time he forsook the low burlesque of his earlier years and aspired to higher cultural levels. He turned to the Bible, Jewish history and legends for themes—revising them whenever he saw fit. Perhaps the best known of all of Goldfaden's musical productions is *Shulamith,* a romantic tale set in the days of the Second Temple. Like any operetta, it has love duets, solo arias, large choruses, intimate scenes with one or two actors, mob scenes of pilgrims and even dances. The score is replete with echoes of contemporaries whom he greatly admired, the well-known composers, Jacques Halevi and Jacques Offenbach.

The hit song of *Shulamith* remains popular to our own day. Goldfaden intended it as an aria with a recitative introduction. His "recitative" is short and metric unlike the usual operatic recitative. His aria is a simple song. Its text is a strange concoction, beginning by setting the scene in a "small room" in the Second Temple (*Bet ha-Mikdash*) where the tragic, widowed "Daughter of Zion" sits all alone, rocking a cradle and singing a plaintive lullaby. Then comes the lullaby itself, with words based on the old Yiddish folk song we encountered in Chapter Twenty-two (Ex. 101)—complete with its little white kid, tethered under baby's cradle, which engages in selling raisins and almonds. Goldfaden's "aria" has become, if anything, more of a folk song than the less sentimental original!

Rozhinkes mit Mandlen
(Raisins and Almonds)

Ex. 114

Words and Melody by
Abraham Goldfaden

In dem beis ha-mik-dosh in a vin-kel he-der
In a dark lit-tle cor-ner of the an-cient Tem-ple the

zitzt di al-mo-neh, Bas Tzi-yon al-layn. Ihr ben yo-hi-d'l, yi-de-le,
daught-er of Zi-on sits wid-owed a-lone. Her child, one and on-ly, she

vigt zie ke - se - der, un zingt im tzu shlo - f'n a
rocks in his cra - dle, and sings him a lul - la - by in

li - de - le shayn. Ah, Un - ter yi - de - le's vi - ge -
ten - der - est tone. Ah, 'neath the cra - dle of my young

leh shayt a klor veis tzi - ge - leh, dos
son stands a kid, a small white one. The

tzi-ge-le iz ge-foh - r'n hand-l'n,
kid far and wide it must wan - der,

dos vet zein zein ba-ruf,
rai-sins and al-monds his wares.

ro - zhin-kes mit
Like him you'll roam hith-er and

mand-l'n.
yon-der.

Shlof - zhe yi-de-le shlof,
Now you must sleep with-out cares,

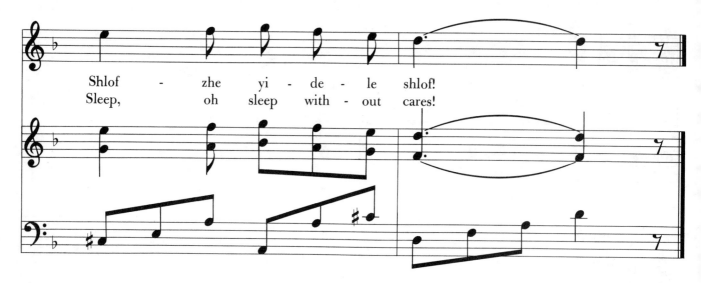

Shlof - zhe yi - de - le shlof!
Sleep, oh sleep with - out cares!

"Rozhinkes mit Mandlen" is the most famous song from *Shulamith,* but here is another song from that same operetta, a love duet which has a quaint charm for today.

Ex. 115
TRANS. BEN ARONIN

Courting Song

WORDS AND MELODY
BY GOLDFADEN

Ah, you are mine, I've caught you, you're mine!

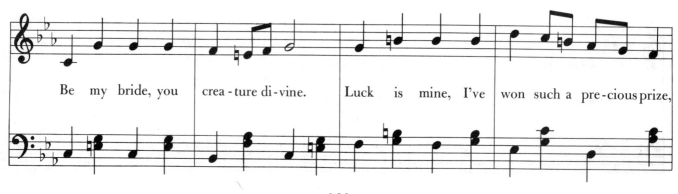

Be my bride, you crea-ture di-vine. Luck is mine, I've won such a pre-cious prize,

gen - tle, pret - ty, no - ble and ve - ry wise, you will be my dear - est. If

you were mere - ly pret - ty I'd sure - ly be de - light - ed, If

you were mere - ly wit - ty our troth would soon be plight - ed.

For it's plain to see, ev' - ry qual - i - ty, joins in cre - a - ting a

being so heav-en-ly, yes it's plain to see, ev'-ry qual-i-ty

makes you dear to me, my dar-ling, O-men se-, o-men se-, o-men

se-loh, o-men se-, o-men se-, o-men

se-loh, o-men se-, o-men se-, o-men se-loh!

2. You are my groom, ah you are mine,
   You've caught me and now love is mine.
   Love is mine; I've found my true happiness,
   Noble, handsome, that I must confess,
     You will be my dearest.
   You say that I am pretty, and truly I'm delighted;
   Here in this holy city our troth will soon be plighted,
     For its plain to see,
     Every quality
   Joins in creating a bridegroom so dear to me;
     Yes, it's plain to see,
     Every quality
   Makes you dear to me, my dearest;
     Omen se . . .

Shulamith was the forerunner of innumerable musical plays in Yiddish—plays filled with sentimental, pretentious arias alternating with cheap dance songs. In the vast migrations from Eastern Europe beginning in the 1880's, Goldfaden and dozens of theatrically-bent actors, producers, singers and aspiring writers immigrated to America where they founded the Yiddish theater on the Lower East Side. Out of that milieu came a host of American popular composers, singers and actors—Irving Berlin, Eddie Cantor, Paul Muni and others. While the Yiddish theater has now virtually disappeared in the United States, it is undergoing something of a revival in Israel. Also, a very strong influence is still evident in American nightclub and TV comedians who are descendants of the old *badhanim*. And of course much of the style and the quality of the Yiddish musical theater lives on in such Broadway productions as *Milk and Honey* and *Fiddler on the Roof*.

It never mattered, in the Yiddish theater, whether the story of the show was set in a nineteenth-century Russian village or in ancient Canaan. The style of the music was invariably the same. Nobody tried to reproduce authentic, historically-accurate music; the audience demanded tunes to hum as they left the theater, and the composers cheerfully provided them. Even in what was at one time the most serious and dignified Jewish cultural center in New York, the Yiddish Art Theater, founded and directed by Maurice Schwartz, the music remained essentially the music of the European *klezmer*. One of Maurice Schwartz's

finest productions was the drama *Sabbatai Zevi*, by Sholom Asch, the story of the false messiah who attracted thousands of Jews with his promise to lead them back to the land of Israel. Sabbatai lived in the seventeenth century, and his story is set, for the most part, in Turkey. Now consider this processional, presumably marched to and sung by followers of the false messiah. You will recognize it as a typical catchy *klezmer* tune, inappropriate, inauthentic and totally out of place in such a drama. (Ex. 116)

2.

An entirely different kind of Jewish theater was born in Europe at the beginning of the twentieth century. During the years of revolution and transition in Russia, a Hebrew theater was founded in Moscow. A group of young, ambitious actors—fired by the thrust of the Zionist dream and by the explosion of new forms of Jewish expression in literature, art and music (which were national in spirit rather than purely religious)—banded together and organized a Hebrew Art Theater known as *"Habimah"* (Hebrew for "the stage"). They succeeded in persuading the great Stanislavski, director of the Moscow Art Theater, to help them organize their theater and to train them in his new and revolutionary methods. (The Stanislavski

A scene from Sabbatai Zevi by Sholom Asch, Yiddish Art Theater

March from *Sabbatai Zevi*

Ex. 116

"method" is still studied by most serious students of the art of acting.)

The talented young actors sought scripts that were rooted authentically in the history and folklore of the Jewish people, and they insisted upon only the highest literary standards. They enlisted the aid of outstanding Hebrew writers who had for some decades been devoting themselves to a re-creation of Hebrew literature: David Frischman, Hayim Nahman Bialik, Saul Tchernichowsky, Zalman Schneur, Jacob Fichman and others. These writers had produced stories, essays and poetry which were being avidly read by a generation of young Jews who had somehow managed to escape the restrictions of the Russian Pale of Settlement and had gone beyond their strict traditional backgrounds and education to study in the great universities of Europe. This new generation dreamed of a new and vigorous existence for the Jewish people. The great Jewish writers were delighted to provide high-level dramas for the young theater, and they also augmented the repertory by translating into Hebrew some distinguished Yiddish plays, written by their gifted contemporaries, which had been considered unsuitable for the old-style Yiddish theater.‡

The Habimah troupe was not interested in producing musical comedy or operetta. However, the very essence of the style they were cultivating was the presence in almost every production of relevant incidental music—music that would be on the same high cultural level as their plays, performed with professional finish, and related, as their plays were related, to the musical lore of the Jewish people. Fortunately, a group of composers, calling themselves the "Society for Jewish Folk Music" of St. Petersburg, were already organized and prepared to fulfill the requirements of Habimah. These composers had long since gone beyond exclusive preoccupation with Jewish folk song. Even before 1900, the task of gathering up and writing down in musical notation the songs of East European Jews had begun for the first time. The St. Petersburg composers were concerned with producing a Jewish art music. They too were buoyed up by the rising tide of Jewish cultural renaissance and Jewish nationalism. They were following another strong current as well— the trend of Russian nationalist music which, in itself, was in line with the nationalist compositions being produced in many other European countries in the late nineteenth century.

One of the Russian Jewish composers in the pioneering St. Petersburg group has appeared earlier in this book—Joel Engel, the editor and music critic of a Russo-Jewish newspaper. His fellow pioneers were Joseph Achron, Moses Milner, Lazare Saminsky, Alexander Krein and Michael Gniessin. All had managed to obtain special passes to live in St. Petersburg—a privilege granted to comparatively few Russian Jews in that day. The young Jewish composers studied at the conservatory under teachers like Rimsky-Korsakov, Balakirev and other leaders of Russian music at the time. The first works of the young men were principally arrangements of folk songs for voice and piano. Soon, however, they began to compose original settings for the poetry—Yiddish and Hebrew— being written by their contemporaries. They went on to instrumental music for solo instruments and chamber music, and even occasionally for orchestra. Much of their work was based on fragments of Yiddish folk song, but they began to feel that this folk song was not sufficiently original for their own creative needs. They therefore turned for musical inspiration to older sources—the *nusah* and the biblical cantillation of the synagogue—while they wrote purely secular material.‡

A clear example of this type of writing is a composition by Joseph Achron—a love song set to a Hebrew poem by Jacob Fichman. If you play the voice line alone, without accompaniment, you will recognize immediately its close similarity to the cantillation of the *Haftarah*. The composition follows. (Ex. 117)

Title page, sheet music of the Society for Jewish Folk Music, St. Petersburg, 1911

Yom Yom Ani Holekh
(Each Day My Steps)

J. Fichman

J. Achron

Yom yom   a - ni ho - lekh li -
Each day   my steps lead to thy

m'o - nekh U - mi - lah al s'fa - tai ha -
dwell - ing, a word on my lips   doth

re - dah.   Ve - te - rem od tu - gad ha - mi - lah
ho - ver.   Oh when shall that small word be ut - tered?

*Transposed 1/2 tone down from original key.

272

V'im   tu - gad   bi - z'man mah, mi   ye - da?
To - day?   Or   who knows, or if   e - ver.

Yom yom   al   ha - de - rekh li - m'o - nekh   Or
Each day   on   the way to thy dwell -   ing   my

273

osh - ri al ro - shi ko lo - het,   U -
joy lights my head   like a ha - lo.   At

v'shu - vi m'nah - me - ni ko kha - vi, ve -
eve - ning re - turn - ing, my star _____ of - fers

kha - mus sod otz - bo bo ro - ed.
com - fort, con - ceal - ing its sor - row.

274

Yom yom be-gan li - bi ba-se - ter
Each day my joy in my heart's se-cret gar - den

tzitz osh - ri ya' - a - dim ye - ha - var
doth blos-som, grows red, and then pal - eth.

275

276

Yom yom a - ni ho - lekh li - m'o - nekh v'ey -
Each day my steps lead to thy dwell - ing, yet

la - yikh lo gu - nav od da - var.
no - thing to thee is re - veal - ed.

pp

Fine ad libitum

Achron's song is far from being theater music. Nevertheless, he was eventually to compose music for the Habimah Theater's production of *Belshazzar*. The first composer to be invited by the troupe was the founder and leader of the musician's group, Joel Engel. He provided the incidental music for their very first production, *The Dybbuk*, by An-Ski—a Yiddish play which was translated into Hebrew by Bialik especially for the new theater.

The play, set in a village of hasidic Jews, depicts the hopeless love of Hanan, a poor and very devout

A scene from The Dybbuk by An-Ski, Habimah Theater

student of *Kabbalah,* for the tragic Leah, daughter of a wealthy merchant, and is based on the lore, superstition and mystical beliefs of the *Hasidim.* The beautiful heroine, Leah, who loves Hanan even as he loves her is forced to marry the son of a rich man against her will. Hanan who is given to fasting, partly out of poverty, partly out of burning hope to reach oneness with God, dies of starvation and heartbreak. But, at Leah's wedding, at the very moment when the bridal veil is being removed from before her face, she rises suddenly. An agonized cry issues from her throat, and she faints. The wedding company is terrified for the voice is not the voice of Leah—it is the voice of the dead Hanan! Hanan's soul, a disembodied spirit, a *dybbuk,* has taken possession of Leah's body. The rabbi tries to persuade and then to command the *dybbuk* to relinquish its new home in Leah's body, but, speaking through the lips of the unconscious girl, the *dybbuk* defiantly refuses. The rabbi finally resorts to the dread ceremony of excommunication, *herem,* driving the soul out of the community of Jewish souls. With one last despairing cry, the *dybbuk* departs. Hanan's voice now calls out from the distance, but Leah's body lies motionless. The girl has died, and the horrified company of rabbis and hasidic elders hear Leah's voice join that of her lover in the receding distance.

The mood of the play was set by an overture based on two motives which symbolize the two themes of the play: the search of the mystic and the love of Hanan and Leah. The first theme, a hasidic meditation, has become very much of a favorite. In the course of the play, it is sung to a text written by Bialik in a vein of genuine Jewish mysticism (Ex. 118):

Why, and wherefore
Doth the soul descend
From a lofty height
To a low estate?

Because, in order
To rise to the heights
One must first descend
To the depths.

(The American composer Aaron Copland used this same melody in quite a different way from Engel in his *Vitebsk Suite*.)‡

The love motive in Engel's *Dybbuk* music is not a sentimental love song. Instead, the composer wanted Hanan's tortured soul to sing out of the prostrate body of Leah in the words and melody which would signify, to his Jewish audience, the very epitome of love song. And what would Jews regard as *the* essential love song? Engel went directly to *The Song of Songs* in the traditional cantillation. (Ex. 119)

Ex. 118

H. N. BIALIK

Mipney Mah?

HASIDIC MELODY

Hinakh Yafah Rayati

Ex. 119
S. of S. 4: 1

VARIANT OF TRADITIONAL
ASHKENAZIC CANTILLATION

Hi - nakh ya - fah ra' - ya -

ti, hi - nakh ya - fah,

ey - na - yikh yo - nim

mi - ba - ad le - tza - ma -

tekh; se - a - ra - yikh ke -

e - der ha - i - zim

she - gal' - shu me -

har gil' - ad.

Other incidental musical pieces for *The Dybbuk* are: *A Beggar's Dance* (based on the *Scherele*, Chapter Twenty-three, Ex. 108); *Wedding March;* and a piece to accompany *The Unveiling of the Bride*, composed in the spirit of *klezmer* music with its trills and runs; a hasidic *nigun* for solo violin; and, finally, a reprise of the two symbolic themes which appeared first in the overture. The closing piece, arranged for four hands at the piano, follows in Ex. 120.

The Dybbuk, together with Engel's music, went on to win world fame. But it was only one of the many outstanding productions created by the gifted acting company in association with creative composers and writers. For example, Moses Milner was invited by Habimah to compose music for *Jacob's Dream* by the noted author, Richard Beer Hoffman, and also for *The Golem* by the great Yiddish writer, S. Leivick. Alexander Krein wrote music for *The Eternal Jew* by David Pinski.

Michael Gniessin, one of the members of the St. Petersburg Society, travelled to Palestine twice, and it was there, in 1921, that he wrote two operas, *The Maccabeans* and *The Youth of Abraham.* Of all the pioneering members of the Society, only Lazare Saminsky did not write for the Habimah Theater. He was interested in the stage, but the ballet form attracted his composing efforts.

The Russian Revolution and the take-over of the government by Lenin, coming on top of disastrous Russian losses in World War I and the bitter civil war, shattered the fabric of Russian life as it had existed before the great upheavals. The promising Hebraist movement in the new Soviet state was doomed, and those actors, writers, artists and musicians who survived the tragic struggles, and who were in a position to leave, migrated either to the United States or Palestine. Joel Engel went to Palestine. Achron and Saminsky chose the West; their American activities belong to a later chapter. Milner, Krein and Gniessin remained in the USSR where they were active in Yiddish musical and dramatic fields until the Communist state clamped down on Yiddish cultural pursuits—and then they were lost to the Jewish world.

The Habimah Theater moved to Tel Aviv in the 1920's, and there it has enjoyed great success and prestige ever since. Indeed, Habimah has given rise to numerous younger repertory companies in Israel over the years. One of the classic productions in its repertory is still *The Dybbuk* with Engel's music.

From *The Dybbuk*

Ex. 120

JOEL ENGEL

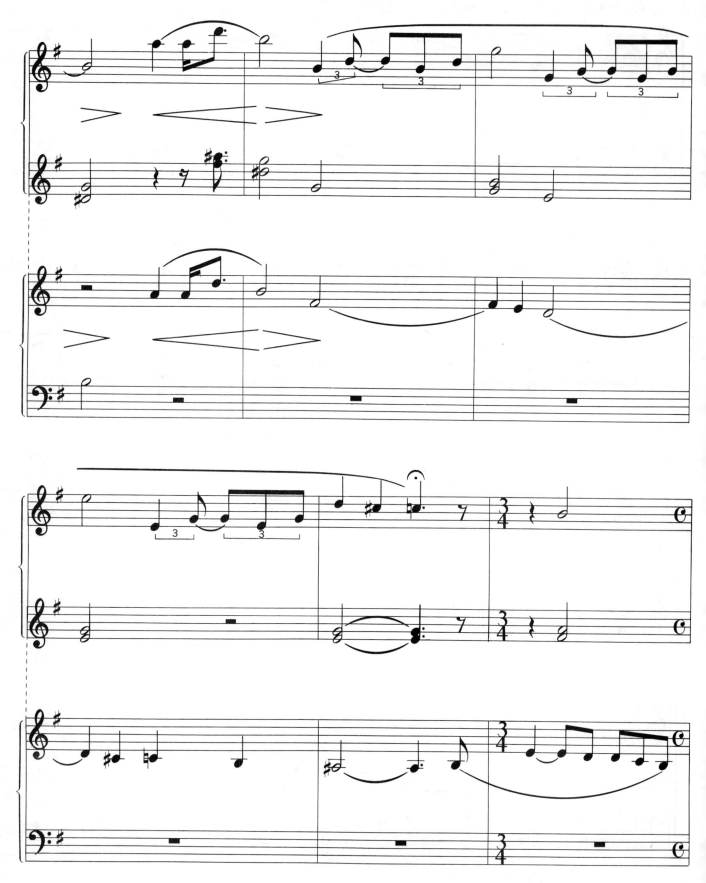

290

291

Twenty-Six
SONG OF EXILE
AND RETURN

IN THE YEAR 586 B.C.E. the Temple of Jerusalem lay in ruins. The leaders of the Kingdom of Judah and masses of other Jewish captives were led in chains into exile in the land of Babylonia. There, they were settled and somehow held together as a separate group, always hoping to return to their homeland. Periodically their hope would dim, and they would be disheartened. Two great prophets, the Second Isaiah and Ezekiel, helped to fan the flames of their hope so that even their second generation remained faithful to the dream of a return.

At some time during that exile, an unknown poet wrote a psalm—part dirge, part avowal of eternal loyalty to Jerusalem:

By the rivers of Babylon
There we sat down, yea, we wept,
When we remembered Zion.
Upon the willows in the midst thereof
We hanged up our harps.

Hebrew captives, wall painting, palace of Ashurbanipal

For there they that led us captive asked of us words
   of song,
And our tormentors asked of us mirth:
"Sing us one of the songs of Zion."
How shall we sing the Lord's song in a foreign land?

If I forget thee, O Jerusalem,
Let my right hand forget her cunning.
Let my tongue cleave to the roof of my mouth,
If I remember thee not;
If I set not Jerusalem;
Above my chiefest joy.

(Psalm 137: 1–6)

Less than fifty years after the Exile, Babylonia itself, and all its vast captured territories, was conquered in turn by the king of Persia, Cyrus, who permitted the Jews to go back to their beloved Judea, now under his rule. Soon after their liberation the Jews began to build the Second Temple. The exultant Psalm 126 may have been one of the new songs of this Second Temple. It is titled *A Song of Ascents* (probably meaning "A Pilgrim Song"):

When the Lord brought back those that returned to Zion,
We were like unto them that dream.
Then was our mouth filled with laughter,
And our tongue with singing;
Then said they among the nations:
"The Lord hath done great things with these."
The Lord hath done great things with us;
We are rejoiced.

Turn our captivity, O Lord,
As the streams in the dry land.
They that sow in tears
Shall reap in joy.
Though he goeth on his way weeping that beareth
   the measure of seed,
He shall come home with joy, bearing his sheaves.

Both of these psalms have inspired innumerable musical settings over the centuries, in many styles and

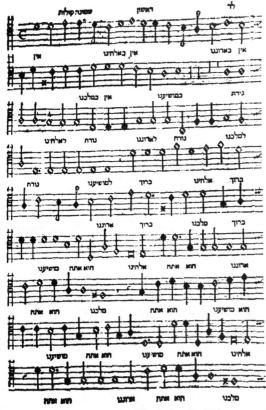

A page from a "tenor-book" of Rossi's Hebrew music

many languages. The first Hebrew choral setting in Western style of Psalm 137 was composed by Salomone Rossi of Mantua, around the year 1600. It is typical of Rossi's religious compositions, all written for *a cappella* chorus and all intended for use in a Hebrew service in the synagogue of Mantua. The music is very much like other Italian music at the turn of the seventeenth century, when all the voice parts were allowed to move along in the same rhythmic patterns to form series of chords. There is no change of mood when the dirge ends and the passionate avowal of loyalty begins. Rossi did not aim to write "expressive" music any more than did other writers of religious music in his time. However, it is impossible to sing it without inserting some restrained dynamics of our own. Following is an abbreviated version of Rossi's Psalm 137. It is adapted for singing by an amateur chorus. (The piano part is intended for rehearsal only. However, if the chorus finds it too difficult to sing *a cappella*, the piano should be played very softly.)

Ex. 121

Ps. 137: 1–6

Al Naharot Bavel
(By the Rivers of Babylon)

S. Rossi

ad - mat ne - khar? Im esh - ka - hekh ye - ru - sha - la - yim tish - kah ye - mi-

ad - mat ne - khar? Im esh - kà - hekh ye - ru - sha - la - yim tish - kah ye - mi-

ad - mat ne - khar? Im esh - ka - hekh ye - ru - sha - la - yim tish - kah ye - mi-

ad - mat ne - khar? Im esh - ka - hekh ye - ru - sha - la - yim tish - kah ye - mi-

ni.

ni, tid - bak le - sho - ni le - hi - ki, im le ez - ke - re - khi, im lo a - a-

ni, tid - bak le - sho - ni le - hi - ki, im le ez - ke - re - khi, im lo a - a-

ni, tid - bak le - sho - ni le - hi - ki, im le ez - ke - re - khi, im lo a - a-

leh et ye - ru - sha - la - yim al rosh sim - ha ti.

leh et ye - ru - sha - la - yim al rosh sim - ha - ti.

leh et ye - ru - sha - la - yim al rosh sim - ha - ti.

Im esh - ka - hekh ye - ru - sha - la - yim tish - kah ye - mi - ni, im

Im esh - ka - hekh ye - ru - sha - la - yim tish - kah ye - mi - ni, im

Im esh - ka - hekh ye - ru - sha - la - yim tish - kah ye - mi - ni, im

lo, lo ez - ke - re - khi, im lo a - a - leh et ye - ru - sha -

lo, lo ez - ke - re - khi, im lo a - a - leh et ye - ru - sha -

lo, lo ez - ke - re - khi, im lo a - a - leh et ye - ru - sha -

lo, lo ez - ke - re - khi, im lo a - a - leh et ye - ru - sha -

la - yim al rosh sim - ha - ti.

la - yim al rosh sim - ha - ti.

la - yim al rosh sim - ha - ti.

la - yim al rosh sim - ha - ti.

After the Roman conquest of Judea in 70 C.E., when Jews were expelled from the land into slavery and exile, Psalm 137 became part of the Jewish liturgy. Each day, after each meal, when the grace was recited, the psalm was chanted, in accordance with the principle that at every occasion of thanksgiving or of joy there must be some reminder of the tragic loss of the homeland. However, on the Sabbath and festivals, the joyous Psalm 126 was substituted, and it is sung just before the recitation of the grace. In most Jewish homes it is sung as a hymn. Its text is divided, sometimes into two, sometimes into four parts which are treated as strophes in a metrical poem. There are a number of hymn-like tunes in common usage. One of them is the following, which has a strong resemblance to many German folk songs:

Shir ha-Ma-alot (Song of Ascents)

Ex. 122
Ps. 126:1

GERMAN MELODY

Shir ha-ma-a-los, be-shuv a-do-noy

es shi-vas Tzi-yon, ho-yi-nu ke-ho-le-mim. Oz yi-mo-ley se-hok pi-nu u-l'sho-ne-nu ri-noh.

Following is a more familiar melody used for Psalm 126. It is of East European origin.

Ex. 123
PSALM 126

Shir ha-Ma-alot

EAST EUROPEAN MELODY

Shir ha-ma'-los, be-shuv a-do-noy es shi-vas Tzi-yon ho-yi-nu ke-hol'-mim. Oz yi-mo-ley se-

hok   pi - nu u - le - sho - ne - nu   ri - noh.

Oz yom' - ru va - go - yim hig - dil a - do - noy

la - a - sos im e - leh, hig - dil a - do - noy

la' - sos i - ma - nu, ho - yi - nu se - me - him.   etc.

Psalm 126 also appears among Rossi's musical works. Like all of his Hebrew compositions, it fell into obscurity and remained so for about 250 years after it was written. Rossi's Mantuan Jewish community was liquidated in 1628, its inhabitants exiled. His music was left to gather dust in scattered libraries. Choral music in his day had been printed in separate voice books, one for tenor, another for bass, etc. All the parts had to be located before the scores could be pieced together. Scholars cannot always be certain

A song of return, a pilgrimage up from Mt. Zion

that they have all the parts, or that they have put them together properly. Also, the words were not written in precisely underneath the notes, so that another aspect of the puzzle is determining exactly how they must be suited to the music. The scholars are still working at it. You can hear one "solution" of Rossi's music for Psalm 126 sung on the recording *Israel Sings*. This one is the work of the eminent Jewish musicologist, Professor Eric Werner.[‡]

There is another version of Psalm 126, which may be more interesting for the circumstances under which it was first sung than for its musical quality. In World War I, a Jewish legion made up of Jewish volunteers from many countries was organized to fight with the British to dislodge Turkish rule over Palestine. Under the British General Allenby, the Jewish Legion succeeded in capturing Jerusalem. The Jewish fighters had their own marching song, and they sang it lustily as they entered the city. The words were none other than portions of Psalm 126, now sung as a song of new return, in the style of a European band tune. But it is not all marching song. The second half of the psalm, "Turn our captivity, O Lord," is a plea and a prayer, sung to a tune in a sentimental, popular ballad style. The martial note returns at the very end with "shall reap with joy."

Shir ha-Ma-alot

Ex. 124

FROM Ps. 126

JEWISH LEGION MELODY

Be - shuv a - do - nai, be - shuv a - do - nai

Et shi - vat Tzi - yon ha - yi - nu ke - ho - le - mim.

Az yi - ma - ley se - hok pi - nu ul' - sho - ne - nu ri -

nah, ri - nah. Az yom' - ru va - go - yim, az yom' - ru va - go - yim, hig -

dil a - do - nai la' - sot im ey - leh, hig - dil a - do - nai la' - sot i -

ma - nu. Shu - vah a - do - nai et sh'vi - te - nu, et sh'vi -

te - nu ka-a-fi-kim ba-ne - gev, ha-zor'-im be-dim'- ah, ha - zor'- im

be - dim'- ah be - ri - nah, ri - nah yik - tzo - ru.

8va

When, in June 1967, Jews reentered the Old City of Jerusalem for the first time in 19 years, another song echoed through its streets and spread like wildfire through the whole country. Only days before the Six Day War, guitar-playing singers had been going from one army camp to another to entertain Israeli troops who had been called up for service against an expected attack. The song the men asked for repeatedly was *Jerusalem of Gold,* which had just won a prize in a national song competition for its composer, Naomi Shemer. It was a wistful song and, after one or two hearings, the young soldiers would join in singing its refrain, a dream of "*Yerushalayim,* shining gold, and shining copper against the sky; for the songs to thy

glory a harp am I!" The soldiers brought the song home to their families, when they went on leave. The radio played the tune over and over again because it had won a prize and had caught the popular fancy. One stanza of the song lamented: "I cannot see your ancient wells, your market place, your crooked alleys or the Western Wall, that last remnant of the ancient Temple."

But here they were, on June 9, 1967—Israeli soldiers, paratroopers, Jews old and young—hearing an enormous *shofar* sounded in the shadow of that very wall and weeping for joy. When the momentous news flashed around the land, Naomi Shemer quickly substituted a new stanza: "The *shofar* calls us from the

Rejoicing at the Western Wall, after the Six Day War, June 1967

Old Wall, 'Come in!' " And, at that moment, a new song of return was born to be heard and sung and loved by Jews around the world.

Jerusalem of Gold, Yerushalayim shel Zahav, musically speaking, could be the direct descendant of the Jewish Legion's *Shir ha-Ma-alot*. A popular tune, part martial, part sentimental—easy to learn, not very original and certainly in no measure equal in quality to the text—it is nevertheless a song of history.

Songs like this have been part of the folk and popular song of Israel from the hard days of the first new settlers, in 1881. Those pioneers, called the *Bilu-im*, were members of a group known as *Bilu*. (In Hebrew, this word is made up of the initial letters of four words, *Bet Ya-akov lekhu ve-nelekhah*, meaning "House of Jacob, arise, let us go up!") The pioneers were university students, young intellectuals, unaccustomed to physical labor or work outdoors, untrained and unprepared for this new life of land-building on a particularly tough terrain. To sustain their spirits, they would sing songs—tunes they had brought with them from the revolutionary underground of Russia and from the German universities. Their words they fashioned out of the Hebrew which they were just beginning to revive, an ancient language, stiff from disuse, filled with great, majestic and classical phrases from the Bible, the Talmud and the poets of the Middle Ages. They still used the Ashkenazic pronunciation of the Hebrew.

Be-mahrashti

Ex. 125

OLD PALESTINE FOLK SONG

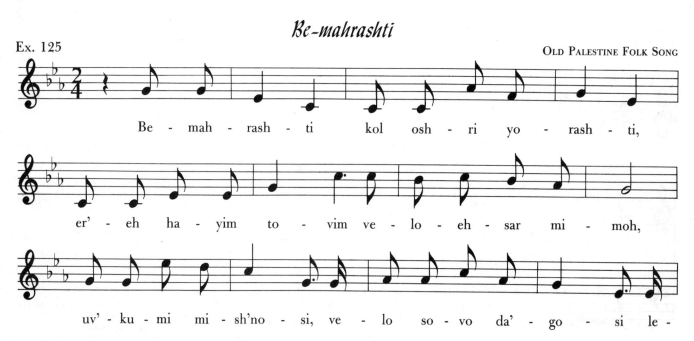

Be - mah - rash - ti   kol   osh - ri   yo - rash - ti,

er' - eh   ha - yim   to - vim   ve - lo - eh - sar   mi - moh,

uv' - ku - mi   mi - sh'no - si,   ve - lo   so - vo   da' - go - si   le -

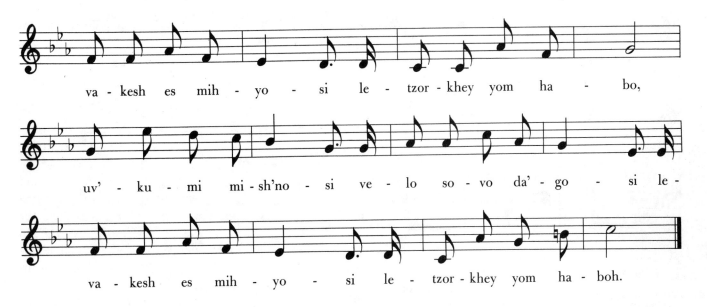

va - kesh es mih - yo - si le - tzor - khey yom ha - bo,

uv' - ku - mi mi-sh'no - si ve - lo so - vo da' - go - si le -

va - kesh es mih - yo - si le - tzor - khey yom ha - boh.

With my plow I earn all my possessions,
I live a good life and lack for nothing.
And when I arise from my sleep, I have no worries
About how to seek a livelihood for the next day.

If one were to pronounce the words of that song with the correct Sephardic accentuation, the verses would not scan and would be totally unsingable. The next song, however, is set to words by the poet Yaakov Cohen; it became one of the best-loved songs of the *Bilu-im*. The melody is probably of Russian origin.

Anu Olim ve-Sharim
(Let Our Song)

Ex. 126

YAAKOV COHEN

OLD PALESTINE FOLK SONG

A - nu o - lim ve - sha - rim al ha - ra - vot uf' - ga - rim
Let our song swell out in waves o - ver ru - ins, o - ver graves

305

A - nu pos' - im ve - hol' - khim u - va - or u - va - ha - she - khah.
Stur - di - ly we find our way in the dark or by light of day.

Uv' - yod' - im uv' - lo yod' - im et ha - de - rekh ne - le - khah
E - ven when we bare - ly know the un - chart - ed way we go

A - nu o - lim ve - sha - rim, a - nu o - lim ve - sha - rim.
Still our song swells out in waves, still our song swells out in waves.

Perhaps you have already surmised that the national song of Israel is of this same musical style and vintage. *Hatikvah* (The Hope) was written in 1886 by a European Hebrew poet, Naphtali Herz Imber, who lived for some years in Palestine. Like the American national anthem, *The Star-Spangled Banner,* and like *America,* Imber's song is derived from an old folk tune. The Jewish musical historian Idelsohn once drew up a table comparing the *Hatikvah* tune to a Basque folk tune, a Spanish pilgrim song, the *Yigdal* hymn of the synagogue (attributed to Leoni), to the *Shir ha-Ma-alot* melody (Ex. 122) and to the Bohemian folk song which is the theme of Smetana's tone poem *Die Moldau.*

Imber's lyrics, written at a time when the modern Zionist return to the land had just barely begun, concluded with the words: ". . . ancient hope to return to our land, to the city where David encamped." By the time the State of Israel was founded, those words had been changed. The song now concludes: ". . . the hope of two thousand years, to be a free people in our land, the land of Zion and Jerusalem."

In the same mysterious way in which *The Star-Spangled Banner* prevailed over many patriotic songs to become the American national anthem, so did *Hatikvah* prevail over a number of other songs to become the official anthem of the new state. Following is the song as it is sung today.

Hatikvah

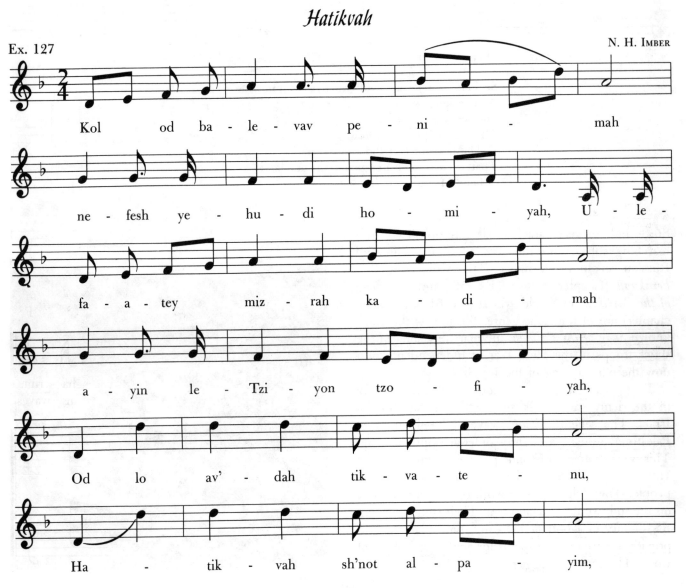

Ex. 127   N. H. IMBER

Kol od ba - le - vav pe - ni - mah
ne - fesh ye - hu - di ho - mi - yah, U - le -
fa - a - tey miz - rah ka - di - mah
a - yin le - Tzi - yon tzo - fi - yah,
Od lo av' - dah tik - va - te - nu,
Ha - tik - vah sh'not al - pa - yim,

307

Li - h'yot am hof - shi be - ar - tze - nu,

E - retz Tzi - yon vi - ru - sha - la - yim.

Li - h'yot am hof - shi be - ar - tze - nu,

E - retz Tzi - yon vi - ru - sha - la - yim.

So long as a Jewish soul still lives within a heart,
And so long as an eye gazes longingly to Zion in the far
   reaches of the East,
Then the hope is not lost,
   The hope of two thousand years,
That we may be a free people in our land,
   Land of Zion and Jerusalem.

Since Imber every Israeli crisis has produced new marching songs, and they are all in the idiom of Russian revolutionary music. The Bialik song *Tehezaknah* (Chapter Sixteen, Ex. 59) and the *Song of the Partisans* in World War II (Ex. 61 in the same chapter) are of the same genre. So, too, is the well-known *Song of the Palmah*, the marching song of the shock-troops in the 1948 War of Independence and now the official song of the Israeli Army.

That particular strain of melody is only one of many in the richly varied folk song and popular song of Israel. The second *Aliyah* (wave of immigration to Palestine) brought a slightly different kind of song. This was the *Aliyah* of young people, beginning about 1907, who believed in labor as the savior of the people. They felt that only work of the hands, work on the soil, would redeem them. Their songs glorified the dignity of labor; at the same time, they had to provide the rhythmic impetus for good, hard physical work. The musical baggage brought by these young

Aliyah

people from the countries of Eastern Europe consisted of hasidic *nigunim* and Yiddish folk songs. Those, then, were what they sang, but they livened the tempos, set new words to them and thus infused an entirely new spirit into the old songs.

Here is a hasidic song transformed into a new *halutz* (pioneer) song. The original words were: "We all give thanks. Happy is he who never sinned. But he who has sinned will repent, and his repentance will be accepted. He who has sinned will repent and be forgiven. How happy are we, how good is our portion, how sweet is our fortune, how beautiful our inheritance." To understand the slight twist which makes the all-important difference in the words of this song, you must know that the Hebrew word for "will repent" is *yashuv;* that same *yashuv* can also be translated as "will return." The new song says, "We all give thanks. Happy is he who works with his hands. And he who comes here will be received [welcomed]. But he who returns, let him return, and his return [to his old country] will be forgiven. Happy are we . . ."

Elu ve-Elu Modim

Ex. 128

PALESTINE FOLK SONG

E - lu ve - e - lu mo - dim, ash - rey mi she - hu po - el! E - lu ve - e - lu mo - dim,

309

ash - rey   mi she - hu po - el! U - mi she - ya - vo

ya - vo,   ya - vo ve - nit - ka - bel, u -

mi she - ya - shuv ya - shuv,   ya - shuv ve - nis - lah

Hundreds of songs like this were based on old hasidic melodies, and many, too, were parodies of old Yiddish folk songs. Perhaps the climax of this type of song making was reached with the best known of all Israeli songs, *Havah Nagilah*. You have danced the *hora* to it. It has been made into a popular American song and is played at every Jewish gathering where there is music. *Havah Nagilah*, too, was originally a *nigun*. *"Lei-di-dei"* or *"bi-bi-bam!"* the devout mystical *Hasidim* sang, at the same time adding physical movement—the narrow restricted steps of ecstatic dance, the snap of the fingers, the clapping of hands. When Allenby took Jerusalem in 1917, the Jews of Jerusalem felt a victory celebration was in order. Abraham Zvi Idelsohn (whom you have already met in his role as scholar and musicologist) was at the time the conductor of a youth choir in Jerusalem and, rising to the great occasion, he decided to present a joyous new song as a tribute to the liberation army.

Idelsohn chose an old melody which once had been sung in the court of his father's hasidic *rebbe* and offered it to his young choir singers. They felt that it needed words, and they held a contest to select the best text. A young boy named Moshe Nathanson won, and from that time on his words have echoed around the world. (Moshe Nathanson later migrated to America and became one of the first to introduce Palestine folk song to the American public.)

"Let us rejoice and be glad. Wake up, brothers, with a joyful heart!" sang the proud youngsters, in a vigorous choral arrangement by their teacher. The syllables of *lei-di-dei* opened up to the broad *havah*. The dance changed from the tiny, mincing steps of the *Hasid* to the sweep and stamp of the *hora*, the circle dance, the symbol of unity and communal living in every *kibbutz* and settlement. It has been sung ever since not only in Israel but, even more, outside of Israel.

A third strain entered Jewish song after World War I and continued during the time of the third *Aliyah*, the third wave of immigration that began in 1920. The settlers began to listen to the sounds of the land itself. They began to respond to the cool of evening with its welcome relief from the burning sun; to the pace of camels with their bells sounding out across desert stretches; to the strange wail of jackals and to the songs of their Arab neighbors and the accompanying Arab drum and 'ud. They listened to the songs of Jews of old Jerusalem whose ancestors had come from Spain

centuries before, of Jews whose forebears long before had made pilgrimages from their remote villages in Bokhara and had remained as inhabitants of the city. This was the time when the first Yemenites, who had somehow got word of the Balfour Declaration in their distant land, began to trickle in small caravans to the Holy Land of their dreams, bringing along their own ancient melodies. All of these sounds found their way into the folk song of the new settlers. The odd rhythms and strange tuning were sifted through Western ears and came out altered, forced into the square rhythms and the tempered tuning to which the Europeans were accustomed.

One of the first to adapt Eastern melody to new texts was that doughty musical pioneer, Joel Engel, who had migrated from Russia in the wake of the Revolution. From his career as a teacher, critic and composer of art music in Russia, he now turned to a new field and earned the reputation of the "father" of Hebrew folk song. During a period of great economic depression and also of danger from hostile Arabs in the 1920's, Engel organized a troupe of young people as roving singers. Along the streets and on the Tel Aviv beach they wandered, trying to cheer the folk with bright new songs. Engel also wrote the first new children's songs to new Hebrew poems by Kipnis and by Halpern. Some of the verses were merely translations and adaptations of old Yiddish folk songs; but others were fresh lyrics singing of the new

Young Israelis learning to play the recorder from a kibbutz instructor

life, the new land and the new outlook. Lullabies told of children who would grow up to be farmers. (Compare this to the Yiddish song by Lazar Weiner discussed in Chapter Twenty-two.) The orchard, the field, the bird took the place of the schoolroom (*heder*), the books, the *alef bet*. And many of the tunes were now to be borrowed from the East. A good example is this song of a little shepherd in the hills of Galilee. The youngster is playing his flute—probably a crude instrument he has fashioned himself out of a reed. He sits alone on the mountainside and watches the dawn. In the distance he hears the cow lowing in the barn.

Engel chose for his melody one of the Yemenite wedding songs we read about in Chapter Twenty-one. Perhaps it may have faintly reminded him of the piano piece "The Little Shepherd" from Debussy's *Children's Corner*. Listen to them both. They make a good pair. Substitute a recorder for the shepherd flute, and play the song; or play only the *"li-li-li's"* while someone sings the rest of the song.

Ex. 129

Shir ha-Roeh
(Shepherd's Song)

HALPERN

J. ENGEL

Bo - ker bo - ker ba - ha - li - li a - ha - lel, li li li,
Ev' - ry morn - ing you can hear me play my flute, li li li,

li li li, li li li li li li. Zar - hah ha - mah min
See the ris - ing sun, in the

he – ha – rim,　　　　li li li li li li li li li li li li li li li
moun-tains night is gone,

8va

Fine

li li li li li li li, li li li li li li li li li.

Fine

Pa – rah sho-me – ah, min ha – re – fet go – ah pa – rah,
I hear her now, From the barn the low – ing of the cow,

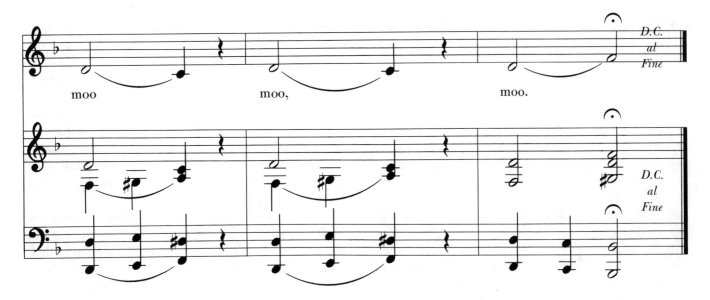

moo   moo,   moo.

Within a matter of years, a considerable number of songs existed—songs borrowed, imitated or adapted, with new Hebrew words, from the Jews of Yemen, Bokhara, Iraq, Iran. This borrowing process began at least two decades before the founding of the State of Israel and was helped along greatly by the discovery of talented young singers among the Eastern new-comers. Gifted singers like Brakhah Tzfirah, Asnat Halevi and Sara Levi were encouraged to present their songs at concerts, gatherings in the towns and in the *kibbutzim*. A few European-trained musicians like Noah Nardi and Jedidiah Gorochov (Amiran) wrote down the tunes and furnished accompaniments for them.

While all these exciting developments were taking place, something else of great importance was gradually occurring: the Hebrew language itself was growing, adding new words daily, losing its antique quality, becoming more "comfortable," more pliant, less classical and more colloquial. In other words, it was now becoming a living, breathing instrument for a living people. The Sephardic pronunciation, slightly changed, was completely accepted and was now universally spoken throughout the country. Adoption of the Sephardic pronunciation required speakers to accent certain syllables not necessarily stressed in the Ashkenazic pronunciation. The change produced a brisk stacatto effect which no longer fitted into the rhythms and melodies of the old songs. At least one of the important folk composers, Jehudah Sharett, modelled his melodies very carefully to conform to the exact sound of the spoken Hebrew. (In effect, Sharett

was doing, on a far more modest level, exactly what the great composer Moussorgsky had done much earlier with Russian language and subsequently Debussy with French poetry.)

Sharett, Nardi, Zaira, Matityahu Shelem—these were only a few of the song makers of the *yishuv* (the Jewish community in the land before the founding of the state). They were truly folk composers. Their songs were printed, passed from place to place and were also collected outside the country. In earlier eras, the composers' names would have been lost or forgotten as in the case of thousands of composers of folk songs in times gone by. But the day of that kind of anonymity is over. In Israel, as everywhere in the West, we know the names of the composers of our current folk songs. In spite of the printing and copyrighting processes today, the songs still undergo some changes as they pass from mouth to mouth, from singer to singer. People learn them by ear, usually, rather than from printed music and are bound to make their individual alterations as they do so.‡

The rise of Hitler and the flight of Jews from the Nazi regime in Germany and Austria brought a new *Aliyah* to the land in the early 1930's. Among the newcomers were many gifted writers, artists, musicians, all highly sophisticated and trained in the most advanced cultural centers of the West. The new arrivals included musicians who had studied under the leading composers in Paris, Berlin and Vienna and experts in the disciplines of musicology and ethnomusicology. These skilled professionals were prepared to engage in scientific research into the exotic and unexplored Middle Eastern kinds of melodies that previous settlers had found vaguely appealing but had not really understood.

A leader among this group of new citizens was Paul Frankenburg who, upon his arrival in Palestine, changed his surname to Ben Haim (pronounced *ha-yim*). Others were Marc Lavry, Uri Boscovitch, Odeon Partos and Moshe Starominsky (known now as Seter). These are today Israel's "older" generation of composers—some of them living, some gone—who devoted their creative energies to art music, instrumental and choral music, piano and string solo virtuoso pieces and art songs—all of which require trained performers to do them justice and which belong in the concert hall. This generation tried to embody in music the sounds, the scales, the rhythms of Eastern Jewish song and the timbres of the Middle Eastern instruments. Listen to the suite *To Israel* by Ben Haim.‡ You will hear how he used conventional instruments of the symphony orchestra to give the feeling of the 'ud, the tanbour, the santura.

A younger generation in the State of Israel today is not copying its elders. They do not seem to be particularly interested in creating a "Mediterranean music." Exactly like their contemporaries in other parts of the world, today's Israeli composers are experimenting in sound in many different ways. They are using every device which the composers of the twentieth century have at their command, and a few more. Some, for example, are writing twelve-tone serial music in the style of Arnold Schoenberg. Others are absorbed in the exciting possibilities of electronic music which is produced in laboratories and performed by tape recorders. Still others are interested in the new form of composition called *aleatory,* or "chance" music. There is also improvisation after the manner of the best jazz musicians. Certain Israeli composers today are experimenting with the cantillation method of composition (a method to which we referred in Chapter Six). This is closely related to the *raga* method of India which you can hear now in the work of Ravi Shankar and other Indian musicians. All these styles are part of an international music style and are all being cultivated by the young generation of Israeli composers.‡

Nevertheless, the song of the return, the song of crisis, the song of courage, the songs for dancing and for popular singing have by no means been stilled. There are always new folk composers to provide them. The songs continue to alternate between pure European tunes and, more and more, authentically Eastern tunes. Folk dancing which, like the song, is devised by people who are consciously creating new folk dances alternates in the same way—between the polka, the waltz-like steps, the Russian stamp and swing, on the one hand; and, on the other, the complicated footwork, the irregular rhythm, the lithe twist of the *debka* in Eastern dance. In addition to all these, there is a growing output of café songs, songs in the latest styles of America, England, France, Italy, etc. Discothèques are set up in nooks and crannies of old sections in the cities of Israel and there one hears and dances to rock exactly as in the Western world. These musical styles are quickly "in" and "out" again, as such things always are. You will find them, as well as the folk songs, in the records which are being made all the time and which are listed regularly in the Schwann *Long Playing Record Catalog.*

316

Twenty-Seven
HERE AND NOW

ALMOST all of the rich heritage of music created out of Jewish living is available in some form in America. Much of it can be heard "live" in synagogues, in meeting rooms or in summer camps. You can find a *hazan* chanting the *nusah* of the Eastern Ashkenazim with his own personal flourishes. You can hear the congregational singing of the Sephardic psalmody. You can visit a hasidic community and even join in their singing and dancing in the joyous *Simhat Torah* celebration, or dance a lively *hora* with a group of visiting Israeli students. There are corners in some of the large cities, especially on the Eastern seaboard, where you might even hear the singing of Ladino *romanzas* or the strumming of the Middle Eastern instruments by Jews from the Arabic lands. What you cannot hear "live" you might find in printed volumes or on records.

Some of the instrumental art music of Israel (and of course of other countries as well) is available to Americans and Canadians in recordings, and occasionally a major orchestra will play a work by Ben Haim, Partos or Lavry. Ernest Bloch's compositions such as his *Shelomo Rhapsody* and his *Sacred Service* (the former composed abroad, the latter composed in America) are well represented in the recorded repertoire. Many exciting works have been published or recorded and allowed to go out of print for lack of awareness or demand by the Jewish public, but your interest and awareness may well restore some of them to the catalogues.

What music is being created out of American Jewish life here and now? The American Jewish community is no different from all the other Jewish communities in all parts of the world. It makes music for Jewish occasions and Jewish needs, drawing partly from the sounds of the surrounding atmosphere, partly from the experience of the past. The first group of Russian Jewish composers had settled here in the twenties, and other groups arrived from Germany, Austria, France and Italy in the thirties, bringing with them the music of European Jewry and the techniques of the continent. It was in America that the first

attempts were made, and are still being made, to compose complete "services"—a fully unified Friday evening service or a Sabbath morning service, a service for the High Holy Days or a midnight penitential (*selihot*) service. These musical works, at the beginning, were all set to the text of the *Union Prayer Book* because composers, migrating to America, were given commissions for such "services" by one or another Reform synagogue.

In spite of efforts to establish a "nationalist" Jewish music which would carry on the movement initiated in Russia, nationalist composers like Saminsky, Achron, Jacob Weinberg and others were provided with their only Jewish audiences in the field of religious music. Abraham W. Binder, the American Jewish composer, also found his opportunity for mu-

NFTY youths perform a rock service

317

sical creativity in the Reform synagogue. Bloch, Frederic Jacobi, Darius Milhaud, Max Helfman, Reuven Kosakoff, Heinrich Schalit, Isidore Freed, Hugo Adler, Frederick Piket, Julius Chajes, Herbert Fromm are among the names of those composers for the Reform service in America whose works are now being heard in various synagogues across the country. Their works are becoming increasingly well known in congregations today; they are as familiar to the new generation as the compositions of the European pioneers of the nineteenth century were to an older generation.

As the years have passed, a native generation has come of age—young men with ears attuned to the sounds of America. What are those sounds, the sounds that penetrate to the hearts and minds of youth? The musical sounds of America have been changing at a dizzying and still accelerating pace. First, we have had jazz: Dixieland, then swing, then boogie-woogie, then modern jazz or cool jazz. Always there was rural folk song but, somewhere around the time when jazz was going through its various metamorphoses, the people of the cities became aware of blues, folk-white, moving on to folk-rock and new rock. On the American scene anything old is old and *dead* even if it has only yesterday sent out an offshoot and of course lives on in that offshoot.

In the music of the synagogue, the first intimations of American sound came in the 1940's in two short commissioned works for the Conservative synagogue. The first was a *Kiddush* for the Sabbath by Kurt Weill, *not* a native American but a German composer of the European version of jazz. With *Three-Penny Opera* in his German past, with *Knickerbocker Holiday, Lady in the Dark* and other stage and film scores among his American works, he was called upon to compose this *Kiddush*. Presumably, he did not set out consciously to write a "Jazz *Kiddush.*" He simply wrote his own lovely, lyrical style of music, complete with jazz chord progressions and blue-note. The second work was by Leonard Bernstein, at that time known as the composer of *Fancy Free, On the Town* and, of course, the *Jeremiah* symphony. He was assigned the Hebrew text from the Friday evening service, *Hashkivenu* ("Cause us, O Lord, to lie down in peace"). Like Weill, Bernstein wrote as he was accustomed to write—jazz harmonies, jazz breaks and syncopation to set one's feet tapping.‡

It was only in the 1960's, after jazz had passed its peak of development and was reaching near-dissolu-tion in extreme modern abstract jazz, that American Jews heard a jazz service *And David Danced Before the Lord* by Charles Davidson. In this case the composer, who had previously written a *Hasidic Service,* set out deliberately to write jazz in an attempt to provide young people with easy and appealing music. His service is a melding of *nusah* with jazz rhythms.‡

But the jazz service was no sooner off the press when rock became the sound of the youth. No longer, in the 1960's, was this American rock the simple natural expression of the folk but a highly sophisticated development, with emphasis on lyrics—lyrics that were being hailed, in some circles, as the "true" new American poetry. From out of the rear ranks of this trend came Jewish composers using the familiar solemn words of the *Union Prayer Book* with the sounds of the old folk-rock. While many young Jews were devoting their talents to the creation of the new poetry, with its overtones of social protest and its strong note of breaking with all traditions, the Jewish composers sang of the Sabbath: "It is an eternal covenant for all generations!" in rock rhythm.‡

(This is not really a new phenomenon in the history of synagogue music. Among some manuscripts of cantorial compositions from southern Germany in the eighteenth century we find melodies marked "Siciliana," "Gavotte" and others. For example, the setting provided for *Melekh Elyon,* "Supreme King," a solemn *piyut* from the *Yom Kippur* service, has the heading "Tempo di Menuetto.")

Another product of the attempt to provide synagogue music which can make an "instant" appeal to listeners has been the introduction of "Israeli style" music. Both Reform and Conservative congregations have commissioned services by Israeli composers, particularly those folk composers who have been discussed in the previous chapter. These composers are speedy and adept in producing short songs for popular "instant" consumption. They have little or no experience with modern worship services and technically lack the sustaining power to write an extended piece of unified music. However, they have contributed to the liturgy a number of fresh and attractive choral and solo songs with the lilt of the shepherd's tune or the liveliness of the *hora.* Two of the more sophisticated Israeli composers, Ben Haim and Mordekhai Seter, have written more highly developed and serious services for the American synagogue.‡

Folk song, too, has been produced by the Jewish

community in America. The hasidic community continues to make songs in the style of its European elders. The Orthodox day schools have helped to spread them among the young people attending Jewish summer camps. In the same genre are the popular songs of Sh'lomo Karlebach, the guitar-playing rabbi whose records have had a wide circulation. All of these songs have texts from the classical Jewish literature—biblical, talmudic, liturgical—with melodies in the hasidic idiom, itself a reflection of the East European environment of its origin.

During these middle decades of the twentieth century, simultaneously with these experiments aimed at making the music of Jewish life immediately appealing especially to young people, an altogether different trend has been developing. A number of highly individualistic composers, very much in the avant-garde of the musical world, are composing with all the technical skill at their command. These are also young people, trained in the conservatories and universities of America, who are at the same time sensitive to the meanings of ancient texts and aware of the musical heritage of the past without being bound to it. In addition to music for the synagogue, they are producing oratorios, cantatas and even short operas. We have mentioned Yehudi Wyner and Robert Starer in earlier chapters. There are other names which should also be noted here so that you can be watchful for performances of their works in concerts, in synagogue services and on radio and television: Samuel Adler, David Amram, Moshe Budmor, Jack Gottlieb, Tzipora Jochsberger, Abraham Salkov, Stephen Richards and Hugo Weissgall.

What will be the enriched Jewish heritage which your generation will hand on to the next? Perhaps you will want new music for the rites of passage. There are already some new American compositions for the occasion of *Bar Mitzvah* and for weddings.‡ There is room for more of this to provide a wider choice and to replace some of the highly inappropriate and often lugubrious music now being used for these important occasions. We have a need for new songs for the Sabbath table and for the home celebrations of all the Jewish festivals of the year. While we do have a rich heritage from the past, it is couched in language—textual and musical—out of the Middle Ages or from foreign shores. This is equally true of songs of lament, of courage, of resistance, of joy or thanksgiving. Surely Jewish life today has its own

struggles, concerns, frustrations and gratifications which need to be uttered in music that we can sing or play together. New theater music on an intimate level—for small operettas and *Purimspiels*—for fun as well as for more serious purposes, will also be welcome.

As we observe the present scene, we notice how few are the large works for chorus and orchestra which are not necessarily part of the conventional religious service. Oratorio, cantata and opera based on the great classics of our literature—whether biblical or contemporary, whether English or Hebrew or Yiddish—could conceivably be incorporated into worship services; and they could also be performed by the important musical organizations of our cities or on the campuses of universities across the country.

Some of you will be the actual composers or the skilled performers of the new music of the Jewish people. Some of our readers will one day be studying in conservatories or in the music departments of colleges. But you will need to know a great deal more about your musical heritage than you have found in this book. Indeed, you will have to know and cherish your total Jewish heritage and to be deeply involved emotionally in the life of the people as a whole. The knowledge can be acquired, to some extent, through reading. For those serious students intent upon a career, it is possible today to get a systematic training in a number of schools which have been established in recent years. In New York City, there are: The School for Sacred Music of the Hebrew Union College-Jewish Institute of Religion which was founded under the direction of Abraham W. Binder and Eric Werner; The Cantors' Institute and the College of Jewish Music of the Jewish Theological Seminary of America under the directorship of Hugo Weissgall; courses in the Department of Music of Yeshiva University and the Music Department of the Jewish Teachers' Seminary. In Los Angeles, the College of Fine Arts of the University of Judaism, directed by Erwin Jospe, includes an active music section. All of these institutions offer courses toward degrees in various aspects of music as well as in general Jewish studies.

Others of you will be the participants in the singing of songs, the playing of some of the music and in listening to professional performances with serious attention. You will require music in your synagogues and concert halls which will make some demand on you beyond the hand-clapping, foot-tapping response, which will engage your minds as well as your bodies. When you require such music, the serious and talented composer will find it worth his while to create music for Jewish life. Perhaps you will be among those who provide the commissions which will encourage experimentation and exploration.

As composer, performer or educated listener, you will be sharing in the creation of the tenth song in the ancient Jewish legend which tells us:

Nine songs there were that the children of Israel sang to God in the course of their history: first, the song they sang in Egypt on the night that they were freed from bondage; second, the song of triumph at the Red Sea; third, the song they sang when the well sprang up in the wilderness; fourth, the song of Moses before his death; fifth, Joshua's song after victory over five Amorite kings; sixth, Deborah's song with Barak over the downfall of Sisera; seventh, David's song of deliverance out of the hands of all his enemies; eighth, Solomon's song at the dedication of the Temple; ninth, Jehoshaphat's song as, trusting in God, he went to battle against the Moabites and the Ammonites. The tenth and last song, however, will be that grand and mighty song when Israel will raise their voice in triumph at their future deliverance, for that will be the final release for all of Israel for all times.

(*Mekilta Shirah* I, 34a–34b.
Mekilta RS 56–57, as told by Louis Ginzburg,
in *Legends of the Jews*, Vol. III)

Twenty-Eight
FOR FURTHER EXPLORATION

In order to learn more about the musical heritage of the Jewish people you might begin with the following basic library:

Idelsohn, A. Z., *Jewish Music in Its Historical Development*. Paperback reprint. N. Y. Schocken Books, 1967.

Rothmuller, A. M., *The Music of the Jews*. Revised Edition. N. Y. Thomas Yoseloff, Ltd., 1967.

Weisser, A., *The Modern Renaissance of Jewish Music*. N. Y. Bloch Publishing Co., 1954.

Werner, E., *From Generation to Generation*. Studies in Jewish musical tradition. Edited by Walter A. Davidson. N. Y. American Conference of Cantors, 1968.

All publications of the National Jewish Music Council, sponsored by the National Jewish Welfare Board, particularly Weisser, A., *Bibliography of Publications and Other Resources on Jewish Music*. Revised and Reedited, 1969.

The notes that follow suggest sources of information to add to specific information provided in the chapters of this book. Wherever it is possible, the exact listing of recordings and of published music is provided, with the caveat that many of these are liable to change or to go out of print. You may need to consult a library: sometimes a Jewish library in a rabbinical school, synagogue or community center; sometimes the music and record department of a public or university library.

Page 6   Detailed information about such archaeological discoveries may be found in a pamphlet by the Israeli musicologist Bathya Bayer. *The Material Relics of Music in Ancient Palestine and Its Environs: An Archaeological Inventory*. Tel Aviv Israel Music Institute, 1963.

Page 7   See Azriel Eisenberg. *The Great Discovery*. N. Y. Abelard-Schuman, Ltd.

Page 8   For an interesting, nontechnical account, look up the handsome quarterly *Ariel*. In the Number 15, 1966 issue of that *Quarterly Review of Arts and Sciences in Israel* you will find an article by Israel Adler called *Synagogue Chants of the 12th Century: The Musical Notations of Obadaiah the Proselyte*.

Page 9   More details about the ancient instruments are given in Werner. Also, read Chapter Five, *The Instruments of Israel*, in *The History of Musical Instruments*, by Kurt Sachs. N. Y., W. W. Norton & Co.

Page 17   This description of the continuity of the tradition is based entirely on the writing of Eric Werner. You can read it in Werner, p. 25, or, in a library, look up the article in its source, *The Interpreter's Dictionary of the Bible*, under "Music in the Bible."

Page 18   Idelsohn issued single-handedly the encyclopedic ten-volume *Thesaurus of Oriental Jewish Melodies*. The first volume is devoted to the music of the Yemenite Jews. This volume has appeared in German, Hebrew and English editions with the introductions in each of the respective languages.

Page 23   *Friday Evening Service* for cantor (tenor), four-part chorus of mixed voices and organ, by Yehudi Wyner. N. Y. Associated Music Publishers, 1963.

Page 25, line 3   Some of the modern *Shavuot* pilgrim songs from Israel are to be found in *The Songs We Sing* by Harry Coopersmith or in *Songs of Childhood* by Eisenstein and Prensky, both published in N. Y. by the United Synagogue of America.

Page 25, line 15   There are many fine recordings of both Handel's *Messiah* and Mozart's *Exsultate, Jubilate*. Consult your Schwann catalogue.

Page 25, line 36   This psalm is only a fragment of the set of psalms called *Hallel*. You can hear the *Hallel* chanted as part of the Passover *seder* of a Yemenite family on the record, *Yemenite Passover*, produced by Eskin (Folkways Records 8291). The melody is a variant of the one given here, but it is similar enough to be quite recognizable. Notice the strange vocal quality of the singing. This is typically Yemenite.

Page 27, left   There are many published editions of Lewandowski's *Halleluyah*.

Page 27, right   If you are to choose a recording of Stravinsky's *Psalms* try to find one conducted by the composer himself or one conducted by Ansermet.

Page 28   There are several recordings of Copland's *In the Beginning.*

Page 33, caption   This notation appears in the great book on Hebrew accents written by the Christian humanist scholar Reuchlin in the early sixteenth century. Note that the music was printed to be read from right to left to conform with the Hebrew text. Note, also, that the chant was arranged in four-part harmony by the notator. This, of course, was not Jewish practice.

Page 35   The standard textbook for this study is *Biblical Chant* by Abraham Wolf Binder, late professor of music at Hebrew Union College—Jewish Institute of Religion, director of music at the Free Synagogue in New York City and himself a composer of much synagogue music. N. Y. Philosophical Library, 1959.

Page 43, line 42   To study some of these compositions, consult the *Out-of-print Classics of Synagogue Music* published by the Sacred Music Press, HUC—JIR School for Sacred Music in New York. Another source is the five-volume *Cantorial Anthology* edited by Gershon Ephros. N. Y. Bloch Publishing Co. This anthology contains contemporary music as well.

Page 43, line 49   You will read about some of these composers in later chapters. Consult the *Bibliography of Jewish Vocal Music,* revised edition, prepared by Lewis Appleton and issued by the National Jewish Music Council sponsored by the National Jewish Welfare Board.

Page 44   The manuscript of Saadyah's *Siddur* from which this is copied is in the Bodleian Library of Oxford University, England.

Page 46, caption   This picture is a detail from a mosaic pavement excavated in Huldah, Israel. The musicologist Joseph Yasser has suggested that the "shovel" is a representation of a mysterious instrument referred to in the Bible and Talmud as a *magrepha.*

Page 46   Herbert Fromm. *Rosh Hashanah Shofar Service.* N. Y. Transcontinental Music Publications.

Page 50   There are many recordings of Bruch's *Kol Nidre.*

Page 52   Schoenberg's *Kol Nidre* may be found in *The Music of Arnold Schoenberg,* Vol. III (Columbia M2S 709).

Page 55   Maurice Ravel. *Kaddish.* Paris, Durand & Cie., 1915. This piece has appeared on a variety of recordings usually as part of a recital of French songs or of songs by Ravel. Available, as of 1971, is one recording sung by Madeleine Grey (Angel COLC 152). This is a remake of an old but authoritative performance. Also, there is a fine interpretation by Gerard Souzay to be found on his

recording of Ravel songs (Philips Sal 3704 839 733Ly).

Page 61   A good, easy arrangement of this song, *Mayim,* for two voices with guitar chordings, may be found in *The New Jewish Song Book* by Harry Coopersmith. N. Y. Behrman House, Inc., 1965. You will find it recorded on a number of folk-dance records listed in Schwann under "Israel Folk Music."

Page 69   The music for this song, *Ha-zor-im be-dim-ah,* with its original Hebrew text may be found in Coopersmith's *The Songs We Sing* (mentioned above).

Page 73   Ravel's arrangement of *Meierke, Mein Zun (Meierke, mon fils),* like his *Kaddish,* is published in Paris by Durand & Cie. The third song which Ravel arranged for voice and piano is the Yiddish song *Die Alte Kasheh (L'enigme eternelle).* All three songs are sung as a group, usually in recital.

Page 77   The *Jeremiah* symphony has been recorded by the New York Philharmonic Orchestra, conducted by the composer with Jennie Tourel singing the solo in the last movement (Columbia MS 6303).

Page 81   The piano score of Mendelssohn's *Elijah* is available in several editions. There are a number of fine recordings of the oratorio, and new ones are always being made. Consult Schwann and follow reviews of recordings in periodicals.

Page 86   Robert Starer. *Ariel* (Piano score). N. Y. MCA Publishing Co. This work has been recorded by the Camerata singers and orchestra, Abraham Kaplan, conductor, with Roberta Peters and Julian Patrick, soloists (Desto DC-1735, as of September 1972).

Page 87   Max Helfman. *Ki Mi-Tziyon.* Transcontinental Music Publications.

Page 90   Leonard Bernstein. *Chichester Psalms.* New York Philharmonic Orchestra, Camerata singers (Columbia MS 3792).

Page 91   Ernest Bloch. *Sacred Service.* New York Philharmonic Orchestra, Leonard Bernstein, conductor, Robert Merrill, cantor (Columbia MS 6221).

Page 98, line 31   You can find Senfl's *Da Jakob Sah (Then Jacob Saw)* on a recording of Senfl's music, *Missa Paschalis* and *Songs,* performed by the New York Pro Musica, directed by Noah Greenberg (Decca 79420).

Page 98, line 35   Honegger's *Roi David* is available on records in a performance by the Utah Symphony Orchestra, Abravanel, conductor, with L. Singher and N. Davrath, soloists (Vanguard 2117, 2118).

Page 99, left The Wolpe lament, *Ha-tzevi Yisrael,* is one of ten songs from the Hebrew recorded by Carmen and Lischner (Columbia 5197).

Page 99, right David Diamond. *David Mourns for Absalom.* N. Y. Mercury Music Corp., 1947.

Page 100 The music of this movement is available in arrangement for mezzo-soprano and piano and could be used for concert programs. Leonard Bernstein. *Lamentations.* N. Y., T. B. Harms Co.

Page 111, line 4 Odeon Partos. *Yizkor* (In Memoriam). For viola and orchestra, Bernstein, Haifa Symphony (Mace S-10033).

Page 111, line 12 A. Schoenberg. *Survivor from Warsaw* is in the album *The Music of Arnold Schoenberg* (Columbia M2S-679). In Vol. VIII (M2S-780) you will find the composer's setting of the Hebrew text of Psalm 130, *De Profundis,* Out of the Depths. This is a much more difficult work than *Kol Nidre* or *Survivor* but a very impressive one.

Page 111, line 22 Michael Sahl. *A Mitzvah for the Dead.* For violin and tape, Paul Zukofsky, violinist (Vanguard— Cardinal VCS 10057).

Page 113 A contemporary composition in the spirit of Levi Yitzhak's protest is the *Kaddish* symphony by Leonard Bernstein, for narrator, solo chorus and orchestra. Bernstein wrote an original text for the narrator. The traditional *Kaddish* provides the text of the sung portions.

Page 119 During the late '60s, we read accounts of singing by Jews in the Soviet Union. Perhaps the most moving of these was Elie Wiesel's in his book, *The Jews of Silence.* In that book he spoke especially of the singing and dancing on *Simhat Torah* and of the old and well-known song *David Melekh Yisrael* (David, King of Israel). Since that time a whole new group of protest songs has reached our ears, smuggled out on tapes by a visiting American. These songs have been edited and arranged by Issachar Miron and are sung by Theodore Bikel on a recording called *Silent No More* (ST-119-18B) which the Star Record Company produced in co-operation with the American Jewish Congress.

Page 127 Castelnuovo-Tedesco's *Lekhah Dodi* may be found in the very interesting volume *Contemporary Music for the Synagogue* edited by David Putterman, N. Y., G. Schirmer. Milhaud's *Lekhah Dodi* is appended, along with other items from the Friday evening service, to his *Sabbath Morning Service* (*Service Sacre*). Paris, Salabert-Ricordi.

Page 146, line 9 For more hasidic songs, see Velvel Pasternak's *Songs of the Chasidim,* Vols. 1 and 2. N. Y. Bloch Publishing Co., 1968-1971.

Both in this country and in Israel there has been a considerable revival of interest in hasidic song. In the late sixties, a musical play called *Ish Hasid Hayah* (Once There Was a *Hasid*) was produced in Tel Aviv. It is based on old and traditional hasidic melodies which are performed in a modified contemporary popular style with guitar accompaniment. The show was a great popular success and has since been produced on the New York stage, in English translation, under the name *Only Fools Are Sad.* A recording is available of the Hebrew production.

Page 146, line 15 Try to find a recording of the complete *Ba-al Shem Suite* by Bloch. There are many recordings of the *Nigun* alone. As of 1969, the best available performance is recorded by Isaac Stern (Columbia CMS-6716).

Page 146, right The scores of three services in hasidic style are: Charles Davidson, *Hasidic Sabbath,* N. Y. Mills Music Corp.; Isidore Freed, *Hasidic Service,* N. Y. Transcontinental Music Publications and Lazar Weiner, *Shir LeShabbat,* N. Y. Mills Music Corp.

Page 149 Lazare Saminsky. *Schir-Haschirim* (The Song of Songs) from *Six Songs of the Russian Orient.* Vienna, 1928. Universal Edition. This song is out of print at the present time, but you might find it in a library. You can hear a fine performance if you can find a record called *Out of the Silence,* songs of Russian Jewry, sung by Reuven Frankel, with Lazar Weiner at the piano (Famous Records Fam 1038).

Page 155, line 20 You will find Bokharan love songs in addition to songs of many other Oriental Jewish communities in the set of four records *In Israel Today* produced by Battarachya (Westminster 9805/6/10/11).

Page 155, line 34 The three acceptable recordings of Ladino songs which have been issued are not listed in Schwann as of 1969. However, they might still be found in shops which specialize in Jewish records or out-of-print records, or in music libraries: Gloria Levy, *Sephardic Folk Songs* (Folkways); Elnadav, *Ladino Songs* (Collector's Guild) and Ron Eliran, *Ladino Songs* (Vanguard).

Be sure to hear the superb recording by Victoria de los Angeles of *Ten Sephardic Songs* (Angel S36716).

Published Ladino songs are hard to come by. A large collection is in preparation. Until it becomes available you might find copies of the following two out-of-print volumes both issued by the World Sephardi Federation in London: *Chants Sephardis,* collected and edited by Leon Algazi and *Chants Judeo-Espagnols,* collected and edited by Isaac Levy. These books contain melody and texts with translations into French.

Page 159   Two basic collections of Yiddish folk songs which contain either explanations in English or English translations as well as piano accompaniments are: Schack and Cohen. *Yiddish Folk Songs.* N. Y. Bloch Publishing Co. and Ruth Rubin. *A Treasury of Jewish Folk Song* (hard cover and paperback). N. Y. Schocken Books. Another excellent collection containing melody line, guitar chordings, English synopses and brief historical backgrounds is *Mir Trogn a Gezang* by Eleanor Gordon Mlotek, published by the Workmen's Circle Educational Dept. To learn more about Yiddish folk song, read Ruth Rubin's *Voices of a People.* N. Y. Thomas Yoseloff, Ltd.

Page 199, line 7   There is a brief and readable account of the background of this Provençal song and other such songs by Armand Lunel, *Lost Jewish Music of the Provence,* in *The Reconstructionist,* Nov. 14, 1958, pp. 25–28. Lunel, a French writer descended of a long line of Provençal Jews and, indeed, bearing the name of one of the old towns in southern France, on many occasions, collaborated with and provided the librettos for the contemporary French composer Darius Milhaud who, like himself, can trace his descent from the Middle Ages in the Provence. If you can find a copy of Milhaud's *Notes without Music: An Autobiography,* translated from the French by Donald Evans and edited by Rollo H. Myers (N. Y. Alfred A. Knopf), you will learn still more about the music of the now defunct community of Provençal Jews.

Page 199, line 23   Saladin. *Canticum Hebraicum.* Edited by Israel Adler. Israeli Music Publications, Ltd., P. O. Box #6011, Tel Aviv. The other selections in this series are: Carl Grossi, *Cantata Ebraico in Dialogo,* for baritone solo, choir and basso continuo, for the annual celebration of the fraternity *Shomrim la-Boker* (Watchers of the Morning) of an Italian community; Volunio Gallichi and Francesco Drei, *Cérémonie musicale pour l'inauguration de la synagogue à Sienne* (Musical Ceremony for the Inauguration of the Synagogue at Sienna), for soloists, choir and orchestra; C. Lidarti, A. Caceres, A. Rathom, *Oeuvres du répertoire de la communauté juive "portugaise" d'Amsterdam* (Works from the Repertory of the Jewish "Portuguese" Community of Amsterdam). By the aforementioned composers plus one anonymous piece, for soloists, choir and orchestra.

Page 207   Judith and Ira Eisenstein. *What Is Torah?* A cantata for unison chorus and piano. N. Y. Jewish Reconstructionist Press. For lists of other musico-dramatic works, consult the *Bibliography of Jewish Vocal Music.* National Jewish Music Council.

Page 223   Lazar Weiner. *Viglied.* Words by Bella Schumiatcher from *Five Yiddish Art Songs by L. Weiner.* Transcontinental Music Publications. This lullaby is sung beautifully on a recording of *Songs by Lazar Weiner: Musical Settings of Yiddish Poetry.* With Bianca Sauler, soprano and the composer at the piano (Naomi 1001).

Page 228   Moses Milner. *In Cheider.* N. Y. Metro Music Co. This song is sung by Reuven Frankel on his recording *Out of the Silence* listed above in this chapter under p. 149. It appears, also, on the recording *Jan Peerce Sings Yiddish Folk Songs.* With orchestra conducted by Abraham Ellstein (Vanguard VSD-2135).

Page 233   There is an effective arrangement of this song for solo, mixed chorus, piano, flute and harp by Leon Algazi (Paris, Salabert & Cie.). This would be eminently suitable for performance by an amateur chorus. The harp and flute may be omitted if necessary. However, if available, they add interest and color to the selection.

Page 234   One source for this *Wedding Ode* is the Naumburg edition of the synagogue songs of Rossi, *Out-of-print Classics of Liturgical Music.* Another, later editing of the same ode may be found in Vol. II of *Ha-Shirim Asher Li-Shlomo* (The Songs of Solomon) edited by Fritz Rikko (N. Y. Mercury Music Corp.). The ode appears on p. 204 under the title *Le-mi Ehpotz.*

For interesting background reading, see Cecil Roth's chapter on *Music and Musicians* in his *Jews of the Renaissance.* Phila. The Jewish Publication Society of America, 1964.

Page 254   Yehoiakin Stutchewsky. *Ha-Klezmorim.* Jerusalem Bialik Institute, 1959.

Page 262   *Forward from Exile: The Autobiography of Shmarya Levin.* Translated and edited by Maurice Samuel. Phila. The Jewish Publication Society of America, 1967.

Page 271, left   For more information about the Habimah Theater, read Raikin Ben-Ari's book, *Habima.* Translated from the Hebrew by A. H. Gross and I. Soref with a foreword by Harold Clurman. N. Y. Thomas Yoseloff, Ltd., 1957.

Page 271, right   A thorough study of this period in the story of the music of the Jewish people is contained in Weisser. Some of the same material is covered in the latter chapters of Rothmuller. In addition, you might read the pamphlet, *The Music of Russian Jewry,* issued by the National Jewish Music Council.

Page 279   There are several recordings of Copland's *Vitebsk, Study on a Jewish Theme.* Consult your Schwann catalogue.

Page 300   Try to hear the recorded album, *Israel Sings.* Edited by Eric Werner. Hebrew Union College. (Out of print but likely to be reissued.)

Page 315   To find some of the older songs of the return, early Zionist songs and songs of the *halutzim,* you will have to consult some out-of-print volumes: Most comprehensive, with melody line and English summaries, is Coopersmith, *Songs of Zion,* Behrman House, Inc. Still available are S. E. and Israel Goldfarb, *The Jewish Songster,* Vols. I and II (Piano edition), Brooklyn Jewish Songster Publishers; Moshe Nathanson, *Manginoth Shirenu,* melody line only, N. Y. Hebrew Publishing Co.; A. W. Binder, *Pioneer Songs of Israel,* with piano accompaniments, N. Y. Bloch Publishing Co. Also, try to find a copy of Silbermintz, *Songs of Israel.* This supplements the above with songs from later decades. For effective piano arrangements of Israeli songs of the 1930s and 1940s, see the series edited by Max Helfman and published by Transcontinental Music Publications.

Page 316, left   The recording of Ben Haim's *To Israel* is out of print as of 1969. Watch issues of the Schwann catalogue for a possible reissue or for any new recording of a Ben Haim orchestral work.

Page 316, right   About a dozen recordings of serious compositions by Israeli composers are available from special sources in this country. Their titles and information about where to purchase them may be had from the National Jewish Music Council. In particular, see the council's resource material for the music festival of 1972.

Page 318, left   These two compositions may be found in the volume *Synagogue Music by Contemporary Composers,* ed. D. Putterman, listed above.

Page 318, line 7, right   Charles Davidson. *And David Danced Before the Lord.* N. Y. Mills Music Corp.

Page 318, line 22, right   Among the first of these are: Raymond Smolover. *Edge of Freedom* (a folk/rock service for the Sabbath). N. Y. NFTY, 1968 (Bell Records, Bell 6021) and Gershon Kingsley. *Shabbat for Today: Oh, Let Us Sing a New Song unto the Lord.* Cantor, orchestra, chorus and moog synthesizer, including the hymn *The World Goes Rolling On.* Lyrics by Bob Larimer and music by Bob Larimer and Gershon Kingsley (KNL-LP-GK-2686). Each of these rock services does include an original text. Since they appeared, many others have been produced.

Page 318, line 48, right   See Issachar Miron. *Kol Rinah be-Chaley Israel: A Sabbath Service from Israel.* With individual numbers by a variety of Israeli composers. N. Y. Mills Music Corp. Also: Ben Haim. *Mah Tovu, Liturgical Cantata.* N. Y. Southern Music Publishing Co., Inc., and his *Kabbalat Shabbat.* Tel Aviv Israel Music Publications, Ltd. Also: Mordekhai Starominsky (Seter). *Sabbath Cantata.* N. Y. Southern Music Publishing Co., Inc.

Page 319   See Gershon Ephros. *Cantorial Anthology,* Vol. V. N. Y. Bloch Publishing Co. From page 201 on you will find new music for a variety of occasions.

TIME CHART

This is an *approximate* "Time Chart"—a chronological listing of the music in this book. The examples included for the early periods are only our guess at how the music of that time may have sounded. They do not include the music for festivity and dancing, processions, work, love, etc., all of which were certainly present in those ancient days. The dating of many chants and folk songs is also, in many instances, pure surmise. Placing the many examples of Ashkenazic synagogue chant in the Middle Ages in Germany, for example, is not necessarily accurate. Much of that chant has come down to us altered and modified through long successions of

hazanim. None of it was written down until the late seventeenth century. For the sake of programming, one could, with justification, move some of the examples forward from the Middle Ages to the sixteenth and seventeenth centuries and from Germany to Eastern Europe.

Where certain examples are listed twice, it is because the melody derives from an early period but the arrangement given here is that of a later composer who wrote in the idiom of his own time: e.g., *Avodah* (Ex. 25) is listed under Middle Ages for its melody and again under nineteenth century for its arrangement by Gerovitch.

DATES	PERIOD	READING			WORDS WITHOUT MUSIC			MUSICAL EXAMPLES	
1300(?)–1000 B.C.E.	Nomadic	Ch.	II	Early narratives Lost collections					
			III	Instruments	P.	98	Jacob's Lament		
			XI	Song of the Well		61	Song of the Well		
						96	*Song of the Sea*		
	Judges							P. 11	Ancient scales
1000–585 B.C.E.	First Commonwealth				P.	98	David's Lament for Absalom		
						98	*Lament for Gilboa*		
		Ch.	III	Psalm headings					
			XVIII	*Song of Songs*	P.	147	*Song of Songs*		
						12, 13	Psalm 92		
						26	From Psalm 118		
						40	Priestly Blessing		
586–347 B.C.E.	Babylonian Exile Return Ezra and Nehemiah	Ch.	XXVI	Exile and return	P.	292	Psalm 137		
						292	Psalm 126		
390 B.C.E.–200 C.E.	Second Commonwealth Early synagogue Mishnaic period	Ch.	III	Psalmody				Exs. 1, 2, 3, 7, 16	
			IV	Psalmody Transition from temple to synagogue					
			V	*Halleluyah*					
			XI	Water-Drawing Festival					
			XVII	Therepeutae					

DATES	PERIOD	READING			WORDS WITHOUT MUSIC			MUSICAL EXAMPLES
200–1000 C.E.	Talmud *Geonim* Palestine	Ch.	VII XXIII VI VIII	Cantors Cantors Accents *Shofar* calls in Saadyah's *Siddur*				
1000– 1500	Middle Ages General	Ch.	VII II VII XXII XXV	Modes 11th-century manuscripts Cantors *Badhanim* Music of the theater				
	Spain and southern France	Ch.	XIX XXII XV XV XVIII	*Romanzas* Wedding songs Mystics of Spain *Kinot* Page from Spanish Bible	P.	167 239 117	*To Queen Sabbath*, Yehudah Halevi *Song of Rain*, Ibn Gabirol (Text only) *If Stone Walls*, Falaquera (Text only)	Psalmody: 4 Cantillation: 10, 41, 52, 71, 72 Synagogue chants: 29, 48, 49, 91, 96, 99 *Selihah*: 62 *Kinot*: 53, 54 Ladino songs: 75, 106
	Northern France and Germany	Ch.	IX XI XXV	*Kol Nidre* Prayers for rain (p. 63) Music of the theater				Cantillation: 9a, b, 11, 37, 38, 39, 47, 51, 70 Synagogue chants: 5, 12, 13, 14, 15, 17, 18, 19, 20, 21, 22a, b, c, d, 23, 24, 25, 26, 27, 28, 30, 31, 55, 80, 93a, b, c, d, 95, 97 *Kinah*: 55 Talmud chants: 33, 35
16th Century	Italian Renaissance	Ch.	II XXII	Manuscripts Pre-Rossi music				
17th Century		Ch.	XXII XXVI XXV XVII XXI	Rossi Rossi Music of the theater Mystics of Safed Yemenite wedding	P.	127	*Sons of the Palace*, Luria	Exs. 63, 64, 65, 84, 89, 98, 121
18th Century		Ch.	XXI XXI XVII XI XVI VII IX	Cantata for *Berit Milah* Provençal hymns Hasidic music Yiddish folk song based on *nusah* Levi Yitzhak Cantors Ahron Beer, *Kol Nidre*				Exs. 32, 34, 57, 66, 67, 87, 92

DATES	PERIOD	READING			WORDS WITHOUT MUSIC			MUSICAL EXAMPLES
19th Century	Germany	Ch.	VII	Cantors (p. 43)				Exs. 8, 21, 25, 43, 69, 82, 90, 122
			IX	Bruch, *Kol Nidre*				
			XIII	Mendelssohn, *Elijah*				
			XIII	Sulzer				
			XXI	Reform hymns				
			XXIV	*Klezmorim*				
			XXV	Theater				
	Eastern Europe	Ch.	XIX	Folk song				Exs. 36, 68, 69, 76, 78, 86, 88, 100, 101, 102, 103, 104, 105, 108, 109, 110, 111, 112, 113, 114, 115, 118, 123, 125, 127
			XXV	Music of the theater				
20th Century	Russia	Ch.	VII	From Morganstern, *Son of the Lost Son*	P.	70	From *Ha-Matmid*, Bialik	Exs. 79, 98, 107, 117, 120
			XXV	Renaissance of Jewish music				
			XXII	Milner				
	Europe, holocaust	Ch.	XV	Music of the holocaust				Exs. 56, 60, 61
			XVI	Music of the holocaust				
	Israel	Ch.	XXVI	History of Israeli music	P.	112	*Do Not Mourn,* Shimoni	Exs. 45, 46, 55, 58, 59, 73, 85, 124, 126, 128, 129
			VIII	*Shofar* in Israel		224	*Lullaby,* Tchernichowsky	
			V	*Halleluyah* songs		69	*Song of Rain*	
			XVI	*Halutz* songs				
			XI	Rain songs				
			XX	Israeli *Shabbat* songs				
			XI	Water celebration				
			VI	Cantillation method of composition				

DATES	PERIOD	READING	WORDS WITHOUT MUSIC	MUSICAL EXAMPLES
	America	Ch. VI Copland, *In the Beginning* VIII Fromm, *Schofar Service* IX Schoenberg, *Kol Nidre* XIV Bloch, *Avodat ha-Kodesh* XIV Bernstein, *Chichester Psalms* XV Diamond, *David Mourns for Absalom* XXVII Music in America XVIII Saminsky XXI Revision of *Union Hymnal* XXII Yiddish art song (Weiner) XVII Bloch, *Ba-al Shem Suite* XVII Hasidic services XXV Music of the theater XV Wolpe, *Lament for Gilboa* IV Y. Wyner, *Friday Evening Service* XIII Starer, *Ariel*		Exs. 40, 44, 94, 116

ALPHABETICAL LIST OF MUSICAL EXAMPLES

331

INDEX

A

Aaron, the High Priest, 189
Abraham He-Hazan, 124
Absalom, 98, 99
Accents, 28ff., 77, 79
Achron, Joseph, 271, 272, 278, 317
Adir Hu, 172
Adler, Hugo, 318
Adler, Israel, 8, 324
Adler, Samuel, 319
Ahasuerus, 262
Ahavah Rabbah, 223
Akdamut, 207
Aleatory music, 316
Alef-beis, 225
Alenu, 55
Algazi, Leon, 323, 324
Al-Harizi, 241
Aliyah, 308, 312, 315
Alkabetz, Shelomo, 127
Amidah, 55
Amiran, Emanuel, 87, 315
Amram, David, 319
Amsterdam, 8
And David Danced Before the Lord (Davidson), 318
Andalusia, 156
Antiphonal singing, 12, 22
Arab, Arabic, 156, 312
Aramaic, 167
Ariel, quarterly, 321
Ariel (Starer), 77
Asch, Sholom, 269
Ashkenazic, 22, 33, 38, 101, 147, 226, 243
Astruc, Rabbi Mordechée, 262
Austria, 315
Avignon, 198
Avodah, 57, 58
Avodat ha-Kodesh (Bloch), 91

B

Ba-al keriyah, 32
Ba-al Shem Suite (Bloch), 146
Ba-al Shem Tov, 132
Babylonia, 5, 241, 292
Badhan, badhanim, 238, 243, 247, 254, 261, 262, 269
Balakirev, 271
Bar Mitzvah, 77, 199, 222
Bar Yohai, Rabbi Simeon, 130
Baroque, 8
Bat Mitzvah, 202
Battle Hymn of the Republic, 24

Bayer, Bathya, 321
Bayonne, France, 207, 220
Beer, Ahron, 50
Belshazzar, 278
Ben-Ari, Raikin, 324
Beneventine neumes, 8
Ben Haim (see Frankenburg), 316, 317, 318, 325
Berditchev, 113
Berit Milah, 194ff., 222
Berlin, 315
Berlin, Irving, 269
Bernstein, Leonard, 77, 79, 90, 100, 318, 323
Bet Am, 178
Bet ha-Knesset, 17
Bialik, H. N., 70, 71, 116, 165, 178, 271, 279, 308
Bikel, Theodore, 323
Bilu, Bilu-im, 304
Binder, Abraham W., 317, 319, 322, 325
Bloch, Ernest, 9, 146, 317, 318
Bohemia, Bohemian, 172, 307
Bokhara, 18, 155, 215
Boscovitch, Uri, 316
Bride, 210
Budmor, Moshe, 319
Buenos Aires, 71

C

Caceres, A., 324
Cairo, 7
Cambridge University, 7
Cantata, 207
Cantigas of Alphonso the Wise, 8, 124
Cantillation, 28, 100, 271, 228
Cantor, cantors (see *Hazan*), 209
Cantor, Eddie, 269
Cantors' Institute, Jewish Theological Seminary, 319
Carpentras, 198
Castelnuovo-Tedesco, Mario, 127
Catalonia, 149
Cavaillon, 198
Chagall, Marc, 228
Chajes, Julius, 318
Chichester Psalms (Bernstein), 90
Chori Spezzati, 233
Cohen, Ethel Silverman, 324
Cohen, F. L., 63
College of Fine Arts, University of Judaism, 319
College of Jewish Music, Jewish Theological Seminary, 319
Comtat Venaissin, 198
Confession, The Great, 59

PHOTO CREDITS

The frontispiece of this book is a Marc Chagall drawing, *The Fiddler and an Angel,* 1941. From the Photographic Archive of the Jewish Theological Seminary of America, N.Y./Frank J. Darmstaedter.

Aaron-Ashley Art Publishers, N.Y. p. 77

America-Israel Culture Center p. 278

Arribas, Luis—Toledo p. 23

Editions Clairefontaine, Lausanne, Switzerland/Izis p. 308

Israel Office of Information pp. 18, 61 (right), 63, 66, 98, 130, 170, 300, 304

Jewish Encyclopedia pp. 90, 100, 107, 113, 126, 183, 193 (upper left), 193 (right), 199, 212, 221

Jewish Museum, N.Y., Harry G. Friedman Collection p. 194 (left)

Jewish Theological Seminary Library pp. 17, 148, 293

Jewish Theological Seminary of America, N.Y./ Frank J. Darmstaedter pp. 7, *33,* 37, 44, 45, 46, 53, 111, 112, 168, 178, 193 (lower left), 209, 222, 225 (right), 233, 238, 254, 256, 257, 293

Kirchner, Paul Christian. *Jüdisches Ceremoniel,* Nuremberg, 1726 p. 50

Louvre, Paris, France/B & G International p. 292

Magnum/Leonard Freed pp. 61 (left), 123, 127, 155, 162, 165, 167, 193 (right), 249

Metropolitan Museum of Art pp. 5, 6 (right)

Mula and Haramaty, Tel Aviv, Israel pp. 24, 213

Photo Researchers, Inc./Jerry Cooke pp. 225 (left), 312

UAHC pp. 28, 317

University of Pennsylvania Museum p. 6 (left)

Vishniac, Roman p. 70

Yivo Institute for Jewish Research pp. 255, 269